D1560042

The
World
Turned
Upside Down

THE
WORLD
TURNED
UPSIDE DOWN

The American Victory in the
War of Independence

Edited by
John Ferling

Contributions in Military Studies
Number 79

GREENWOOD PRESS
New York • Westport, Connecticut • London

Library of Congress Cataloging-in-Publication Data

The World turned upside down : the American victory in the War of
  Independence / edited by John Ferling.
      p.   cm. — (Contributions in military studies, ISSN 0883–6884 ;
  no. 79)
  Bibliography: p.
  Includes index.
  ISBN 0–313–25527–X (lib. bdg. : alk. paper)
  1. United States—History—Revolution, 1775–1783. 2. United
States—History—Revolution, 1775–1783—Campaigns. I. Ferling,
John E. II. Series.
E208.W87 1988
973.3—dc19   88–15482

British Library Cataloguing in Publication Data is available.

Library of Congress Catalog Card Number: 88–15482
ISBN: 0–313–25527–X
ISSN: 0883–6884

First published in 1988

Greenwood Press, Inc.
88 Post Road West, Westport, Connecticut 06881

Printed in the United States of America

The paper used in this book complies with the
Permanent Paper Standard issued by the National
Information Standards Organization (Z39.48–1984).

10 9 8 7 6 5 4 3 2 1

For
My Parents
Ernie and Ruth Ferling

Contents

Preface

Why did America win the revolutionary war? Each essay in this volume seeks to answer the question.

The question is not new, of course. Only since World War II, however, has it been commonplace for academic historians to attend to such an inquiry, previously having been more than content to leave such concerns to professional soldiers and popular nonfiction writers. If professional historians were slow to take up military history, they swiftly made up for lost time. The quarter century after World War II witnessed a voluminous outpouring of literature on the War of Independence; the Vietnam War and the celebration of the bicentennial of the American Revolution in the 1970s prompted an even greater explosion of studies on the revolutionary war.

Each essayist in this volume has benefitted from the impressive scholarship of the past fifty years. Indeed, the objective of the contributors to this anthology has been both to synthesize the disparate strands within those earlier studies and, through fresh research, to offer new insights into the outcome of this conflict. The result, hopefully, is an enriched understanding not only of the complexities of the worldwide struggle that erupted in a sleepy Massachusetts hamlet in the spring of 1775, but to comprehend the many factors that led the diplomats a world away in Paris in 1782–83 to recognize the reality of the American victory.

Several persons have assisted in the progress and completion of this work. Albert S. Hanser offered insightful suggestions that were of value in the conceptualization of this collection. Theodore Fitz-Simons, James T. Gay, and Steve Hanser graciously and unfailingly provided teaching schedules that made available the time necessary both for the completion of my own essay and for the perusal of the contributions of others. Nancy Farmer and

Anne Manning of the Irvine Sullivan Ingram Library at West Georgia College cheerfully assisted in the procurement of important research materials, while Deborah Campbell and Nancy Steinen helped with the immense correspondence involved in putting together this volume. More than to anyone, however, I am grateful to Darlene Jones, who patiently, amiably, and competently typed the manuscript.

The
World
Turned
Upside Down

1

The Colonial Background
to the American Victory

Fred Anderson

By the rude bridge that arched the flood,
   Their flag to April's breeze unfurled,
Here once the embattled farmers stood,
   And fired the shot heard round the world.[1]

You know the rest. In books you have read,
How the British regulars fired and fled,—
How the farmers gave them ball for ball,
From behind each fence and farm-yard wall,
Chasing the red-coats down the lane,
Then crossing the fields to emerge again
Under the tree at the turn of the road,
And only pausing to fire and load.[2]

Even though they partake more of myth than fact, these lines by Emerson and Longfellow have told generations of Americans all they really wanted to know about the colonial background to victory in the War of Independence. Historians have long known that it was hardly so simple—that there was much more to winning this long and bloody war than sniping at redcoats from behind each fence and farm-yard wall. Although thousands of Massachusetts militiamen did indeed begin the war by responding to the Lexington Alarm in 1775, there would never again be a comparable episode: the war was won not by citizen-soldiers from the militia, but by the long-suffering professional troops of the Continental army. Continentals, not militiamen, stayed in the field against great odds, often receiving barely enough support from Congress and the states to keep them alive. But it is precisely because the war was fought in a way so radically different from the way it began that we are obliged to pay special attention to the military background of the colonists. If we hope to comprehend how thousands of ordinary colonists could take the extraordinary step of engaging units of their sovereign's regular army in combat, we must begin by understanding the colonial military tradition and the forces that shaped it, and in particular we must understand the influence on New England of the last of the colonial wars. Only then will it be possible to see why only the New England militiamen were capable of beginning the War of Independence, yet why militiamen alone were incapable of achieving the final victory.

Viewed from the broadest institutional perspective, the formations of the New England militia and the British regular army that confronted each other on April 19, 1775, were the descendants of a common ancestor, the Elizabethan militia.[3] Two centuries earlier, Queen Elizabeth had sought to increase the effectiveness of the English militia by abandoning what seemed to be the obsolete and probably dangerous principle on which it had rested, the universal military responsibility of a "nation in arms." Fearing an armed peasantry and distrusting a militarily powerful nobility, Elizabeth turned over responsibility for England's territorial defense to a new, selective, and predominantly middle-class militia of "trained bands." Each county had such organizations made up of yeomen and burghers, administered by royal officers called lords lieutenant, who were drawn from the county aristocracy. Poorer subjects received neither arms nor training, but were regarded as a manpower pool upon which the monarch could draw for foreign expeditions. Elizabeth's reforms succeeded in disarming the least trustworthy segments of the population and turning powerful nobles into royal administrators, even as it made the militia a more manageable institution. Whether or not the trained bands would have proven a match for a professional army from the Continent, however, was tested neither in Elizabeth's reign nor that of her successor, James I, for Elizabeth's navy (and luck) forestalled foreign invasion, and James proved a markedly unmartial monarch.

James's more bellicose son, Charles I, took the next step in increasing the effectiveness of England's military institutions. He ascended the throne in 1625 intent on achieving a greater military role abroad and on modernizing the arms and training of the militia within the realm. Not only seeking to create a "perfect militia," Charles tried for the first time in English history to raise conscript armies in peacetime, forces which would stand ready for service overseas, or, his adversaries in Parliament feared, for repression at home. The expense and unpopularity of Charles's military measures touched off a long struggle between king and Parliament over who would control England's militia, and raised the larger issues that would eventually pitch the country headlong into civil war.

In the course of fighting its war with the king, Parliament found it necessary in 1645 to create England's first permanent professional military organization, the New Model Army.[4] This force proved so effective that it not only defeated the king and drove his son into exile, but also came to dominate the Parliament that had created it. During the period of the Protectorate, the New Model Army became the de facto ruler of Great Britain; indeed, it was only at the sufferance of the army's leading commander, General George Monck, that the exiled Stuarts returned to the English throne in 1660. Following his Restoration, Charles II prudently decided to make Monck his lord general, the commander of a small standing army formed in 1661 out of elements retained from the New Model Army and remnants of the royalist troops who had supported Charles in exile. From the curious marriage of former enemies was begotten the British regular army, an apolitical permanent military establishment paid by Parliament and controlled by the crown, used abroad as an instrument of foreign policy, and employed domestically, when needed, as a constabulary force.

Along with the regular army, the Restoration Parliament in 1661–63 also established an updated militia, a system intended like its Elizabethan predecessor to be a predominantly middle-class home guard, available if needed to preserve civil order and to defend against invasion, but also to provide a territorial reserve infrastructure for the support of the regulars.[5] However, now that he had an effective standing army, Charles II had little practical use for a cumbersome militia; moreover, he was unnerved by the prospect of a sizable share of the civil population in arms. Accordingly he neglected the militia. His successors followed suit, and from 1670 through the mid–1750s the institution endured a prolonged decline. In functional terms the militia remained the preserve of local gentlemen, and in political theory it represented a quasi-republican counterbalance to the standing army. In fact, it was a joke: a social organization whose musters and sham battles caricatured the professional maneuvers of the regulars. Only when invasion really threatened did the militia become animated enough to gain a semblance of efficiency, and then only by becoming an adjunct of the army. Thus, since the Restoration, the defense of the realm has been the job of the regular armed forces.

From the sixteenth through the eighteenth centuries, then, the trajectory of Great Britain's land defenses was toward greater professionalism, greater control by the Crown, and greater segregation of the military from civilian society. By the middle of the eighteenth century, the regular army had become a highly effective military organization, which in cooperation with the Royal Navy was capable of forcibly projecting British policy almost anywhere in the world. In the Seven Years' War (1756–63), the army did exactly that, fighting with great success in Europe, North America, the Caribbean, India, West Africa, and the Philippines. As the reach, size, and effectiveness of the regular army grew, the English militia atrophied, becoming an essentially vestigial institution. In Great Britain's North American colonies, however, the trajectory of military development from the English militia of Elizabeth's reign was entirely different.

England's first North American colonists, settling along the Chesapeake and the shores of Massachusetts Bay, adapted the militia system of the mother country to meet the special challenges they faced in the New World. In America the military functions that Elizabeth had tried to restrict to a limited, propertied segment of the population were generalized almost immediately to virtually all able-bodied male colonists. From the beginning the Virginia militia differed from its English counterpart in that nearly every white male resident within the colony was compelled to serve in a trained band. Similarly, within two years after the Puritans' initial settlement, Massachusetts's government required that all men except ministers and magistrates acquire and maintain arms for the colony's defense. This was the first in a long series of acts that would eventually incorporate every town and almost every able-bodied man between sixteen and sixty in the Bay Colony's militia system. All of the seventeenth-century colonies except Quaker Pennsylvania required military duty of most healthy white freemen and, in many cases, of white male servants. In extreme emergencies even slaves might be given military responsibilities. The earliest phases of settlement in almost all of the English colonies were thus marked by "regression" to the inclusive medieval model that Elizabeth had abandoned in 1573.[6]

As the colonies grew, their populations increased, their societies and economies evolved in distinctive directions, their military requirements changed, and the character of their military institutions altered accordingly. Virginia's militia, like those of the other southern colonies, became less inclusive as the colony matured. In part this was because the militia had proven so effective in the early wars that native Americans posed no direct threat to the survival of the colony after about 1650; in part it was because population growth enlarged the supply of potential soldiers beyond Virginia's ability to employ them en masse; and in part it had to do with the leading planters' growing fear of their poorer neighbors. These fears were not merely paranoid. The insurgents in Bacon's Rebellion, an uprising that forced Governor Sir William Berkeley to flee the colony in 1676, manifested no small degree of class antagonism. "How miserable that man is," Berkeley complained, meaning himself, "that Governes a People where six parts of seven at least are Poore Endebted Discontented and Armed." In the last quarter of the century Virginia's militia systematically excluded from its membership such discontented debtors, finally becoming "nearly as exclusive as the [militia] in England."[7]

The growing exclusiveness in the militia reflected changes in its military function that responded to deeper changes in Virginia's society and economy. Although enslaved Africans were present from the 1640s or even earlier, Virginia's tobacco planters preferred to use English indentured serv-

ants to grow their crops during most of the seventeenth century. Toward
the end of century, however, shifts in the English market for indentured
servants increasingly turned Chesapeake planters toward black slave labor
to work their fields, launching a trend that would make Virginia's labor
force predominantly black by the first decades of the eighteenth century.
With the transition to slave labor, planters' fears came to focus on the
dangers of slave rebellion, and the most critical duties of the militia shifted
from defense of the frontiers to control of slaves. Soon squads of militiamen
patrolled roads and searched slave quarters to "take up" blacks traveling
or meeting without permission from their masters.[8]

Soon, too, as they assumed responsibility for the internal police of the
slave system, the southern militias forfeited their military capabilities. Virginia, for instance, faced no serious external threat between 1700 and 1750,
and on the single occasion that a governor tried to raise the militia to resist
a potential Indian incursion, so few men responded that he was compelled
to negotiate a peace. Similarly, South Carolina's planters eventually found
themselves unable to contemplate the use of militia for anything except the
control of slaves. Less than twenty years after the Yamassee War of 1715,
which had posed so grave a threat to the colony that even slaves had been
armed, South Carolina's government maintained in a memorial to the king
that "the presence of three Negroes for every white man made provincial
self-defense impossible." It would not be until the outbreak of the Seven
Years' War, or even the onset of the revolutionary crisis itself, that the
southern colonies would seek to reanimate their moribund military institutions. In the meantime, the southern militias so much resembled their
English counterpart in ineptitude and conviviality that a touring Englishman
in 1746 found Dryden's earlier jibe at the English militia appropriate to
describe a Virginia muster:

> And raw in the fields the rude militia swarms;
> Mouths without hands, maintained at vast expence,
> In peace a charge, in war a weak defence:
> Stout, once a year they march, a blust'ring band,
> And ever, but in times of need, at hand;
> Of seeming arms, they make a short essay,
> Then hasten to get drunk, the bus'ness of the day.[9]

In New England, by contrast, the militia neither decayed so drastically
nor lost its inclusive character. The first settlers of Massachusetts and Connecticut sought a system of universal participation in the "trainbands" which
was deeply consonant with the convenantal principles on which Puritan
society was organized.[10] Reacting against the elitist, centralizing military
system of Charles I, the Puritan system permitted militiamen to choose their
own officers and made military leaders subject to the control of elected civil

officials. The election of militia officers lasted until 1668 in Massachusetts, into the eighteenth century in Rhode Island, and to the end of the colonial period in Connecticut. Although blacks and Indians were excluded from militia training by about the middle of the seventeenth century, the idea of universal military responsibility was never seriously questioned in New England. Principally this was because the New England provinces were steadily engaged in fighting foreign enemies, the French of Canada and their Indian allies.

The New Englanders never enjoyed the kind of surcease from warfare granted to Virginia from the late seventeenth century to 1754. Following King Philip's War of 1675–76, a bitter, costly war with the Wampanoags and their allies, further conflict struck New England in five intensifying waves, in 1689–97 (King William's War), 1702–13 (Queen Anne's War), 1722–25 (Governor Dummer's War), 1744–48 (King George's War), and 1754–63 (the French and Indian War). Massachusetts towns within forty miles of Boston remained subject to attack until early in the eighteenth century. Under such conditions, provincial militias attained levels of military competence evident nowhere else in the Anglo-American world. Within the space of ten days during the campaign of 1757, for example, the New England provinces mobilized 20,000 or more militiamen in response to the French and Indian destruction of Fort William Henry, a strategic post at the south end of Lake George, New York. Because the attack seemed to portend a full-scale invasion of New England, several thousand Massachusetts and Connecticut militiamen actually assembled near Lake George before it became clear that Fort William Henry had fallen to raiders, not invaders, and the alarm was cancelled. That so many units could take the field on such short notice testifies to an extraordinary vitality—at least in wartime—in the New England militia systems. Yet this incident also suggests why, active as they might be in an emergency, these militias were no longer organizations capable of sustained combat operations.

As the New Englanders themselves had realized as early as King Philip's War, mobilizing a high proportion of the able-bodied men in any region and marching them off to fight left the militiamen's own homes defenseless. Militia units, in other words, might make a reasonable force to defend against attack, but they could not be used offensively without bringing whole towns to an economic standstill and exposing them to enemy marauders. The necessity of mounting forces for extended campaigns in King Philip's War and in the imperial wars that followed thus led to the most important adaptation in northern colonial military institutions, the creation of short-term provincial armies.

Provincial armies were entirely separate from the militia and were comprised principally of volunteers, although men might be "impressed," or drafted, from militia units if it proved impossible to fill the ranks voluntarily. During wartime the colonies annually raised provincial forces, enlisting men in the spring of each year and discharging them in the fall, after six or eight months of active service. Since little active campaigning occurred in the winters, only a comparatively small number of soldiers, usually garrison troops or rangers, served throughout the year. As a result nothing resembling a permanent military establishment ever emerged in New England. Despite the fact that for years thousands of men might be under arms, the provincials remained preeminently summer soldiers, never far removed from civilian life.

As war followed war in the eighteenth century, provincial units came to perform virtually all of the active defense, as well as the offensive military functions of the New England colonies. Under these circumstances, the militia assumed a variety of supportive roles. Militia units provided the manpower pool from which provincials could be recruited or drafted. Militia magazines comprised a rear-echelon supply network. Militia officers trained their townsmen in the rudiments of drill and maneuver. Finally, militia regiments constituted each province's last line of defense in case of invasion.[11] The result was a two-tiered, flexible, and often quite effective system that was not sharply divorced from New England society. Through it, the vast preponderance of adult male New Englanders experienced military training in the militia, and a substantial minority of the young men of the region saw active service as provincial soldiers, especially in the last colonial war.

By the middle of the eighteenth century, then, military institutions in England and the English colonies of North America had diverged sharply, despite their common ancestry. The form that each system had assumed reflected both the military needs and the essential structure of its parent society. In England the persistent efforts of the crown to minimize the military responsibilities of the populace at large had succeeded largely because English society was so strongly divided by class. The population of permanently poor and socially marginal people in Great Britain was sufficient to generate a steady supply of recruits for the regular army, men whose prospects in civilian life were no better than those they could find in the ranks. Similarly, the aristocracy and the middle classes produced more than enough sons willing to officer the army. Military careers were indeed attractive enough to sustain a steady market in commissions, which officers bought and sold as a species of private property. The price of commissions offers a convenient barometer of the desirability of military careers. In 1720, when a good Surrey farm of a hundred acres would rent for about £76 per year and earn the farmer an annual profit of perhaps £35, the price of a subaltern's billet in an ordinary infantry regiment was from £170 to £200 sterling. The colonelcy of a first-class infantry regiment might run as high as £9,000.[12] Such a system clearly helped to maintain the boundary between officers and enlisted men, which was otherwise enforced by a ferocious disciplinary system designed to insure subordination whenever it was not willingly rendered. Thus the patterns of English social relations, formalized and institutionalized by the regulations and habits of the military subculture, were permanently incised in the character of the British army.

In the North American colonies, military institutions evolved into their definitive form under the pressure of the French and Indian War, and reflected the structure and nature of American societies as accurately as the regular army mirrored those of British society. Virginia, again, offers the best example of the southern military model. Faced in 1754–55 by a direct threat to its froniters for the first time in a half-century, the Old Dominion found its militia unable to mount an effective defense and began to grope toward the creation of a provincial force, the Virginia Regiment. Under the command of Colonel George Washington, a young planter ambitious to make the regiment comparable to any in the British army, this unit ultimately did a creditable job of defending Virginia's long, exposed frontier. For all his professional ambition, however, Washington could never precisely replicate the British regimental model he so admired, because Virginia's society was in no sense identical to Great Britain's. Although finding officers with gentlemanly credentials was no problem at the margins of Virginia's planter elite, there was no large pool of permanently impoverished men on which to draw for enlisted volunteers. Virginia was not without its poor working men, but most of its agricultural laborers and many of the artisans were slaves, and thus unavailable for service. The province first sought to solve its recruitment problems by conscripting men "with 'no visible way of getting an honest Livelihood,' " but failed miserably, raising only 25 percent of the Regiment's authorized strength. In 1755 and thereafter, it resorted more successfully to a combination of land bounties and threats of impressment to induce enlistments. The men who came forward always were fewer in number than the provincial government wanted, and showed no particular disposition to remain long in its service. In general they proved to be men disadvantaged by Virginia's slave system. Most were either recent immigrants whose skills competed directly with those of slave artisans or poor young men from the Tidewater; both kinds of recruits evidently saw military pay and land bounties as means to acquire land and a competency in the West. For most of these soldiers, in other words, military service was a temporary occupation, a potential avenue around the obstacles that Virginia's highly stratified slave-holding society placed in their paths. Thus in spite of Washington's earnest efforts to retain men from year to year, the Regiment was continually plagued by high annual turnover. Between 75 and 80 percent of the men in its ranks from 1755 through 1757 were first-term soldiers, which meant that the unit had no chance to develop professionalism through continuity, as the British army did.[13]

The New England provinces were much more heavily engaged in fighting during the French and Indian War than Virginia or any of the other southern colonies, and there the demand for recruits was truly extraordinary. The lowest possible estimate places one-third of the most eligible Massachusetts men in the Bay Colony's provincial armies during the war, and an even higher proportion of Connecticut men may have served their province in a similar capacity.[14] Although the New England colonies, like Virginia, provided statutes for the impressment of vagrants, provincial military duty was in fact both more widespread and more thoroughly voluntary in New England than anywhere else in the Anglo-American world. This was a consequence of the structure of rural New England's economy and society, in which the distribution of wealth was much more a function of age than of class. Lacking a sufficient number of permanently impoverished men to meet their military needs, the New England colonies turned instead to their temporarily poor population for soldiers. That is, these colonies drew mainly on young men, especially those between the ages of sixteen and twenty-six. Such men were usually still single and, because most of them had not yet accumulated or inherited sufficient resources to begin life as household heads, they remained in some measure the dependents of their fathers or employers. For these men, serving for a campaign or two as provincial soldiers offered a break in the routines of dependency and a way to make money. New England wages and bounties were high, offering provincial privates at least as much as they were likely to earn in civilian life as laborers or journeyman artisans. With savings from their wages and bounties, they could hope to finance—or to complete the financing of—their prolonged transition from dependent bachelorhood to householdership.[15]

In keeping with their society's strongly age-graded nature and its comparative lack of stratification, the New England officers differed from the provincial privates in their companies primarily in age, not in class. Captains were not infrequently the fathers of men serving as privates in their companies. Officers received commissions almost entirely on their ability to enlist men to serve under them. Thus loyalties between provincial officers and men could be intensely personal, for soldiers who volunteered for service were in effect choosing their leaders for the coming campaign. Armies constituted in this way clearly had to be held together by something other than the draconian discipline that British regular officers favored. What provided the cohesion for New England provincial forces was not deference enforced by terror—which the regulars assumed was the only reliable system—but rather personal loyalty to the officers, as well as the pervasive understanding that the soldier's relationship to his province was contractual and reciprocal. So long as the province fulfilled its obligations to its soldiers, and so long as the leaders remained popular, effective, and loyal, New England provincial armies could function reasonably well. But the voluntary ties of personal loyalty and contractual obligation could be, and often were, severed, in which cases the provincials began rapidly losing their efficiency and cohesion, and might even mutiny or desert en masse. The high pay, instability, and evident indiscipline of the New England provincials stunned the regular officers who served alongside them during the French and Indian War. What the regulars did not understand was that a professional military system on the English model could never have worked in the colonies. If the New England governments intended to fill the ranks with ordinary young men from ordinary families—the only men in New England's comparatively unstratified society numerous enough to serve their region's voracious military needs—they simply had no choice but to offer high wages and to accept high turnover and imperfect discipline.[16]

Thus the last of the colonial wars brought together in North America three strikingly different military systems, each the descendant of a common ancestor, and each the product of a different social, economic, and cultural system. In structure and ethos, England's professional army mirrored its class-divided society and, indeed, could not have existed apart from it. In Virginia a different system had emerged from Colonel Washington's efforts to replicate Britain's regular army in miniature in his Viriginia Regiment. Although Washington ultimately succeeded in creating an effective organization, it was never as professional as he would have wished, for the Virginia Regiment could never recruit its men from the kind of immiserated population that furnished long-service enlisted men for the British army. He was forced to rely instead on his ability to build up a core of gentleman officers and committed enlisted veterans by emphasizing professionalism and esprit de corps, and to deal as best he could with constant turnover in the ranks. Virginia's provincial force thus reflected—and suffered from— the character and problems of Virginian society. In New England's provincial armies the annual turnover was even more pronounced than in Virginia, but it was accepted as part of the price of raising large forces year after year; and in New England its effect was to blur the boundaries between officers and enlisted men, and even between soldiers and civilians. Among the thousands of New Englanders who served in provincial armies between 1754 and 1762, comparatively few men ever aspired to professionalism as did Washington and his fellow officers of the Virginia Regiment. If as a result the New Englanders never were as effective in the field as the regulars or even the Virginians, it was because the New England provincials always represented average members of their society much more fully than either the regulars or the Virginians represented the average members of theirs.

As different in character and capacity as the British and colonial American systems were, they were in fact complementary, and under the right circumstances could be made to cooperate to achieve striking successes. The record of the colonial wars, indeed, afforded no examples of military success without cooperation and coordination between the British and the colonial systems. The greatest achievement of American arms in the first half of the eighteenth century—the instance usually cited as proof of the colonies' military maturity—in fact illustrates this point. In 1745, 3,000 provincials from

Massachusetts and Connecticut successfully besieged the greatest French fortress in the New World, Louisbourg on Cape Breton Island; but Louisbourg never would have capitulated had not Commodore Peter Warren's Royal Navy squadron been present to choke off all supplies and relief. What King William, Queen Anne, and King George's Wars most consistently demonstrated was the colonies' inability to cooperate among themselves in matters of defense. Again the case of Louisbourg furnishes the best example. New York's policy of maintaining de facto neutrality in King George's War, and its refusal to stop trading with the French through Albany after 1745, essentially neutralized the advantage the New Englanders and the Empire had gained by conquering the fortress. This policy of neutrality made eminent sense for a colony susceptible to French invasion but too weak to mount a reliable defense on its own. Besides, neutrality offered a splendid opportunity to make money from the war. Viewed from the perspective of New England or the Empire, however, New York's neutrality was self-interestedness tantamount to treason.

The American colonies succeeded against New France only in the French and Indian War, the one conflict in which they managed to achieve a degree of cooperation in matters of defense. But it is important to realize that the Anglo-American forces began even that notably successful conflict by recapitulating the flaws and failures of the previous colonial wars. The Albany Congress in 1754 was supposed to produce an intercolonial union for defense; it created only heightened suspicions among colonial assemblies. The Crown, realizing that the Americans would never unite of their own free will, tried next to remedy their chronic disunity by appointing for North America a commander-in-chief who possessed such vast legal authority that he was in effect an American viceroy. The result was not unity, but opposition. The colonial assemblies resisted the will of the commanders-in-chief so resolutely that the war effort all but came to a halt by late 1757. Lord Loudoun, the supreme commander in that year, had expected the colonies to fund the prosecution of the war and to accept his strategic direction without question, and the assemblies would do neither. It was only the decision by England's charismatic war minister, William Pitt, to abandon the vice regal system of directing the war that finally turned military failure in America into spectacular success in the years following 1757. Pitt understood that the war could not be won without colonial cooperation, but that cooperation could never be compelled; he therefore set out to obtain it by subsidizing the colonies' military efforts and requesting—rather than ordering—colonial support for the cause. In return for their voluntary cooperation in raising provincial troops to serve jointly with the regulars, and for participating in the conflict in innumerable other ways, the colonies received reimbursements for a substantial share of their expenditures. The colonies responded eagerly, particularly in New England, which recruited armies of unprecedented size to undertake the conquest of Canada alongside the thousands of regulars whom the Crown had dispatched to North America.

As victory followed victory from 1758 through 1760, the colonies achieved a degree of cooperative wartime unity unprecedented in American history. Pitt had succeeded in harnessing colonial self-interest and patriotism to realize the latent military potential of the Empire in North America. With the highly disciplined regulars available to do the bulk of the fighting, the provincials could be used to perform all sorts of strenuous support functions, such as cutting roads, hauling supplies, constructing fortifications, and digging siege works, all of which were necessary for the successful prosecution of the war, but none of which required high levels of training or discipline. At the same time, provincials also remained available to act as scouts, as tactical reserves, as garrison troops to man strategic forts, and as occupation forces to hold conquered territory. The regulars had military skill and staying power; the provincials, who lacked both, provided sufficient temporary strength to enhance the regulars' effectiveness in the field. The Anglo-American victory in the French and Indian War was thus primarily a British victory, in the sense that it was achieved under British direction, in battles won primarily by British arms. But it was a victory that the British could never have achieved without American participation. It also was a victory for which the Americans were eager to claim more credit than the British regulars (who despised the provincials for their amateurism) were willing to allow.

In light of all this, the British by 1763 could only conclude that the American colonies were incapable of defending themselves without direct leadership from the mother country. Judged from a purely political and military standpoint, American disunity was so extreme that no other conclusion could reasonably be drawn. But for the Americans, the last two colonial wars offered entirely different, paradoxical lessons. New Englanders especially, but to some extent colonial Americans in general, developed a very high opinion of themselves as soldiers, even though the battlefield successes in fact had been gained mainly by the British. New Englanders could believe that they were largely responsible for victory in the French and Indian War because their principal mode of understanding the meaning of battles and wars was a providential one. They tended to interpret great victories, such as the capture of Louisbourg in 1745 or the collapse of French resistance in Canada in 1760, as signs both of the Lord's approbation for Anglo-American Protestants and of His wrath against the French papists. "It is evident," wrote a Massachusetts major (a blacksmith in civilian life) following the capitulation of Louisbourg, "that God has both begun and finished this great work, even the reduction of Louisbourg; and given it into the hands of the English; and glory be to the great name of Jehovah for it."[17] Fifteen years later another Massachusetts blacksmith, serving as a provincial captain in the invasion of Canada, made a strikingly similar entry in his diary when a French force fled ahead of his unit. "The enemy are gone to Montreal," he observed; "thus Heaven apparently fights for us, and therefore it is our duty to acknowledge it's the hand of Divine Providence, and not done by any force of ours or arm of flesh."[18] The frequent appearance and the stylized similarity of such observations in provincial soldiers' journals bespeaks a view of the world that virtually required those who shared it to discount the contributions of the regulars to victory over the French. British soldiers and sailors, as everyone who had been near them understood, were prodigious blasphemers and swearers, inveterate whorers, profaners of the Sabbath, and notorious for relying on the arm of flesh rather than the hand of God. If victory came from the Lord, it was impossible not to believe that God was showing His mercy and favor to His faithful servants, the New Englanders, and that battles were being won in spite of the godless regulars who served beside them. This popular providentialism, casting the New England provincials as soldiers of the Lord, formed part of a vital tradition that placed New England in a special convenantal relationship with the Almighty. In the most profound sense the defeat of New France ratified New England's special position in God's favor and its special responsibilities in helping to fulfill His plan for mankind.[19]

On a more mundane level, New England and New Englanders especially were powerfully affected by the manpower requirements and financial demands of the last colonial war. In Massachusetts at least, the personnel demands were so great that virtually every family was touched directly by the war, through provincial service or through the civilian employment of one of its members with the armies as an artificer, wagoner, or sutler. Those men who returned from the war brought home memories of service with the British regulars; those memories were not particularly positive ones.

Most New England soldiers had not previously met the kinds of Britons who filled the ranks of the regular army, much less the type of men who comprised the British officer corps. There was no parallel for the harshly disciplined relations between regular officers and men in the provincials' own units, or in their society at large. In general Americans were shocked by the severity of floggings (which frequently ran to hundreds of lashes with a cat o' nine tails) and other punishments they witnessed while serving with the regulars. "Three men," one witness to a flogging wrote, "were tied up to be whipped. One of them was to receive eight hundred lashes, the others five hundred apiece. By the time they had received three hundred lashes, the flesh appeared to be entirely whipped from their shoulders, and they hung as mute and motionless as though they had long since been deprived of life."[20] Five to eight hundred lashes were not unusual penalties. An average provincial on General Jeffery Amherst's Crown Point expedition in 1759, for instance, could have witnessed seven executions and at least sixteen floggings of from three hundred to one thousand lashes between the middle of May and the middle of October. One colonial soldier described a typical execution laconically enough, but not without showing revulsion: "This day there was a regular shot to death. He seemed to be very obstinate and would not kneel to be shot. They were obliged to tie him with a rope to a tree and then shot him. Oh, what a dreadful sight it is to behold men used after such a manner!"[21] Since the provincials had no reason to believe they would be exempt from such treatment, their relations with the British were marked by fear and mistrust. Not fully realizing that the regulars were representatives of what was in fact a culture different from that of New England, the provincials tended to judge the British in moral terms, and to conclude that they were at best callous, at worst brutes. "There is no spare here of the whip," a provincial private grimly noted in his diary when he realized that he would be under regular command in the garrison at Louisbourg. The passage of time did nothing to lighten his mood. Three months later he reflected: "We now see what it is to be under martial law and to be with the regulars, who are but little better than slaves to their officers. And when I get out of their [power] I shall take care of how I shall get in again."[22]

Victory over the French brough rejoicing in the colonies and a massive surge of pride at having participated in the greatest military venture in Anglo-American history. Ministers in His Majesty's government, however, found themselves faced with problems of peace after 1763 that were nearly as vexing as the problems of the late war. Many of the difficulties that these officials faced arose from Pitt's subsidy-and-requisition policy, which had granted Americans substantial rewards for cooperation while allowing the colonial assemblies control over provincial finances. The subsidies had succeeded in procuring colonial cooperation, but they also had succeeded in nearly doubling Great Britain's national debt, which at the end of the war stood at over £130 million sterling. Once the Peace of Paris was signed, Whitehall concluded, it was time for the colonists both to cooperate with the ministry—that is, to obey it in its new resolve to run a tight imperial ship—and to help pay the bill for the war. These were not unreasonable expectations, but given postwar conditions in the colonies they could only have had seriously disruptive effects.

New Englanders in particular were convinced, with good reason, that they had already paid their share, and more, of the costs of the French and Indian War. Massachusetts, for example, had passed province taxes that were the highest in its history. The war, in fact, had brought the colony to the verge of bankruptcy in 1758, from which it was narrowly rescued by the arrival of a Parliamentary reimbursement; thus what from the imperial British perspective seemed largesse looked from the New Englanders' standpoint to be critically necessary, and indeed barely sufficient, aid. And New Englanders had expended the lives of their sons no less prodigally than they had given of their treasure. Although casualty figures were not systematically recorded, a highly conservative estimate would place the toll among the provincials from Massachusetts at between 1,500 and 2,000 dead. In proportion to its population the death rate for Massachusetts in the French and Indian War therefore was more than five times as high as that for the United States in World War I, three times as high as that in World War II, and about one-half that sustained by the Union during the Civil War.[23]

Nor did the coming of peace in 1763 alleviate the burdens of war. New Englanders continued to pay extraordinarily high province taxes to discharge the public debts their colonies had incurred during the war. Indeed, taxes stayed at all-time highs in Massachusetts from 1762 through 1772, despite a severe postwar depression and the aggravation of the hard times by the scarcity of currency in the province's hard-money economy. The numerous and geographically widespread veterans of the French and Indian War, in other words, found that it was even more difficult to establish themselves as independent householders than it would have been in ordinary times. It hardly was accidental that the British ministry's decision to tighten the screws on the colonies ignited a particularly vigorous reaction among New Englanders who already believed themselves to be taxed to the limits of their ability to pay.

The singular concatenation of its people's experiences in the French and Indian War and in the postwar period made New England the one region in the colonies best suited to sustaining widespread, popular resistance to British attempts to reform the Empire after 1765. The Stamp Act, Great Britain's initial attempt to raise taxes directly from the American populace, produced opposition throughout the colonies because it touched all colonists directly, regardless of their region; but following its repeal the fragmenting localism and self-interest of the colonists surely would have reasserted themselves had it not been for the actions of Massachusetts' radicals. Their stubbornness in the face of imperial authority, and the intensifying violence of the confrontation in and around Boston between 1768 and 1775, provided radicals in all the colonies with a focus for their attention and anxieties. The stationing of regular troops in Boston in 1768, the Boston Massacre in 1770, and the Coercive Acts in 1774 all furnished evidence to republicans throughout the colonies of a ministerial conspiracy to smash the virtue and the liberties of the Bay colonists. This supposed evidence of Britain's tyrannical intentions eventually persuaded many of the inhabitants of other colonies that they confronted a similar peril, too grave to meet except with cooperation. But the British never would have pressed so hard as they did in Massachusetts, and the Bay colonists never would have resisted so vehemently, without the experience of the last of the colonial wars to draw upon.

The British ministers and subministers who struggled to impose order on a burgeoning, chaotic empire had derived a set of lessons from the painful experiences of the recent wars, and those lessons gave them their program for imperial reform.[24] The colonists had proven themselves to be unreliable.

They would trade with the enemy, resist the legitimate authority of His Majesty's representatives, shirk responsibility for paying their fair share of the costs, and insist on what they called their rights and liberties all the while. The Americans needed, therefore, to be controlled. Colonial commerce in particular, which had always benefitted the colonists more than the Empire, required regulation. Parliament had to assert its sovereign authority over the colonies in an unequivocal way. Royal governors and other officials had to be made independent of the colonial assemblies and thus turned into effective agents of the Crown. The colonists had to be made to pay a reasonable share of the expenses of administering the Empire, which had, after all, been expanded to their great benefit in the late war.

But the French and Indian War had taught a very large number of New England men a set of lessons too, lessons that made the conspiratorial rhetoric of republicanism seem particularly plausible. Slavery was no abstraction to men who had seen British military discipline at first hand and concluded that regulars were "but little better than slaves to their officers." The tyrannical potential of taxation without representation was terribly real to men who had faced a decade of crushing province taxes imposed with their own consent, only to be faced with the prospect of further levies over which they could exercise no control. The shared experience of the French and Indian War made it possible for thousands of ordinary rural New England farmers, artisans, and laborers to rally to the aid of the Bostonians, providing support with an enthusiasm that under ordinary circumstances would have been unimaginable. The Bay colonists' steadily growing resistance to Parliament's authority was what made it possible in turn for other colonies to come to the aid of Massachusetts when its liberties seemed doomed. Thus the British ironically supplied the Americans with the crucial element that they had always provided when colonies had achieved military success. Great Britain supplied the intercolonial unity.

Finally, the colonial wars also provided a repertory of military responses for the colonists to draw upon when the dispute finally came to blows. The New England militias, which routinely came to their highest states of readiness in wartime, once again were training frequently in 1774 and 1775, selecting their most committed and proficient members as a rapid deployment defense force, the Minutemen. With the Lexington Alarm of April 19, 1775, thousands of these men took up arms against the British and improvised the siege of Boston even before formal command and control could be established. As the New England governments imposed order on the units that had marched to Boston, they reflexively adopted the provincial model of the colonial wars, enlisting men for a single campaign, with each colony responsible for supplying, paying, and maintaining control over its own troops. Even after the Continental Congress adopted the forces that were besieging Boston as a Continental army and appointed George Washington as commander-in-chief on June 15, 1775, the military system that emerged bore a striking resemblance to the hybrid system in which regulars, provincial armies, and militias had fought the French in the last of the colonial wars. Washington, who had been among the most professional in ambition and orientation of all the American provincial officers of the French and Indian War, set out to create as regular an army as circumstances would permit, for he knew that only a professional force made up of men serving long enlistments could have the skill and staying power to face the British in battle. But the Continental army by itself would never be large enough or powerful enough to stymie the British regulars in the field. It would need the help of state troops, recruited on the model of the provincial armies of the colonial wars, as well as the aid of temporary militia levies to meet emergencies and to control the countryside and the population at large. Indeed, even the first offensive strategy that occurred to the Americans— the invasion of Canada—directly derived from the experience of the colonial wars. It would be too much to say that the revolutionary war was merely the last and largest of the colonial wars, for it evolved into a conflict different in character and vastly greater in consequence than any of its predecessors. But it would not be too much to say that the French and Indian War was an indispensable precondition to the resistance that finally led to American independence. If not in the ultimate victory, then at least in its beginnings, the revolutionary war demonstrated the dominating influence of the last of the colonial wars.

2

The Continental Army and the American Victory

James Kirby Martin

Some forty years after the American War of Independence, Joseph Plumb Martin, who had served for seven years in the Continental army, prepared a remarkable narrative in which he described his experiences as a revolutionary soldier. He reminisced about the unending privation that he and his comrades endured, and he spoke of his pride at having stayed in the ranks through several years of rigorous campaigning. Yet he was angry as he wrote, for his Maine neighbors were claiming that the Continental army was a "useless appendage to the cause" of American liberty. These "wise-acres" maintained that "it would have been *much* better" and more economical had the patriots depended solely on militia units for victory, rather than having Martin and other long-term Continentals "eating so much provisions and wearing out so much clothing when our services were worse than useless."[1]

Martin had fallen into the trap of arguing the relative merits of short-term citizen-soldiers in comparison to long-term regulars. As students of United States military history well know, that heated issue has plagued the American military tradition, from before the era of the American Revolution to our own time. Today most scholars agree that both Continentals and militia played crucial parts in the patriot victory over Britain. Each type was necessary and, without the other, an American republic might not have come into existence, at least not in the eighteenth century.[2]

This essay will not offer yet another investigation of the militia-regular controversy. Rather its purpose is to look at the ways in which Private Martin and his comrades in the Continental army helped to defeat the British and secure an independent American republic. Taking issue with Martin's neighbors, the argument will be that the Continental army not only was essential to military victory, but to making a stable new nation. Victory depended upon the willingness of General George Washington's soldiers to endure for an extended period of time the "hardships of fatigue, starvation, cold, and nakedness" so movingly described by Martin.[3] Certainly, too, militia, naval forces, and privateers were also essential to victory, as was the material and martial assistance of allies like France. But while all were of consequence, winning the war and making a new nation depended primarily upon the actions of the Continental army.

This essay will explore some of the ways in which the Continental *armies*—there was more than one Continental establishment between 1775 and 1783—provided an array of victories—success on the battlefield was only the most obvious form of victory—for the new American republic. General Washington's armies contributed to internal unity, national identity, and political stability, essential elements in the creation of a republic dedicated to the enshrinement of popularly-based political institutions and human liberty. Indeed, the greatest victory of the Continental armies was the securing of that political freedom.

To subdue its rebellious colonists, Great Britain had to reconquer and hold a vast territory stretching 100 or more miles inland along 1,500 miles of Atlantic coastline running from Maine to Georgia. It had to do this with the small-scale, conventional military forces characteristic of this era of more "civilized" limited warfare. The spatial problem may have made the war unwinnable for the British even before the shooting started.[4]

Making matters even more difficult for His Majesty's forces, the colonies lacked a strategically-vital geographic center which, if conquered, would have ended the war. This problem involved more than space. The colonists had not, as John Adams claimed in 1818, bonded together in one mind and heart before the commencement of the war. Certainly a majority believed that Britain's imperial policies had become too restrictive after 1763, but otherwise the colonists had little in common. Rhode Islanders were Rhode Islanders, Pennsylvanians were Pennsylvanians, and Virginians were Virginians. To defeat one group or to conquer one geographic area would not guarantee the capitulation of colonists elsewhere.[5]

Seeking to take advantage of colonial parochialism, the British in early 1775 tried to isolate and defeat the Massachusetts incendiaries before they received succor from other quarters in New England. Despite widespread protest against the Coercive Acts of 1774, king and Parliament declared only the Bay Colony citizenry to be in rebellion, and Lord Dartmouth, the secretary of state for American affairs, ordered General Thomas Gage, the commander of the British army in America, to employ his 4,000 redcoats in Boston to "arrest and imprison the principal actors and abettors" of sedition. If they could not be run down, he was to demonstrate the brutal power of British arms to the "rude rabble" in eastern Massachusetts, a people "unprepared to encounter with a regular force."[6] That lesson would not only end local resistance but it would also destroy patriot attempts to build intercolonial unity of purpose. Surely, leaders in London believed, the colonists would retreat into long-ingrained habits of localism rather than face massed British arms.

General Gage feared the consequences of such precipitous action. He was not quite so convinced that his redcoats were invincible, or that the Bay colonists were that unskilled in military matters. But his superiors in London had ordered him to act, and he did so in the worst sort of way. He dispatched a column some twenty miles into the countryside to capture and destroy patriot arms and gunpowder at Concord. Resisting militia had an easy time of it, almost casually ambushing the retreating redcoats from behind trees and fences. April 19, 1775, the day of the Lexington and Concord confrontation, represented an embarrassing defeat for proud British arms. Worse yet, the failure of Gage's initiative had the psychological effect of inflaming much of New England, and within a few days over 10,000 New Englanders had Gage and his troops trapped on Boston Peninsula.

Britain's attempt to isolate and militarily humiliate Massachusetts had gone awry. The stunning victory over Gage's force had helped to unify the patriot populace, at least temporarily. Dr. James Thacher, later a surgeon in the Continental army, perceived exactly what had happened. "The maxim adopted by our enemies is, '*Divide and Conquer*,' " he explained, but in response to Lexington and Concord all true patriots took to "the command, '*Unite and be invincible*.' " Each person now had "to encourage and promote a more perfect union among the colonies.... '*Liberty or death*,' '*Unite or die*,' are the mottoes which blazon the chronicles of the day, and embellish the military standards of almost every militia company."[7] Despite their intentions, then, the British had made their first critical mistake. The difficulty that now faced provincial Americans was to maintain, preserve, and expand the feeling of comradeship and indivisibility until king and Parliament redressed their grievances.

In the first exuberant months of the war thousands of New Englanders did come forth in militia companies to defend their families and communities. Their presence, concluded an optimistic Dr. Thacher, was proof that "the voice of liberty cannot be stifled."[8] Most hoped to fire a musket ball or two at the British regulars, then quickly return to their homes. Most soon found camp life boring, and they disdained rigorous training and discipline. Yet these militiamen, as property-holding citizen-soldiers, assumed that their virtuous commitment to so noble a cause would easily sweep away Britain's American army.

The assembled Yankees-in-arms, acting like a regional constabulary, were the harbingers of the first, or republican, Continental army of 1775–76. Before mid-June some of them even volunteered to serve for the remainder of the year, if the British did not back down before then. No longer technically militia, they formed into regiments representing their respective colonies. In most cases they elected their officers, forming a loose chain of command up to General Artemas Ward, a veteran of the French and Indian War. But this was no standing army acting capriciously without overriding civilian control. These patriots served under the auspices of the Massachusetts Provincial Congress and its executive body, the Council of Safety. Neither Ward nor any other general officer gave serious thought to initiating military actions without first securing the approval of civilian patriot leaders.[9]

By the end of May 1775 another reality was emerging. The war was already spreading beyond New England. Rebel partisans under Ethan Allen and Benedict Arnold had captured Fort Ticonderoga at the southern end of Lake Champlain in New York, and citizens in New York City were pressing the second Continental Congress for protection from redcoats rumored to be crossing the Atlantic. The need for central planning and direction had become obvious.

In mid-June, therefore, Congress "adopted" the New England constabulary as its own, calling it "the American Continental army" and naming a committee to draft regulations governing service. Congress also selected general officers and voted in favor of George Washington to serve as commander-in-chief. Naming a Virginian to direct the Continental army encouraged the involvement of the southern colonies, at least symbolically, in what at this juncture was a war affecting only the northern provinces.[10]

With the war spreading, leaders in Congress and general officers in the army had to find some way to turn America's geographic vastness to advantage. They also had to search for the means to keep the inevitable pull toward localism in check, should the war continue for a lengthy period. Both depended upon maintaining ample supplies of troops in the field, units which would go anywhere in the colonies to counter British military offensives. Yet in the summer of 1775 neither matter seemed too pressing. After all, the *rage militaire*, or what "the French call a passion for arms," a Philadelphian explained, was running at high tide. Patriots everywhere repeatedly talked of giving their all, no matter how long it took, to preserve liberty for themselves and posterity.[11]

Caught up in the popular mood, congressional delegates approved only short-term enlistments and proclaimed very generous "Articles of War." The maximum corporal punishment was thirty-nine lashes, as compared to 500 in the British army, and treason was a crime without penalty. Hard rules, logic dictated, were for the dregs of society pressed into the ranks of standing armies, not for freedom-loving patriots.[12]

Optimism prevailed into the autumn. Washington had over 22,000 volunteer troops in eastern Massachusetts. Detached columns, moreover, under Richard Montgomery and Benedict Arnold were striking deep into Canada.

The most obvious problems were those of training, discipline, and supplies, but on these counts pessimists could always hope for improvement.

But then, as the British remained inactive in Boston, war weariness set in. Short-termers by the hundreds refused to reenlist for another year's service. Civilian and military leaders pleaded with them to stay in camp. Everything "is at stake," including "your reputation and property, your safety, your very existence." Quit the service, their arguments went, and "those instruments of ministerial villainy will be at liberty to stalk at large, to satiate and glut their brutality, avarice, and cruelty."[13] Only a vigorous new recruiting campaign kept the numbers of Continentals near the 20,000 mark.

Disconcerting as was this waning of enthusiasm, it did not affect the outcome of events around Boston. In Canada, however, a number of short-termers under Montgomery and Arnold insisted upon returning home as soon as their enlistments were up, January 1, 1776. The two American commanders decided to storm the fortress-like city of Quebec while they still had the troop strength to consider such a bold move. Early on the morning of December 31, in the midst of a driving snowstorm, the partriots tried to execute their battle plan. A debacle resulted. Montgomery was killed, Arnold was seriously wounded, and nearly 500 soldiers were casualties, most of them captured. Patriots naturally concluded that the two commanders, facing an enlistment crisis, had rushed the assault and in the process lost the main chance to turn Quebec Province into the fourteenth colony in rebellion against Britain.

The fiasco at Quebec convinced some rebel leaders that Continentals needed to become much more like Britain's regular, long-term soldiery. Washington described the "evils" of short-term enlistments as "more extensively hurtful than any person...can form any idea of." By the time recruits had received "a tolerable degree" of training, he said, enlistment periods were expiring, and to secure reenlistments officers had to "relax... discipline" and "curry favor" with the very soldiers they were training. If the patriots wanted to succeed, concluded Washington, they had to be willing to go anywhere and stay there as long as necessary until achieving total victory.[14]

Until the British massive land and sea offensive of 1776 however, Washington's words fell on deaf ears. Most congressional delegates remained committed to the tradition of militia service. A virtuous, liberty-loving yeomanry, they repeatedly claimed, would reenlist until they had secured their property and political rights. After all, the *rage militaire* was still evident, despite the setback in Canada.

The martial enthusiasm evaporated when General William Howe unleashed a series of powerful blows beginning in August 1776. With 45,000 soldiers and sailors in his command, he struck at Brooklyn Heights, White Plains, and Fort Washington, and sent the Continentals reeling through

New Jersey, across the Delaware River, and into Pennsylvania. As they retreated, the republican army collapsed, losing 50 percent or more of its manpower base of 19,000 effectives. The ill-trained, poorly-disciplined Continentals proved a feeble match for British regulars, and the *rage militaire* died an inglorious death.

Washington was despondent. He wrote his brother in mid-December 1776 that "*I think the game is pretty near up.*" "No Man, I believe, ever had a greater choice of difficulties and less means to extricate himself from them," and he referred to the "accursed policy of short enlistments" as a key reason for the rebellion's perilous prospects.[15] What he did not discuss were plans to recross the Delaware and strike at British outposts, which he accomplished with a force of 2,400 early on the morning of December 26. In overwhelming some 1,000 Hessians still in their cups from celebrating Christmas, and with a second victory at Princeton a few days later, Washington's gambles pumped a new breath of life into the cause, but there was no raising the republican army from the dead.

The Continental army of 1775–76 had not been a total failure. Although unprepared for combat, it had functioned as a common rallying point for citizens with enough conviction to defend their liberties by taking up arms. It had provided a base on which to overcome localism and to build internal unity, and it had become a foundation for a national identity separate from the British Empire, as it drew citizens from the middle and southern colonies into the bond of military fellowship with New Englanders. It had also demonstrated that the rebellion could continue as something more than an endless series of unfocused guerrilla forays without beginning or end.

British military leaders perceived some of these points. They concluded that the Continental army had become a type of strategic vital center of the revolution. To overcome American resistance completely, the army had to be destroyed. As the campaign of 1777 beckoned, General Howe, who had blundered by not taking his opponent seriously enough in 1776, decided to atone for his error. His first goal, if chance permitted, would be to lure Washington into a set piece battle, knowing that his veteran regulars could carry the day in close order combat. If Washington proved too elusive, then Howe would seize the enemy's capital of Philadelphia, the more traditional type of strategic vital center, and win in that manner.

In June, Howe tried to bait the Continentals into coming out of the Watchung Mountains of north-central New Jersey and engage in a winner-take-all battle. Washington refused to cooperate. Instead, the American commander assumed the role of Fabius Cunctator, the Roman general who wore down the invading Carthaginians by staying on the defensive. Washington sent out raiding parties that poked cautiously at the British, but he kept the bulk of his troops in the hills until Howe finally gave up, pulled in his Jersey outposts toward New York City, and prepared to execute yet another variant of his scheme to crush the rebellion.[16]

Necessity had dictated Washington's Fabian tactics. He lacked the troop strength to fight in a general engagement. Because of the collapse of the *rage militaire*, he accepted that the cause "may remain for some time under a Cloud" until *"every nerve is . . . strained* to recruit the New Army."[17] With fewer than 3,000 troops on hand in late winter and only 10,000 at the end of May, his first priority was to construct Continental forces that could, in time, stand up to and defeat the British hosts.

Indeed, Washington's reference to a new army had specific meaning. During September and October 1776, as Congressional delegates received reports of Howe's destructive course, they acceded to Washington's pleas for a regular force, one consisting of soldiers with more than patriotic resolve to keep them in the field. The new Continental army would be made up of disciplined long-termers serving for a minimum of three years or the duration of the war. They would be rigorously trained to withstand close order volleys and bayonet charges until they became fully proficient at the art of war.[18] Then Washington, with his Europeanized army, would accept an all-out battle, knowing that the results might well bring American independence.

Establishing this regular force flew in the face of the colonists' traditional fear of standing armies. A standing army of long-term Continentals, Whig ideology held, could easily wipe away the very liberties that Americans sought to gain. Long-term "soldiers are apt to consider themselves as a Body distinct from the rest of the Citizens," Samuel Adams had counseled before the military setbacks of 1776. "They have their Arms always in their hands. Their Rules and their Discipline is severe. They soon become attached to their officers and disposed to yield implicit obedience to their Commands." "Such a Power," Adams had warned, "should be watched with a jealous Eye."[19]

Only military necessity caused Congress to regularize the Continental establishment, and to risk the formation of an army that might turn against American civilians and the cause of liberty. The change had to be taken, since it was obvious before the spring of 1777 that patriotic appeals would not lure respectable citizens of property into long-term service. To secure adequate troop strength, Congress now sought to draw the poor, dependent, and unfree classes into military service. They would be enticed by enlistment bounties, regular wages, and promises of free land at war's end.[20]

These new soldiers, however, would be subject to more rigorous rules governing their behavior. Congress revised the Articles of War in September 1776 so that more brutal levels of corporal punishment (up to 100 lashes well-laid-on) could be administered for minor infractions, and the delegates expanded the list of major crimes for which soldiers could be executed. These penalties were still milder than those of the British code, but the toughened Articles reflected increased concern about controlling the propertyless persons who would now fill the ranks of the Continental army.[21]

The benefits of such an army appeared to outweigh the dangers. For one thing, a soldiery of rootless persons would not object to marching from one geographic locale to another, wherever British armies threatened. Their presence, moreover, would serve as a rallying magnet in these war zones for militia units, which hopefully would come out for short periods to protect families and property. In this way, Washington's hard-core regulars would be deployed to overcome the obstacles of defending so much space and the revived localism of most colonists.

Once fully devised, this system of defense, predicated upon a new, standing force of Continentals, worked masterfully, as Howe learned before the end of the 1777 campaign season. After failing to engage Washington in central New Jersey, he put 15,000 regulars on troop transports and sailed for Philadelphia. Howe had reckoned correctly about one matter. Washington would lead his troops out of the hills in an attempt to protect the rebel capital, and Howe got his set piece battle in mid-September at Brandywine Creek. A well-planned flanking maneuver almost finished the Continentals, but they managed to escape after suffering 900 casualties, as compared to 550 for the British.

Howe entered the enemy capital without opposition later in the month, only to discover over the next few weeks that he had gained absolutely nothing. Unlike London or Paris, Philadelphia lacked critical strategic value, so capturing it really meant nothing. Congress simply moved elsewhere. Washington's army, moreover, was still in the field. Worse yet, another Continental army, one that Howe had not reckoned with, had rendered the whole British campaign a shambles.

The seeds of the British disaster of 1777 were sown two years earlier. In July 1775, upon Washington's recommendation and the need for specific oversight of the Canadian invasion, Congress established a command department separate from the main army. This New York Department, more commonly known as the Northern Department, first fell under the purview of General Philip Schuyler of Albany, who although subordinate to Washington, had permission to communicate directly with Congress.[22]

Congress had acted to protect the many vulnerable stretches of American territory, assuming that enough troops could be assembled. The Continental army could function in coordinated parts, rather than as a massed whole, making it possible to have vital centers of resistance in more than one locale at any time. Thus, while Washington's army had besieged Boston in 1775, the northern army had invaded Canada. In 1776, shortly after Howe began the New York campaign, a second British force numbering 10,000 under General Guy Carleton, Quebec's governor, sought to invade New York from the north.[23] Carleton's army never made it. In the face of stout resistance offered by a hastily assembled Northern Department naval fleet under the command of General Benedict Arnold, Carleton retreated to Canada, thereby delaying for another season the invasion of northern New York.

British strategy focused on gaining control of the Hudson River/Lake Champlain water corridor running north from New York City to Montreal. Once secured, British forces were to sweep eastward and crush resistance in New England. With these troublesome rebels back under imperial control, King George and his ministers assumed that resistance would collapse everywhere else.

For some reason, perhaps Washington's daring sorties against Trenton and Princeton, Howe decided not to support the British troops scheduled to drop out of Canada in 1777, but to focus on the "principal" rebel army and Philadelphia, Anyway, he did not think that the northern British army would need much assistance. As he wrote to Carleton in April, "the friends of Government in that part of the country [upper New York] will be found so numerous and so ready to give every aid and assistance in their power, that it will prove no difficult task to reduce the more rebellious parts of the province."[24]

Thus Howe dismissed as inconsequential a second vital center of rebel resistance, the Northern Department of the Continental army. General John Burgoyne, in many ways, never had a chance. In July, when his force of 8,000 overran Fort Ticonderoga, General Schuyler had 5,200 Continentals around with which to rally the regional populace. As these soldiers impeded Burgoyne's progress, Schuyler sent out pleas for militia support. Congress's decision to relieve Schuyler in favor of Horatio Gates as Northern Department commander helped to bring in some 10,000 militiamen from New England. Before Burgoyne surrendered in mid-October, Gates had a three-to-one advantage in troop strength. Continentals, effectively supported by militia under the command of a regional Department, had confounded Burgoyne, Howe, and the British Highlands strategy.[25]

The crushing patriot victory at Saratoga changed the war. France entered the conflict in 1778, turning what had begun as a civil rebellion into a world war. In response, the king's ministers redeployed British troops to protect West Indian sugar islands and to guard the British Isles against a possible French invasion. Sir Henry Clinton, who replaced Howe following the disastrous 1777 campaign, received orders to pull out of Philadelphia, to retreat to New York City, and to prepare to evacuate the continent, if necessary.

In marching across New Jersey, Clinton clashed with pursuing Continentals at Monmouth Court House. At day's end, the American long-term regulars controlled the field. Clinton had learned that Washington's regulars now possessed the training to duel evenly with British regulars in open field combat. There is irony here. At last Washington had a proficient Continental force, one that even knowledgeable European military authorities could admire. It was the type of army that he lacked when Howe urged him to battle in New Jersey a little over a year before. Now it was Clinton's turn to avoid an all-out fight. Just as Washington stayed in the hills during the spring of 1777, Clinton repeatedly refused to come out of New York City to engage the Continentals in a climactic, set piece battle. Frustrated by these circumstances, Washington kept devising plans for a showdown assault on Clinton's New York base. But with the intervention of other European nations, and with Britain's decision to disperse some of its troops to other parts of the globe, the major battles in the North were over.

Even before they abandoned Philadelphia, the British swung their strategic focus southward. Lord George Germain, serving as secretary for American affairs, had the capacity, unlike Howe, to reckon with the way that the decentralized Continental army had stunned Burgoyne. "It cannot be expected that farmers or men of property accustomed to a life of ease will engage in the military service for an indefinite time, or expose themselves ... to places remote from their own possessions," he wrote to Clinton in a "most secret" letter of March 1778. They would, however, "take up arms as an embodied militia," if directly threatened by an unfriendly force. "Such appear to be the methods taken by the rebels for strengthening their army," concluded Germain, "and I am commanded to recommend the experiment to your consideration."[26]

Britain's southern strategy, then, took some of its form from the Continental army's primary method of resistance. Germain urged Clinton to deploy a small force of regulars from New York to serve as a rallying point for southern loyalists, whom British officials erroneously believed were far more numerous than in the North. Local loyalists, gathering into militia and special forces units, would serve as substitutes for regulars now being drawn off to other parts of the globe. The king's friends would provide the numerical strength for pacifying their own communities. Once geographic areas had been secured militarily, these same persons would then be charged with reestablishing royal government while the regular British force moved forward into new areas and began the pacification process all over again. In time, the whole South would be made secure and could then serve as a staging arena for reconquering the northern provinces.[27]

Clinton followed the script. In November 1778 he sent out 3,500 troops to capture Savannah, Georgia. This force did draw out loyalist militia, and by early 1779 the southernmost of the rebellious colonies was back under British control. During that year Germain continued to encourage Clinton to take the next step and launch an expedition against Charleston, South Carolina. But the British commander, perplexed by Washington's possible assault on New York, delayed. Finally, however, he sailed south with an expeditionary force of 7,600 and put Charleston under siege in April 1780. Waiting for him was the Southern Department commander, General Benjamin Lincoln, with 3,000 Continentals and 2,500 militia.

Back in February 1776, Congress had established the Continental army's Southern Department in response to a detached British force under General Clinton, then threatening the Carolinas. Congress named controversial General Charles Lee as the first Southern Department commander, and he provided invaluable leadership in checking Clinton's assault on Charleston in mid–1776. For the next thirty months, with British forces concentrating on the North, the Southern Department was not active, but rebel militia units neutralized both loyalists and Indian nations.[28]

When the war shifted to the South in late 1778, Congress reactivated the Continental command structure for that region. General Lincoln arrived too late to help organize Georgia's populace against the British invaders, but he worked tirelessly throughout 1779 to prepare Charleston for an expected assault. Lincoln's efforts were unavailing, however. As Clinton tightened his siege lines during April and May of 1780, the local populace grew weary of the British cannonade, which they feared would destroy their town and their property. They exhorted Lincoln to submit.

On May 12, as formal surrender ceremonies took place, the British celebrated their capture of the whole of the Continental army's Southern Department. At last, it seemed, they had seriously wounded the rebels, beating them at their own game. And without a regional command structure to focus patriot resistance, pacification of South Carolina could proceed quickly. But there was a snag. Clinton and his immediate subordinate, Charles, Lord Cornwallis, had not reckoned with yet another type of Continental army—one that functioned with replaceable parts. In mid-July Congress named General Gates to take over the Southern Department. Within a matter of days Gates raised his standard in North Carolina, where 1,200 regulars waited. Some militia units did rally, and Gates rushed into South Carolina, only to see his "grand army" of 4,000 destroyed at Camden in mid-August by a smaller force under Cornwallis, whom Clinton had placed in charge of the British southern campaign. Fewer than 1,000 of Gates's soldiers made it back to North Carolina.

In little more than three months, the British had mastered two regional Continental forces. Now too confident with success, Cornwallis, rather than focusing on pacification, moved into North Carolina, allowing his loyalist regiments to torture and kill local rebels, as well as pillage and burn their property. Then, as his left wing, mostly loyalists under Major Patrick Ferguson, approached the Appalachians, "over-the-mountain-men" gathered their guns and began to stalk this column. Ferguson retreated and chose a defensive site atop King's Mountain, where in early October 1780 the frontier partisans attacked from all sides. They wiped out Ferguson's loyalists before melting back into the woods.

The American victory at King's Mountain, reflecting the brutal nature of partisan warfare in the vicinity of Cornwallis's army, was the first setback for Britain's southern strategy. Loyalists had learned that the presence of British arms could not guarantee them complete safety, and they were less willing to join Cornwallis's ranks in the days ahead.

In early December General Nathanael Greene arrived in Charlotte, North Carolina, and yet again raised the Continental standard—for the third time in seven months. Greene's presence and strategy amazed Cornwallis. Rather than concentrating what few troops he had, Greene divided them into three groups. "It makes the most of my inferior force," he wrote to Washington, "for it compels my adversary to divide his, and holds him in doubt as to his own line of conduct."[29] All three columns would employ harassing tactics, but they were to treat the local populace with respect, not only to procure food and supplies but to get citizens to support them, perhaps even in arms.

Thus began a most incredible chase scene. When a detached force from Cornwallis's army under Banastre Tarleton caught up with General Daniel Morgan's troops at Hannah's Cowpens early in 1781, the "Old Wagoner" wheeled around and all but annihilated this British adversary. Meanwhile, the second column, consisting of cavalry under "Light Horse" Harry Lee, swept southward around Cornwallis to link up with rebel partisans under "Swamp Fox" Francis Marion, and they helped to loosen the loyalist grip on South Carolina. Greene, for his part, retreated northward, with Cornwallis pursuing him all the way into Virginia before turning south and squaring off for a fight in mid-March at Guilford Court House in North Carolina.

After this indecisive engagement, Cornwallis broke off the chase and retreated with his exhausted army to Wilmington, North Carolina, where he rested his soldiers and considered further actions. Like Howe in late 1777, Cornwallis had become hopelessly confused. In a year's time he had engaged three different Southern Department Continental armies, and the third one had the audacity to divide itself into three parts. But unlike Howe, who could only promise defensive operations, Cornwallis decided to go completely on the offensive. Unilaterally abandoning the strategy of pacification and careful forward advances, he bolted into Virginia, and dared the Americans to test his troops in a climactic battle. Cornwallis was about to get what he wanted, but not in the fashion intended.[30]

For three years Washington had hoped for a combined Franco-American offensive against the British in New York City. Finally, the opportunity for combined operations presented itself, but in a different location—Yorktown, Virginia. With a French fleet under the Comte de Grasse sealing off a water escape route through Chesapeake Bay, and 7,800 French soldiers under the Comte de Rochambeau joining 5,800 Continentals and 3,200 militia, Washington had Cornwallis's army of 8,000 surrounded by late September 1781. Traditional siege tactics accomplished the rest for this allied version of the Continental army. Cornwallis's troops marched out of their Yorktown defenses and surrendered on October 19, 1781, as their musicians played "The World Turned Upside Down."

Having endured many defeats, the Continental armies had finally set the stage for a favorable peace settlement. But as Joseph Plumb Martin was to write, their triumph came in the wake of enormous pain and suffering. No revolutionary group had put up with worse treatment than Washington's long-termers. Martin stated that America's yeomen farmers showed much greater concern for the welfare of their cattle than the civilian populace did for the Continentals. At the Battle of Monmouth, he claimed, "a fourth part of the troops had not a scrip of anything but their ragged shirt flaps to cover their nakedness"—this after the terrible winter at Valley Forge in which hundreds of Martin's comrades had died from exposure to the elements and starvation.[31]

Scenes like those at Valley Forge explain why so many long-termers gave up and deserted. The British reported a total of 4,347 rebel soldiers and sailors fleeing to their lines during their eight month occupation of Philadelphia. Hundreds more just disappeared from camp and headed into the countryside, asking themselves why they should continue to suffer when the propertied civilian populace seemed so uncaring.[32] The majority stayed, but they seethed with anger, the kind that Private Martin still could remember forty years later.

In many ways, the post–1776 Continentals viewed themselves as the condemned of their society. Civilians and many of their officers continually labeled them the "rabble" of America, the scrapings of humanity, the natural cannon fodder of war, the real social expendables who should be happy to get by on virtually nothing, even if that meant going naked into battle, despite the bloated rhetoric of recruiters about regular pay, decent food, and plenty of clothing. If they did not like their circumstances, they were not to complain, and if they retaliated, they knew that they would be cast as the dupes of some tyrant wanting to exploit their combined military muscle to grab political power and destroy the cause of liberty. It was an unenviable, unwinnable situation for Washington's regulars.

Such civil-military tension soon was obvious to the British. Trying to take advantage of circumstances after their embarrassing campaign effort of 1777, they actively stirred up as much discord as possible, thinking that the patriot cause might collapse from the inside. In 1778 Lord Germain instructed Clinton to encourage desertions by guaranteeing that "loyalty will not be suffered to go unrewarded," and by the next year Clinton reported that "signs of disunion among the rebels are apparent; great discontent is said to prevail in the army owing to the insufficiency of pay, and the supply of provisions." Through Major John André, Clinton courted Benedict Arnold, one of Washington's most talented lieutenants, and encouraged him to renounce the cause that had treated him and so many others, whether of high or low rank in the Continental army, so ungratefully. The Arnold-André plot to seize West Point failed in the fall of 1780, but its existence reflected Arnold's disgust with a hypocritical civilian populace that kept professing a deep commitment to liberty while allowing the army "to starve in a land of plenty," as he wrote just a few days before fleeing to the British.[33]

The Continentals themselves became increasingly restive. A near revolt in the Connecticut line in 1780 came to a halt only after the soldiers had exacted promises of better food and fairer treatment. Then on January 1, 1781, the Pennsylvania line mutinied, followed three weeks later by an uprising in the New Jersey line. All of these Continentals would have agreed with a "A Jersey Soldier" who complained in 1779 about "the ungrateful disposition of the people" who, while "sauntering in idleness and luxury . . . are among the foremost to despise our poverty and laugh at our distress." As the Pennsylvanians marched toward Philadelphia from their camp near Morristown, New Jersey, two British agents joined their ranks and encouraged them to return their allegiance to the parent state. The mutineers hanged the spies. They despised American civilians, but, fortunately for the cause, these Continentals hated the British even more.[34]

Through all of these crises, Washington struggled to keep the army together. "Unless this dangerous spirit can be suppressed by force," he wrote to Congress in reporting the Jersey uprising, "there is an end to all subordination in the Army, and indeed to the Army itself."[35] Without a Continental military establishment to provide vital centers of resistance, the Revolution would be dead. Thus Washington retaliated against the Jersey mutineers, even though they had returned to camp after their grievances had been redressed. He had their leaders seized, and they were ordered to draw lots to determine which three would die at the hands of the others by firing squad. It was a harsh punishment for committed long-termers, but Washington saw no other choice if the army was to complete its agreed-upon assignment of defeating the British and securing American liberties.

Despite these mutinies, most of Washington's regulars who bore arms showed considerable restraint, lest attempting anything too threatening might permanently damage the cause. Washington's officers were also restrained, even though they, likewise, had taken to asking: "Can the Country expect Spartan Virtue in her army, while the people are wallowing in all the luxury of Rome in her declining State?"[36]

The grievances of enlistees centered on their current deprivation, but the officers sought postwar rewards. Beginning during the harsh winter at Valley Forge, they demanded pensions in recognition for their self-sacrifice, and two and a half years later they threatened Congress with mass resignations should half-pay pensions not be guaranteed. In late 1782 the officers sent a strongly worded petition to Congress demanding commutation of pensions to five years of full pay at war's end. Nationalist leaders in Congress seized upon the officers' threatening words—the officers had written of "fatal effects" for the cause, if something were not done—to exact taxation authority from the sovereign states. The nationalists went so far as to suggest to Washington, and then to Horatio Gates, second in command at the army's Newburgh, New York, cantonment, that a demonstration of the Continental army in the field, directed against the civilian populace, might result in

Congress gaining the necessary revenue sources to settle debts with the army.[37]

Washington, however, refused to play his assigned role. In a masterful presentation before the assembled officers at Newburgh, he asked how they could turn against the country "in the extremist hour of her distress." He chided them for having considered a mutiny which would result in the elevation of military over civil authority, and perhaps even dictatorship. Reminding them of their sacrifices, he urged the officers to stand by their ideals as selfless republicans. Then he pulled eyeglasses from his pocket, announcing that he wanted to read a letter. The officers were caught off guard, not knowing that their aloof, distant commander had need for spectacles. Seizing the moment, Washington calmly said: "Gentlemen, you must pardon me. I have grown gray in your service and now find myself growing blind."[38]

Washington captured the moment with that stunning phrase. To have sacrificed the energy of one's life for something less noble than free political institutions—and human liberty as opposed to military slavery—was unthinkable. The Continentals, officers and soldiers alike, had repeatedly set a higher example in the face of self-serving, parochial civilians. Now, once again, they needed to demonstrate the virtue that had been theirs all along as the real republican citizenry of revolutionary America.[39]

It would be years before the aging Continentals who peacefully laid down their arms in 1783 received pensions for essential services rendered to the new nation. Yet when these veterans looked back, they could do so with pride. They had stood after the *rage militaire* was dead and gone. They had marched all over the landscape, far from their homes (for those who had homes) to counter every major British offensive during the war. They had been ravaged by disease, inadequate shelter, food and clothing shortages, and cruel weather, but they had endured. This was their personal victory indeed.

Because they stood for the long-term fight, and because they displayed virtuous restraint at critical moments, they made a mockery of civilian fears of a standing army. By keeping their most serious group protests, like their line mutinies, within the bounds of moderation and by not staging a military coup, they established the principle that civil authority must always be superior to military might, never the obverse. Further, by choosing to lay down their arms in 1783, they cleared the way for a national frame of government, the Constitution of 1787, predicated on law rather than on the whims of those who would foment tyranny in their lust for power. Hence the Continental army endorsed and provided a critical precedent for developing a tradition of political stability in the United States.

As they endured in the field, the Continentals served as a magnet for those in militia units with the fortitude to defend specific locales. Each time militiamen appeared in camp, they became part of an American Continental force with the charge not only of protecting homes and property, but of making a distinct, separate nation. Thus Washington's regulars helped to expand the localist-oriented horizons of countless numbers of Americans. By war's end, allegiances were still primarily local, but the beginning of an identifiable national consciousness was germinating in the minds and hearts of the people.

The Continental army, everywhere it went, worked to promote national legitimacy. Washington repeatedly punished soldiers who plundered from the populace, understanding that to rob and pillage a family was to make an enemy for the republic. In the Carolinas, Greene likewise exhorted his troops, no matter how desperate for supplies, not to steal from civilians. Cornwallis, on the other hand, in abandoning his supply lines to chase after Greene, let his troops do as they pleased. They grabbed everything in sight, from friend and foe alike. The Continental army, because of its constraint, won many friends among neutrals, and even some loyalists concluded that there was substance to the Whig cant of improving the lot of humanity. As a result, the army convinced thousands that they should identify with the nation that the Continentals were fighting to build.[40]

Even though it would be naive to assume that Washington's soldiers never plundered—numerous court-martial hearings document their frequent un-savory conduct—the consistency of the army's restrained behavior toward the civilian populace was impressive. Perhaps that was because Washington's long-termers, most of whom were originally lured into the army for such mundane considerations as enlistment bounties, free food, and clothing, came to understand how essential they were to the realization of the ideals of the cause. If it was to be a revolution devoted to preserving life, liberty, and property, they could have no license to steal, pillage, maim, and kill. No matter how bitter they became toward civilians, they had to set a more noble example by becoming the embodiment of such ideals. That they did so may well have been their greatest victory.

As the years passed, they had to endure one more test. In the inevitable flood of postwar patriotism, everyone, it seemed, including Joseph Plumb Martin's neighbors, wanted to take credit for the Continental army's vic-tories. The words varied, but the message was usually similar to the July 4th New Jersey orator who, in 1793, thrilled his listeners with rhetorical flights of fancy about citizens "who have fought side by side—who have mingled their blood together," and whose sacrifices had resulted in "a union cemented in blood."[41] What was emerging with the passage of time was a national mythology about a virtuous, united populace that had stood as one through the eight years of frightful war. Private Martin and his comrades knew better, and they grumbled among themselves. Yet they accepted this pious disfiguration of reality with the same restraint that they had exercised during the war, hoping that it would bury forever the self-interested, self-serving, localist mindset that had made their victories so difficult to obtain in the first place.

3

The American Soldier
and the American Victory

Paul David Nelson

It is difficult to generalize about the typical American soldier during the revolutionary war, for in fact there were many types of American soldier, each serving the cause at different times for different reasons. Some enlisted in the Continental regulars, while others did their duty in the militia or in state units. Some were in the ranks early in the war, others later. About the only thing that they had in common was a burning desire to defeat the British and secure for the United States independence under a republican form of government. While it might be argued that their triumph was due as much to blundering British leadership as to their own martial qualities, they were far superior to their foes in one respect: their willingness to suffer deprivation, lackadaisical leadership, civilian neglect, and even a military discipline that was antithetical to personal liberty in order to secure victory. This motivation, the distinguishing characteristic of the American revolutionary fighting man, was his most precious contribution to the American victory.

At the outbreak of the war in 1775, a vast military enthusiasm prevailed in America. Many people expressed their strong conviction that the defense of liberty and the people's moral rectitude were determined by the individual citizen's willingness to fight personally for these principles. According to this logic, to be free required the risk of death, and the loss of liberty was just as surely a loss of life as dying in battle. Caught up in a *rage militaire*, as historian Charles Royster has characterized this phase of the war, America's soldiery in 1775–76 came from a wide spectrum of American society, including substantial farmers, tradesmen, and mechanics.[1] "After the battle at Lexington," said surgeon James Thacher, "such was the enthusiasm for the cause of liberty, and so general and extensive the alarm, that thousands of our citizens, who were engaged in the cultivation of their farms, spontaneously rushed to the scene of action." One of these enthusiasts, Sylvanus Wood, a shoemaker from Woburn, Massachusetts, belonged to a "minute company" that served both at Lexington under Captain John Parker and at Concord. Later Wood was at New York under Generals John Sullivan and Lord Stirling, and only after being wounded in fighting at Throgs Point did he leave the army "with great reluctance." Mothers and sisters were also infected with this early enthusiasm. The mother of four enlistees wrote her sons: "Let me beg of you, my children, that if you fall it may be like men; and that your wounds may not be on your back parts." Another woman wrote that she had sent her only brother off to the war and, she added, "had I twenty sons and brothers they should go."[2]

Many officers—especially those from outside New England—were scandalized by their soldiers' lack of discipline. David How, a leather worker from Methuen, Massachusetts, described incidents such as two troopers who "Drink'd So much That one of Them Died in About an hour or two after," and the discovery of "a man found Dead in a room with A Woman." Another New England soldier, Aaron Wright, told in his journal of an incident in which an officer over him was sent packing by the privates and replaced by one of their own. Although the officers were convinced that these "lower class" practices were destructive of military discipline and weakened the cause, the more democratic New England soldiery was not impressed with these concerns. They did not think themselves a rabble. They would have agreed with Jesse Lukens, a volunteer in Colonel William Thompson's battalion of riflemen at Boston who concluded that "the men being employed will yet, no doubt, do honor to their provinces, for this much I can say for them that upon every alarm it was impossible for men to behave with more readiness or attend better to their duty: it is only in Camp that we cut a poor figure."[3]

By the end of 1776 the widespread military enthusiasm of the first two years of the war was at an end. "The noble spirit of patriotism," said Thacher, was "in a considerable degree extinguished," and even troops already on duty were anxious to get home and let others take their turn at soldiering. Simeon Lyman, a Connecticut soldier, and his fellow citizens from that state refused at the end of 1775 to reenlist, despite the fact that General Charles Lee "curst and swore at us." Some Virginia soldiers also decided a year later to leave the army at the expiration of their enlistment, agreeing with one of their comrades "that repose should be ours," since they had served their country well and earned their rest.[4]

While these events were taking place, officers such as George Washington and Nathanael Greene, among others, were encouraging Congress to institute a policy of long-term enlistments. A more stable army of trained regulars, they maintained, could better fight the British. American officers had become convinced, said Thacher, that more "discipline and subordination" were needed among the regulars. Dependence upon militia was totally impossible, he added, what with the citizen soldiers' constant coming and going, their democratic way of electing officers, their short terms of service, and their waste while in camp. General John Lacey complained that departing militia "left their camp equipage strewn everywhere—Muskets, Cartouch-boxes, Camp Kettels, and blankets." And General Greene observed that the militia was too tenderhearted and lacking in courage "to stand the shocking scenes of war," not having been "steeled by habit or fortified by military pride" to stomach such sights. Hence, when Congress responded to the officers' pleas by voting a 75,000 man army to be enlisted for three years or the duration, and when America's more substantial citizens showed great reluctance to serve in this "new modeled" army (preferring instead to do their duty in local militia units), the makeup of the Continental army changed dramatically.[5] Thereafter, its membership came predominantly from the ranks of indentured servants, apprentices, young landless men, hired substitutes, recent immigrants, deserters from the enemy, prisoners of war, vagrants, criminals, and free blacks and slaves. In a word, the army now was drawn overwhelmingly from the bottom ranks of society, with its social origins much the same as those of the British army; more substantial citizens were only too happy to let the poor do all the fighting.[6]

After 1777, better off Americans still piously yearned for an army of citizen-soldiers, but as Royster remarked, "the hope for interchangeable citizens and soldiers no longer described the Continental Army." Its composition now was hardly likely to inspire pride among America's revolutionary citizenry. In mid–1777, Sergeant Jeremiah Greenman observed that his Rhode Island Continentals were "all most ye biger part of them old Country men [i.e., born in England or Ireland] which are very bad we are [forced] to flog them night and morning.... Sum will git drunk stab the genl horse's wen on Sentry ... others ... will leave ther post and git drunk." Joseph Plumb Martin, a private from Connecticut, graphically described the Continental Army in 1780 as "A caravan of wild beasts.... Some with two eyes, some with one, and some, I believe, with none at all ... their dialect, too, was as confused as their bodily appearance was bad and disgusting. There was the Irish and Scotch brogue, murdered English, flat insipid Dutch and some lingoes which would puzzle a philosopher."[7]

Black soldiers also began to enlist in large numbers after 1776, whereas before they had been severely restricted in their opportunities to serve. It is estimated that by the end of the war some 5,000 blacks had served in the American forces. Some free blacks fought at Bunker Hill, and according to Colonel William Prescott, one man among them, Salem Poor, "behaved like an experienced officer as well as an excellent soldier." Beginning in 1777, Massachusetts declared that blacks, both slave and free, were eligible for the state draft. Rhode Island quickly afterwards began recruiting two black battalions, and other states, such as Maryland and Virginia, allowed slaves to serve as substitutes. Only in the lower South were blacks excluded entirely. Despite distinguished service by black soldiers, prejudice against them remained high among white Continentals. Private Joseph Plumb Martin, for instance, described a "shocking" incident in which he entered a tavern in Delaware owned by "a great pot-bellied Negro," only to discover that the proprietor was married to a white woman. "I was thunderstruck," said Martin.[8]

When the war began, America's populace contained at least 100,000 potential soldiers, yet probably no more than 25,000 of these ever bore arms on the patriot side. What was it that motivated this minority of citizens to enlist? This is a question that perplexed contemporaries and has continued to fascinate scholars. Despite a vast amount of speculation, there is still no consensus. In general, there are two interpretations. The first, which may be labeled "traditional" because it has been most prevalent until recently, holds that the soldiers were motivated by devotion to the cause of liberty, by a desire to remain true to Whig virtue, by nationalism, by religion, by freedom, in sum by altruistic motives.[9]

Private Joseph Bloomfield expressed these sentiments early in the war when he said that "many young Men whose Parents are Men of good Property, Family & Circumstances... who could not be induced to enter into the Service from Interest," were quite willing to enlist "purely to Serve their Country." As for himself, Bloomfield had left a prosperous law practice in order to serve as a private, "and this purely from Patriotic Principles." George Ewing, a New Jersey soldier who enlisted in 1775 and was discharged in late 1776, arrived home just in time to hear a call to assist Washington in his retreat across the Jersies. Commenting in his diary that he was "more regardless of my own ease than my Countrys safety," Ewing joined Washington "and marched to oppose the unjust invaders of our rights." Similarly, Enoch Anderson of Pennsylvania, who fought with the Continentals in 1777, remarked that the defeat at the Brandywine had not disillusioned the American soldier: "Had any man suggested, merely hinted the idea of giving up,—of relinquishing further opposition,—he would have been knocked down, and if killed it would have been considered as no murder! Such was the spirit of the times,... such were my views."[10]

He was not alone. Joseph Hodgkins, a Massachusetts cobbler in the army at Bunker Hill and during the siege of Boston, reenlisted in 1776 because he thought it was his duty to do so, even though his wife was entreating him to come home. Private Martin reenlisted in 1777 for three years or the duration, despite having "learned something of a soldier's life, enough, I thought, to keep me at home for the future." However, one winter at home changed his mind and he reenlisted, knowing full well that his country again would fail to adequately pay and feed him. The situation, he mused, "was much like that of a loyal and faithful husband, and a light-heeled wanton of a wife. But I forgive her and hope she will do better in the future."

Although he was too old, the elderly father of James Collins expressed a willingness to serve because he believed "the nature of the case requires the best energies of every man who is a friend to liberty"; he also encouraged his son to volunteer. Early in 1781 James Thacher commented almost with amazement on the large number of soldiers who continued to reenlist in the regulars, "notwithstanding the numerous difficulties and discouragements with which our army have been compelled to struggle." Although "it may seem extraordinary" to an outside observer, he said, the soldiers who "voluntarily engage again in the same service" had good reasons for their behavior. First, "there are charms in a military life: it is here that we witness heroic actions and deeds of military glory." More importantly, he added, "there is to be found... in the bosom of our soldiers the purest principles of patriotism: they glory in the noble cause of their country, and pride themselves in contributing to its successful termination." "Nothing but Virtue [and] that great Principle, the love of our Country," declared Lieutenant Colonel John Brooks in 1777, could account for so many officers and soldiers remaining in the service.[11]

Despite the evidence adduced by the "traditional" interpreters to account for soldiers' motives, a second group of scholars has marshaled quite different arguments. These historians maintain that after 1776 the Continental Army was composed principally of lower class persons who had little political or economic stake in society, and who were motivated to service primarily by economic necessity or by a belief that joining a long-enlistment army would improve their social or economic status.[12] This was the view of General Washington, who even maintained that "whoever builds upon [patriotism] as a sufficient Basis for conducting a long and bloody War, will find themselves deceived in the end. I do not mean to exclude altogether the Idea of Patriotism. But I will venture to assert, that a great and lasting War can never be supported on this principle alone. It must be aided by a prospect of Interest or some reward." Many contemporaries agreed with Washington. Surgeon Lewis Beebe declared in 1776 that if all who fought for "the cause of Liberty" went home, "our army would be reduced to a small number." At about the same time, Sergeant William Young of Pennsylvania observed that if "Salvation comes to our guilty Land it will be through the tender Mercy of our God, and not through the Virtue of her people."[13]

Analyzing the motivation of thousands of soldiers over a nine-year period is a tricky matter at best, and proponents of one or the other of the two interpretations admit that there is considerable complexity to the question. Charles K. Bolton, an early advocate of the "traditional" point of view, soberly observed that some soldiers no doubt were moved to enlist by material and tangible considerations rather than patriotism. In fact, he said, not a few enlisted after having been gotten drunk by recruiters. Also, when volunteer enlistments fell off, authorities often were compelled to fill the

ranks of the regulars by drafting militiamen. On the other hand, Mark
Edward Lender, a proponent of the new interpretation, gives due weight in
his studies of the rank and file (especially in the period 1775–77) to patriotic
motive, while continuing to maintain that other considerations were more
important. In the final analysis, however, important criticisms of the new
interpretation have been raised by recent "traditional" interpreters such as
Charles Royster, Don Higginbotham, and Allan Millett and Peter Maslowski.

These scholars admit that new studies show the Continental army indeed
was composed of young, poor men, a fact that Americans observed while
the war was being fought. What they find problematical with the new studies
in what they call, in the words of Royster, the unwarranted inference "that
when they have shown the soldiers' poverty, they have also established that
men enlisted under the influence of economic need and ambition and not
of revolutionary ideals." This is a "misleading dichotomy," says Royster,
for none of the studies establish any correlation between a person's poverty
and his adherence to or lack of revolutionary ideals. Additionally, critics
point to a major problem with the argument that the young, poor soldiers
after 1776 joined the army in search of economic advancement, noting that
if money were their object they could have turned to alternatives such as
privateering or farm labor, either of which offered more money, food, and
comfort than service in the regulars—and usually at much less danger. Final
proof of the Continental soldier's patriotic motive, however poor his economic or social background, conclude Millett and Maslowski, is to be found
in his willingness to endure hardships almost continuously and still persev-
ere. These authors quote with appreciation Baron von Closen's statement
about American troops: "I admire [them] tremendously! It is incredible that
soldiers composed of men of every age, even children of fifteen, of whites
and blacks, almost naked, unpaid, and rather poorly fed, can march so well
and withstand fire so steadfastly." Thus, concluded these historians, "Money
could not buy, and discipline could not instill, the Continentals' type of
loyalty; an ideological motivation that promised a better life for themselves
and their posterity held them in the ranks," even though they were from
the lower ranks of American society.[14]

Also, it was this ideological motivation that compelled the Continental
soldier to subordinate his personal freedom—the very thing for which he
fought—to the necessities of military discipline. From the comments of
General Washington and some other observers, one would be led to believe
that the American regular was a rather undisciplined, poor fighter. The
commander-in-chief, in fact, believed that he faced a paradox in trying to
mold his soldiers into effective combatants. It was a desire to preserve their
freedom that had brought his men to rebellion and military service in the
first place, but this same freedom made them poor fighters. Although personally courageous, they were impatient of restraint and discipline, and

discipline was at the heart of any well functioning army. This "problem" was never resolved to Washington's, or to any other general's, satisfaction, because the American soldiers' independent spirits were never subdued during the war. The best America's officers could hope for, as Robert Middlekauff has noted, was that they might create a standing army "composed of free men broken of some of the worst habits freedom engendered."[15]

Despite the rather gloomy assessment by the generals, the soldiers gradually learned from hard experience in combat that they needed to accept military discipline and training. So when General Friedrich von Steuben commenced drilling the Continentals at Valley Forge, they bemusedly went along with him, prompting the Prussian volunteer to remark that "the genius of this nation" was not to be compared with the European mentality. In Austria or Prussia, he added, "You say to your soldier, 'Do this,' and he doeth it, but [here] I am obliged to say, 'this is the reason why you ought to do that,' and he does it." Only the militiamen never willingly subordinated their freedom to the self-restraints necessary to function as an army, and they were branded by General Nathanael Greene as "Ungovernable." Militiamen insisted on electing their own officers, serving short enlistments, coming and going from camp at will, and resisting military discipline. Ultimately, not only the officers but also the Continental soldiers mistrusted them.[16]

Private Joseph Plumb Martin, for instance, scoffed at those who believed the war could have been won with militia soldiers. Such troops, he declared, never would have endured the suffering and hardships that the regulars bore with fortitude; "they would have considered themselves (as in reality they were and are) free citizens, not bound by any cords that were not of their own manufacturing," he wrote, "and when the hardships of fatigue, starvation, cold and nakedness . . . began to seize upon them in such awful array as they did on us, they would have instantly quitted the service in disgust, and who would blame them?" Perhaps Martin was too hard on his militia comrades, for in fact some did hold and fight, as at Bunker Hill and Princeton. On these occasions, the key to their successful performance, according to Middlekauff, seemed to be that they were standing on the battlefield in proximity with their neighbors and were unwilling to "disgrace" themselves or besmirch their "honor" by breaking in front of those persons whom they most wanted to impress. Later, in the South, the militiamen were much less familiar to each other and they did not do so well in battle. Inadequately trained, poorly disciplined, and lacking the personal bonds with their fellow combatants that might have held them to their duty, the trainbandsmen often failed when confronted with the horrors of the battlefield.[17]

What was it that caused the American soldier, once he had become a member of the regular forces and accepted military discipline on the drill field and in camp, to risk death or mutilation in battle? Why did he choose to stand and fight once he had engaged the enemy? Some scholars have suggested that factors such as fear of their own officers inspired leadership, and even the lure of plundering those killed in battle largely determined the conduct of the soldier. Additional factors may have been more significant, however. In some cases, a soldier's fear was artificially suppressed by extra rations of rum just before battle; according to a sergeant who fought at Princeton, some patriot soldiers used "rum . . . to promote courage" during that battle. Often soldiers were sustained by a belief in the protection of Divine Providence, and in diaries and letters of ordinary troopers there are many references to God's power. A significant number of the men—including even those not given to "an orderly, decorous piety"—believed that the cause itself was sacred, that God had given His blessing to the Revolution. Chaplains were not loath to remind their flocks that the war was just and providential. It was not unusual for a soldier to declare that he was fighting for "the sacred cause of freedom," or for chaplains to choose sermon texts that reinforced the soldier's surety that he fought for a noble cause. Other men were convinced that they enjoyed God's protection of their persons in battle and that they were fulfilling His will by serving in the Revolution. Joseph Hodgkiss, in his letters to his wife, Sarah, referred often to "gods Providence and hope in his mercy for Salvation & Deliverance from all the Eavels," and he confidently asserted, "as I am engaged in this glories Cause I am will to go whare I am Called."[18]

One very important factor contributing to the soldier's willingness to fight was his deeply felt sense of loyalty and responsibility to his nearest military colleagues and his desire not to let them or himself down. In a sense, this attitude was like that held by successful militiamen, although the Continental soldier's closest comrades were not his civilian neighbors. Yet if soldiers' testimony may be relied upon, the troops who served together became closer than neighbors. "We had lived together as a family of brothers for several years," said Joseph Plumb Martin of his most intimate military colleagues, and "had shared with each other the hardships, dangers, and sufferings incident to a soldier's life; had sympathized with each other in trouble and sickness; had assisted in bearing each other's burdens . . . ; had endeavored to conceal each other's faults. . . . In short, the soldiers, each in his particular circle of acquaintance, were as strict a band of brotherhood as Masons and, I believe, as faithful to each other." These close relationships sustained individual soldiers upon the battlefield, for the arena of conflict in the eighteenth century was narrow enough to allow individual soldiers to see his near comrades and sustain personal relationships even in battle. More importantly, as Middlekauff has pointed out, the limited battlefield robbed the entire process "of some of its mystery" and "permitted the troops to give one another moral or psychological support." Hence, the soldiers did not feel the terrible loneliness that has come to characterize the empty battlefield of the twentieth century.[19]

The patriot soldier also believed that he was the only source of "virtue" left in a revolutionary movement that otherwise had been corrupted by civil and political vice. He felt martyred to the cause, but he also felt that only he could, or would, see things through to the end. Hence, the Continental army, which was recruited more and more from the poor and dispossessed, fought better as it came to resemble its apolitical British counterpart. Its members were infused with a "tough professional ethic." They were proud of themselves and challenged one another to behave bravely, to be courageous, honest, and gallant in the service of liberty. In battle they placed greater emphasis on virtuous behavior—which they defined as devotion to the public trust—rather than upon saving their own lives.

Even though the Continental soldiers thought themselves to be little more than hired killers for an uncaring civilian populace, they were compelled to make a moral choice between standing firm and upholding their own and their comrades' honor, or of running away and serving only themselves. The rank and file, as one contemporary put it, could either accept "the hazard of dying like heroes, or be certain of living like cowards." James P. Collins, a soldier at King's Mountain, described his personal struggle with conflicting demands of duty and self-preservation. Before the battle, he wrote, each "leader made a short speech in his own way to his men, desiring every coward to be off immediately. Here I confess I would willingly have been excused, for my feelings were not the most pleasant... but I could not well swallow the appellation of cowards." He stayed and fought. Private Martin, expressing his disgust at seeing a lieutenant in hysterics during the battle of Long Island, declared, "I would have then suffered anything short of death rather than have made such an exhibition of myself."[20]

The American soldier's decision to fight, even if for the noblest of motives, was not to be made lightly. Battles could be sanguinary, ghastly affairs. Indeed, a greater percentage of the soldiers succumbed in the revolutionary fighting than in any conflict other than the Civil War. During the battle of Bunker Hill, Amos Farnsworth, a young corporal from Groton, Connecticut, was twice wounded, but he proudly recorded in his diary, "I did not leave the entrenchment until the enemy got in." During that same fight, Joseph Hodgkiss and his unit were "Exposed to a very hot fire of Cannon & small armes about two ours But we whare Presarved I had one Ball went under my arme and out a large hole in my Coate & a Buck shot went throue my coate & Jacket But neither of them Did me any harme." Private Jeremiah Greenman, with the patriot army at Quebec, remembered how the soldiers "With hearts undaunted [decided] to scal the walls" of the citadel, but after their commander, Colonel Benedict Arnold, was wounded, they were captured and "marched... into a french Jesseuit College." Describing the same events, Private John Joseph Henry cryptically recorded in his diary: "About nine o'clock, A.M., it was apparent to all of us that we must surrender. It was done."[21]

Some soldiers found it extremely difficult to write about the horrors of battle. Others did so almost matter of factly. Michael Graham, who fought at Long Island in the summer of 1776, found it impossible "to describe the confusion and horror of the scene . . . the artillery flying . . . , our men running in almost every direction, and run which way they would, they were almost sure to meet the British or Hessians." Describing the same battle, Enoch Anderson recollected that the "British pressed hard upon us with far superior numbers . . . I was wounded,—a bullet struck me on the chin and run down into my neck. Many fell, many were wounded. About three o'clock in the afternoon a retreat was ordered. We crossed over a mill-dam on a foot bridge" and thereby reached relative safety. Another soldier in the battle asserted, more pugnaciously, that he "had the satisfaction of dropping one of [the enemy] the first fire I made; I was so near that I could not miss. I discharged my rifle seven times that day as deliberately as ever I did at a mark, and with as little perturbation." Jabez Fitch wrote in his diary that it took Captain Joseph Jewett thirty-six hours to die of bayonet wounds after the fighting at Long Island.[22]

Enoch Anderson, a veteran of the battle of White Plains, wrote that a "soldier of our regiment was mortally wounded. . . . He fell to the ground;— in falling, his gun fell from him. He picked it up,—turned on his face,— took aim at the British, who were advancing,—fired,—the gun fell from him,—he turned over on his back and expired." Elisha Bostwick, a Connecticut soldier who was in the same battle, observed a cannon ball plow through "Lt. Youngs Platoon, which was next to that of mine the ball first cut off the head of Smith . . . then took Taylor across the bowels, it then struck Sergeant Garret of our Company on the hip took off the point of the hip bone . . . Oh! What a sight that was to see . . . those men with their legs and arms and guns and packs all in a heap." Sergeant Thomas McCarty, later remembering a skirmish with a British foraging party in New Jersey, wrote that his unit "attacked the body and bullets flew like hail. We stayed about 15 minutes and then retreated with loss." British soldiers then proceeded to slaughter American wounded that had been left on the field. "They dashed out their brains with their muskets and run them through with their bayonets. . . . This was barbarity to the utmost." The battle of the Brandywine was graphically described by Private Elisha Stevens, who recalled that the engagement had lasted an entire day "with out much Seasation of arms Cannons Roaring muskets Cracking Drums beating Bumbs Flying all Round. Men a dying Woundes Horred Grones which would Greave the Heardest of Hearts to See Such a Dollful Sight." Joseph Clark, a New Jersey soldier in the same battle, remembered that "the valley was filled with smoke, and now I grew seriously anxious for the event. . . . About sunset I saw a column of the enemy advance to one of our batteries to take it, . . . an engagement began with musketry, and the enemy gave way."[23]

James P. Collins a soldier at Cowpens in early 1781, recorded his horror at being charged by Banastre Tarleton's cavalry. " 'Now,' thought I, 'my hide is in the loft,' " he reminisced. But he was saved by William Washington's horsemen, who put Tarleton's men to flight. Exhorted by Daniel Morgan to " 'Form, form, my brave fellows [and] give them one more fire,' " Collins and his compatriots "advanced briskly" and forced a great victory. Private Josiah Atkins wrote proudly of his conduct upon the battlefield at Green Spring Farm, "We were often broke, often formed; several times almost surrounded; and yet...came off again in heart!....I cannot forget the memorable action....The fatigues of that day I cant describe." One of the most graphic and horrific battle descriptions came from a Connecticut militiaman, Jonathan Dickerson, who in 1781 was with a militia party that got cut off just below White Plains by a loyalist cavalry patrol. "The horse," he remembered later, "came upon the party full speed...calling out, 'Surrender, you damned rebels, surrender!' " But when Dickerson sought to surrender, he "was struck down to the ground, his skull fractured, and cut through the bone for four inches or more, and, while lying on the ground, was rode over and struck four strikes in the head and several in the body with a cutlass." After being plundered of his possessions, Dickerson was forced to ride with the cavalrymen about half a mile, whereupon he fainted from loss of blood and fell from his saddle. "Someone asked, 'Shall we kill him?' The captain said, 'No, let him alone. He will die soon himself.' " The Tory was wrong, however, for Dickerson was taken in by some local inhabitants and nursed back to health.[24]

The horror of battle was only one problem among many that the patriot soldier had to face, once he had decided to serve the cause to the last extreme. The ubiquitous Private Martin believed that service in advanced parties near enemy lines was almost as bad as full-fledged combat. "No one who has never been upon such duty," he declared, "can form any adequate idea of the trouble, fatigue and dangers which they have to encounter." The only thing that eased the monotony and terror of such activity was the opportunity to banter with enemy pickets, or sometimes to call local cease fires in order to exchange goods and to visit with British soldiers. Marches could be times of especial woe for the American soldier. Arnold's long trek to Quebec in 1775 was one of the most horrid episodes ever faced by American fighting men. Likewise, Joseph Hodgkiss penned a graphic description of his retreat from Long Island across New Jersey. "I am a good deal Tird of Marching," he told his wife; "I Cannot Express the hardships & fetegue we have undergone on our March from Place to Place." Another soldier sardonically described a march in which "quantities of young women" came out "on the Road to see the Glorious life of a Soldier, ragged, dirty and fainting with thirst and Drinking water out of every puddle he comes by [and eating] with as good a stomach as a dog whatever the Commissary allows him." But worse for the rank and file than any of these problems was captivity, a calamity that according to Jeremiah Greenman was at best "dismal" and at worst lethal.[25]

Camp life also could be unpleasant. While in no way comparing to the terrors of military actions or to the arduousness of long marches, the every-day routine of camp life was usually displeasing and sometimes harsh. Privates with a religious turn of mind found life in camp to be corrupting. "Wickedness prevails Very much," Joseph Hodgkiss told his wife, "to the astonishment of any that Behold them." Homesickness was a problem for others. Private Daniel Barber, noting that before the war most of the men in his company "had not been twenty miles from home," observed that they all missed their loved ones greatly. The maintenance of a healthy atmosphere was a concern of all, but personal hygiene among men in camp usually was extremely poor. Soldiers "eased themselves" wherever they wished, and one Massachusetts man was reported to have gone two months without washing his face and hands. Not surprisingly, disease was always a problem. The itch was a soldier's constant companion, as were other maladies such as the measles and smallpox. Many soldiers underwent inoculation against smallpox, in order deliberately to induce a (hopefully) mild case of the disease and head off a later, more severe one. All hospitals were dreadful places, and soldiers feared being sent there, no matter how debilitating their diseases or wounds, because they considered admission to a hospital tan-tamount to a death sentence. Sometimes sectional tensions ran high in the army contributing to the disagreeable camp life milieu. Yankees were often belabored by their comrades from east of the Hudson River for cowardice or incorrect political views, and many New Englanders certainly lost no love for Southerners.[26]

Soldiers filled their leisure time in camp with many diversions, not all of which were physically or morally salutary. A large number of the men partook to excess of strong drink, and oftentimes their imbibing led to brawling, or even murder. Some men used their free time for reading, others for dancing and music making (especially on holidays), swimming, playing games, hunting, or chasing women. Boredom was always a problem for men in camp, and Jesse Lukens, a Virginia rifleman at Boston, observed that when troops were fed up with their everyday tedium, they were "ren-dered . . . rather insolent for good soldiers." General Washington recognized the dangers of such inactivity, noting that men with time on their hands had "leisure for cherishing their discontents and dwell[ing] upon the hard-ships of their situation." Therefore, he admonished his officers to keep their troops occupied as much as possible.[27]

A great amount of the soldiers' time in camp was spent on matters of mere survival, for their living conditions during much of the year were horrendous. A sergeant described the "destitute and deplorable condition" of the army in early 1777, noting that "Our men . . . were without shoes or other comfortable clothing; and as traces of our march toward Princeton, the ground was literally marked with the blood of the soldiers' feet." Surgeon Albigence Waldo, bewailing his own lot at the end of the same year, moaned,

"I am sick, discontented, and out of humor. Poor food. Hard lodging. Cold weather. Fatigue. Nasty clothes; Nasty cooking. . . . Smoked out of my senses. The Devil's in it, I can't endure it. . . . A pox on my bad luck." At about the same time, Elijah Fisher wrote of the army's plight, "We had no tents, nor anything to Cook our Provisions in, and that was Prity Poor . . . and the Water we had to Drink and to mix our Flower [with was] very Dirty and muddy." Private Martin, suffering at Valley Forge, complained that he was in danger of perishing "in the midst of a plentiful country." What minuscule amounts of beef he did manage to procure, he snarled, were "not many degrees above carrion."[28]

The lot of the soldiery did not improve with time. In mid–1778 Jeremiah Greenman still could complain that the soldiers "suffered grately for Provisions," and Private Martin, a few months later at Morristown, New Jersey, observed sarcastically that the troops "went on in our old Continental line of starving and freezing." Describing conditions in 1779, he said, "We were absolutely, literally starved. I do solemnly declare that I did not put a single morsel of victuals into my mouth for four days and as many nights, except a little black birch bark, which I knawed off a stick of wood. . . . I saw several . . . men roast their old shoes and eat them." The duty at Morristown, according to Greenman, was "very hard, we are ordered to exercise twise a day & two battalions to parade . . . twise a Week for the purpose of exersiseing." By the summer of 1780, Samuel Cogswell said that the army was "destitute of tents and encamped in a wood with no other security from the inclemency of the weather than the boughs of trees, or now and then a bark hut." As if the soldiers did not have enough problems, they were also not being paid, at least after August, 1777, except for a single payment in specie in 1781 and promissory notes when they were furloughed at the end of the war.[29]

As if not troubled sufficiently by life in the army, the soldiery eventually discovered that even the general populace had grown unfriendly toward those who bore arms, especially after 1776, when the Continental army began to resemble the British units that Americans had come to dislike in the 1760s. Civilian suspicions, however, were based on reasons more substantial than traditional contempt for regulars. The soldiery's frequent necessity to forage aroused the greatest bitterness within the civilian sector. In 1776 a Continental soldier in New York noted that his colleagues were pillaging property in their off-duty hours. Another soldier, Daniel Barber, slyly observed that the "Devil now and then tell us, that it was no harm sometimes to pull a few potatoes and cabbages, and pluck, once in a while, an ear of corn, when we stood in need." Private Martin admitted that from time to time he pilfered "a few articles of light clothing." " 'Rub and go,' " he said jocularly, "was always the Revolutionary soldier's motto." James Thacher wrote that Washington often heard complaints that his men were "pilfering and plundering the inhabitants of poultry, sheep, pigs, and even their cattle," and the commander-in-chief always reacted vehemently against such practices, declaring repeatedly that stealing was "disgraceful." Despoilation only increased civilians' distress, he argued, when it was the army's "business to give protection and support."[30]

Several states responded to the pillaging with laws designed both to prevent the soldiers from "encroaching" upon civilian houses and to regulate indebtedness among the soldiery. Meanwhile, many soldiers received short shrift from civilians. One mean-spirited civilian even refused Sergeant John Smith a little straw with which to make a bed upon the hard, cold ground. Private Martin, also unlucky in his treatment by noncombatants, complained that "If I stepped into a house to warm me when passing, wet to the skin and almost dead with cold, hunger, and fatigue, what scornful looks and hard works have I experienced."

The soldiers thoroughly resented the neglect and haughtiness that civilians directed their way, and in time those who bore arms became almost totally isolated from the larger society, forming attachments largely within the ranks of the army. Thus, the civilians' endemic fear of regular soldiers and standing armies, manifesting itself as a contempt and fear of their own troops, might have resulted in the creation of the very monster they wished away. However, the soldiers did not lash out against their "tormentors" by becoming militaristic or by using armed might against them, but they did blame civilians for many of their woes. They were convinced, with reason, that congressional neglect of their salaries was improverishing their families at home. Sarah Hodgkiss wrote her husband in 1776, urging him to come home and attend to his family's needs. "Let Some body else take your Place," she implored. It took Hodgkiss two years to relent to such entreaties, but relent he did, for he at last became thoroughly disgusted at having to spend his entire salary just to keep himself in the field, leaving nothing to send home.[31]

The soldiers also believed that civilian apathy and venality contributed to their distress. Years later Joseph Plumb Martin bitterly recollected what the government provided for the soldiers' Thanksgiving dinner in 1777: "our country, ever mindful of its suffering army opened her sympathizing heart so wide, upon this occasion, as to give us something to make the world stare. And what do you think it was, reader? Guess. You cannot guess, be you as much of a Yankee as you will. I will tell you; it gave each and every man *half* a *gill* of rice and a *tablespoonful* of vinegar!!"[32]

The soldiers also profoundly resented what they perceived as the rapacious profiteering among civilians while they perished from inattention. General Washington warned congressmen about this widespread feeling among both officers and enlisted men, asserting that "the large Fortunes acquired by numbers out of the Army, affords a contrast that gives poignance to every inconvenience from remaining in it." The Continentals' viewpoint on this matter was expressed by a "Jersey Soldier" who wrote in 1779 that it was "truly mortifying to the virtuous soldier to observe many, at this day, displaying their cash, and sauntering in idleness and luxury," while the long-suffering soldier, who "has been generous and patriotic beyond a parallel in history, in serving three active and difficult campaigns, without the compensation of pay, and destitute of those enjoyments which make life tolerable," had received neither the thanks nor the approbation of his ungrateful countrymen.[33]

If the soldiers stayed with their duty because of singular devotion to honor and virtue, and if they did so in spite of civilian neglect, they did not romanticize their military existence or pretend that it was a superior way of life. On the contrary, the average soldier remained a civilian at heart, wishing with all his soul to be rid of his dreary martial routine and forever resisting any and all attempts by his officers to "regularize" him. In fact, most troopers had a hearty contempt for officers, especially for those with pretensions to "gentlemanly" status but with no military ability. Private Elisha Stevens thought his company commander, Captain Peter Mills, "Voyd of all grace," and Sergeant John Smith was critical of officers who left camp when they should remain with their men. Joseph Plumb Martin spoke the feelings of most of his comrades when he roundly condemned the officers for their unfeeling and contemptuous attitude toward the rank and file: "We might have been [dead] for aught they knew or cared.... [T]hey did not feel the hardships we had to undergo, and of course cared but little, if anything at all, about us." Usually, if soldiers liked an officer they did so despite his airs and because he had merit. Private David Barber remembered Lieutenant E. Fitch Bissel as a gentleman not of "familiar turn," but still "steady and correct [in his] attention to the duties of his station."[34]

Although patriot soldiers were willing to put up with a great amount of privation and scorn, they were sometimes pushed beyond endurance and protested their lot in diverse, and at times ingenious, forms. As a general rule, the soldiers' discontents manifested themselves in mild dissent. Corporal Lemuel Roberts, who was disgusted at a general for working him too hard, took night sentry duty outside the offender's tent in order to keep up "such a stamping on the loose boards of the stoop, as to prevent his sleeping." The general sent out a colonel to quiet Roberts, and this officer, "judging rightly of the existing facts," gave the soldier a whiskey jug, "with a request" that he be quiet. "His politeness," said Roberts, "very much favored the churlish general's repose." Sometimes, soldiers would use swearing as a form of protest, because they knew it annoyed their officers; although Washington in general orders called profanity "a vice productive of neither Advantage or Pleasure" and subversive of "decency and order," the soldiers continued merrily to employ the most horrific oaths and cursing in their conversations. Wearing long hair and hats with irregular and asymmetrical shapes also became favorite ways for the men to vex their superiors. The more commanders such as Anthony Wayne railed against "unmilitary" hair styles, and the more they insisted that their men wear "soldier-like" hats, the more the troops resisted such pressures. Some men used excessive drinking as a form of protest, deliberately inebriating themselves in order to irritate their officers and get out of work. General Peter Muhlenberg observed in 1777 that it was "a practice" of a few of his troops to get drunk "once a Day" in order to "render themselves unfit for duty."[35]

On occasion soldiers adopted more serious forms of protest. Sometimes they simply refused to work. Private James Stevens described an instance wherein a captain "spok very rash concerning our chusing a sargent... which displeased the soldiers very much they went of and did no duty that day." Not until the offending captain made "sum recantation" did the soldiers return to their duty. At other times, soldiers deserted in protest of unfair treatment, taking to swamps and woods to avoid having to serve under what they perceived as unfair conditions. Often, as Private Martin noted, the soldiers took more spontaneous and direct actions against cruel treatment meted out to one of their fellows. At Peekskill in 1779, a "rag-amuffin" hangman was recruited by the officer in charge to execute a deserter. The soldiers, as was customary, were made to assemble and watch the punishment, but when the executioner, as also was the custom, began to strip the corpse, the outraged soldiery revolted, forcing an end to the hangman's vulturous endeavors. Soldiers sometimes conducted mutinous parades, refusing to disperse after the officers had dismissed them. On one such occasion in 1780, described by Martin, "We...kept still upon our parade in groups, venting our spleen at our country and government, then at our officers, and then at ourselves for our imbecility in staying there and starving in detail for an ungrateful people who did not care what became of us."[36]

The most potent weapon of protest in the soldiers' arsenal was mutiny, and from 1777 to 1783 Continental troops availed themselves of this last resort on twenty-eight occasions. However, its terror was lessened for officers and civilians alike by a general recognition that the enlistees did not want to go to such extremes, even under the harshest of conditions. Private Martin, commenting on the ease with which a near-mutiny in the Connecticut line was suppressed in 1780, noted that while the soldiers were "unwilling to desert the cause," they were caught in a dilemma. "What signified our perishing in the act of saving [the country]," he asked, "when the very act would destroy us" and bring the nation to ruin as well? The fault for mutinous infractions of military discipline, he said, lay not with the mutineers but with uncaring civilians that had allowed the situation to come to such a desperate pass. As for the troops, they "saw no other alternative but to starve to death, or break up the army, give all up and go home. This was a hard matter for the soldiers to think upon. They were truly patriotic, they loved their country... but to starve to death was too much also." So, on parade they stood "growling like sorehead dogs," only calming down a little after receiving some provisions. Even in the great Pennsylvania mutiny of 1781, the majority of soldiers wanted to remain in the service if they could but acquire some food and clothing, and they were more devoted to the ideal of revolutionary virtue than to brotherly solidarity. Hence, the mutiny was quelled more easily by officers than many had thought possible when the troubles commenced.[37]

After suffering virtually every imaginable travail, American soldiers finally prevailed in the revolutionary war, winning for the United States both independence and a republican form of government. Although most who enlisted after 1776 were drawn from the lower social economic orders, those soldiers had proved themselves to be devoted to both republican virtue and the desire to avoid the "corruption" of militarization. When the fighting ended, therefore, they looked forward to quick demobilization and a return to civilian life. They also hoped, without much conviction, that they might at last be rewarded in some small way by their fellow citizens. Not only were they convinced that victory had been achieved largely because of their dedication and suffering, but they also felt that they alone of all Americans involved in the Revolution had upheld republican virtue and honor.

At war's end, however, the soldiers met with disappointment. According to Private Martin, the Continentals returned to society "starved, ragged," with no money "and no means or method in view to remedy or alleviate their condition. This was appalling in the extreme." As far as neglectful officers and civilians were concerned, he added, "It was, soldiers, look to yourselves; we want no more of you," and the rank and file considered it "cruel to be thus vilified." Perhaps Martin exaggerated the degree to which the soldiers went unrewarded, but not by much. It was to be many years before he and his colleagues received any compensation, partly because America's postwar governments were financially straitened, but largely because the citizenry and its political representatives did not think the issue very important. Therefore, military pay and bonus certificates, which were issued in lieu of salary to soldiers at the time of their dismissal from service, were not redeemed until the 1790s. Even then, the money from those redemptions often went to speculators who had bought the certificates at greatly reduced rates. Also, bounty lands promised by Congress to veterans at the end of the war were not forthcoming for more than a decade, and by then land warrants, like pay and bonus certificates, often had been sold to second parties and outsiders. Not until 1818 did Congress vote a pension for all veterans who could prove need, and it was 1828 before the veterans' pensions were made equal to their former military pay.[38] However, the nation's gratitude to its long-suffering Continental soldiery, so long in coming, was too late for those who had died during the wait.

4

George Washington
and the American Victory

John Ferling

Before June, 1775, George Washington had never commanded more than 1000 men. Only once before had he taken an army into battle against a conventional European force, and he had lost that engagement. But his fellow delegates in the Continental Congress believed that he had "great experience and abilities in military matters."[1]

Washington's fellow congressmen gave many other reasons for entrusting him with command of the provincial army. He was modest, discreet, polite, sober, patient, composed, and generous, they said. Some also had heard that he was courageous, and still others had been told of his reputation as an efficient and resolute administrator. That he was willing to risk his great fortune in the common cause was still another positive factor. To John Hancock, the new appointee was simply "a fine man." To Eliphalet Dyer, Washington's selection was essential primarily because it would "more strongly Cement the Southern with the Northern Colonies."[2]

Other colonists had served as officers during the French and Indian War, and some even had soldiered in King George's War thirty years before, but none had commanded as many men for such a long period as had Washington. There also were men available with a background of command in the British army, but that very experience tended to disqualify them in the eyes of many. Moreover, of all the men who could have been considered for the commander's post, Washington alone had attended both the First and the Second Continental Congress. He alone had been present to be scrutinized and evaluated by the congressmen; Washington, they were confident, could be trusted not to misuse the awesome power entrusted to the commander.

Congress did not just name a commander on that warm, summer day in Philadelphia. It created an army, transforming the New England militia force that besieged occupied Boston into a national army. To broaden the resistance, Yankee political leaders sought a non–New Englander to take command of the new army, while powerful southern congressmen, especially those from the Chesapeake, yearned to place one of their own—particularly one who, like themselves, was interested in western expansion—in a position of authority.[3]

Thus, on June 15, 1775, Washington was Congress's choice "to command all the continental forces."[4] Time would tell whether Congress had correctly judged this man who was naturally reserved and aloof, and difficult to fathom.

Some ambitious young men of middling status in eighteenth-century Britain and its American colonies sought economic and social mobility through a military career. Horatio Gates, born in Maldon, England, to parents of low rank, chose a career in the British army in an attempt to escape the obscurity and financial scantness likely to be his lot. Seeking to make a name for himself and to escape the shadow of his famous father, William Franklin volunteered at age nineteen or twenty to serve in a provincial force raised to invade French Canada. Youthful John Adams knew that soldiering was the quickest means by which a young man could "cut a flash," and he later admitted that he had "longed more ardently to be a Soldier than I ever did to be a Lawyer." But he could never make the decision to bear arms. Young Alexander Hamilton would have given anything for such an opportunity. Unlike Adams, who was twenty-one years old when the French and Indian War broke out, Hamilton reached maturity a few years after the conflict ended. "I contemn the grovling and condition of a Clerk or the like, to which my Fortune, &c., contemns me. I wish there was a War," he bleated in the peacetime year of 1769.[5] George Washington had better luck, and unlike Adams he displayed no hesitancy in seizing his opportunity.

The third son of a prosperous planter and businessman, Washington seemed fated for a comfortable existence, albeit one as a modest and obscure Virginia planter.[6] Only eleven when his father died, George inherited ten slaves and a spent farm on the Rappahanock, as well as some underdeveloped lands elsewhere. Without liquid assets or a profitable plantation, and without a formal education, Washington's prospects appeared limited. By age fifteen or sixteen he had come to see his likely destiny as intolerable.

It was young Washington's growing awareness of the very different world inhabited by his half brother, Lawrence, that most profoundly altered his aspirations. Educated in England, owner through inheritance of Mount Vernon, a promising estate on the Potomac River, and related through marriage to the Fairfax family, the wealthiest and most powerful clan in the Northern Neck of Virginia, Lawrence must have cut a dashing figure for George. That he had served as a Virginia officer during Britain's ill-fated invasion of Cartegena in 1741 only added to his luster.

Despite the differences in their ages—Lawrence was about fourteen years older, approximately twenty-four to George's ten when he returned to Virginia from his military service—George was made to feel welcome at Mount Vernon. He visited frequently, observing his brother's power and luxurious life-style, and noting the urbane demeanor not only of Lawrence, but of his friend George William Fairfax, the master of neighboring Belvoir plantation.

The visits affected Washington in significant ways. He soon longed to become a grandee on the magnitude of these Potomac planters, and he was no less interested in acquiring their educated habits and tastes. On the other hand, he soon must have become keenly aware of his limitations, his awkwardness, his inelegance, his inarticulateness. Washington's immediate response was to labor tirelessly to make himself over in the image of his new role models. He took music and fencing lessons; he developed a passion for appealing, fashionable clothing; so that he might participate in their discussions, he began to read, perusing both self-help books and the essays of the London literati. Mostly, however, he fell into the habit of quiescence, watching, listening, seldom speaking in the presence of others, and all the while discreetly preparing and polishing his behavior and expression into an accommodating style.

Reality was unkind, however. Washington lacked the financial means to live as did Lawrence and the Fairfaxes, or to acquire the respect and notice that their wealth commanded. Late in life he would remember his youth as a time when he had suffered for "the want of money." He also would remember that as a youngster he had felt "a natural fondness for Military parade." Thus, when his powerful friends counseled a military option as a means of escaping his Rappahanock fetters, Washington listened eagerly, and at age fourteen he sought to go to sea to become a midshipman and eventually an officer in the British Royal Navy. His mother refused his entreaties. Two years later he began to study surveying, and in 1749 he was commissioned the surveyor of Culpepper County. It was not an exalted calling, but it was an honorable profession, and its remunerations were such that a frugal man could acquire a considerable domain along the frontier. It was the path to becoming a Virginia planter that was taken by Thomas Jefferson's father, and it almost certainly would have remained young Washington's avenue toward greater wealth and status had not fate intervened.[7]

In the early 1750s the premature deaths both of Lawrence and his only surviving child gave Washington control of Mount Vernon. In addition, in the years between those two tragic events, Virginia raised an army to wrestle control of the Ohio Country from the French. Although only twenty-two years old, Washington, aided by the influential Fairfax family, was appointed commander of the Virginia Regiment.

Colonel Washington served from 1754 to 1758, four of those years as commander of Virginia's army, one as a volunteer without pay at the head-quarters of General Edward Braddock, the commander of Britain's army in America. The few months alongside Braddock were important. He ob-served a large professional army at first hand, made acquaintances with several young British officers, kept the general's orderly book and ran his errands, and beheld the folly of the redcoat army's endeavor to campaign on the American frontier in the same manner that it might have gone to battle in Europe.

Washington learned from errors of his own contrivance as well. Foolish immaturity led him obstinately to commit his first army to battle against an overwhelmingly superior French force. At the Great Meadows in July, 1754, his little garrison was overrun by a force nearly three times as large as his own.

His relationship with Virginia's civil authorities was almost equally dis-astrous. He grumbled and complained incessantly, until his petulant habits and his niggling, caviling tone caused Governor William Dinwiddie, once a benefactor, to turn on him, charging him with deceit and ingratitude.[8]

Washington's life-style in the midst of this war also aroused bitterness. Between September, 1755, when he reassumed command of the Virginia Regiment following his stint with Braddock, and the following spring, he was with his troops only about one-quarter of the time. During much of this period he was elsewhere courting authorities whom he believed could commission him an officer in the British army. Although casualties were considerable—one-third of his men were killed or wounded in 1756—Wash-ington frequently made trips to Mount Vernon and Belvoir, or even to examine property that he had purchased. It was whispered that while he was at headquarters he lived apart from his troops, that he frittered away his time with parties and indulgences.[9]

Public criticism soon followed. A newspaper critic denigrated him as a rakish nabob unsuited for a command post. Dinwiddie, too, blasted Wash-ington. Headquarters is "with't doubt...the proper place for the Com'd'g Officer," he once churlishly advised. On another occasion he ordered his young colonel to remain with the army. "Surely the Commanding officer Should not be Absent when daily Alarm'd with the Enemy's Intent's to invade our frontiers," he had to admonish.[10]

Washington left the army in 1758 convinced that he possessed the mettle to command other men. So did the officers who served under him. In a "humble Address" signed by each of his officers, a cadre that included many tough, older men, some already experienced soldiers when they came under Washington's command, the young colonel was lauded for having taken "us under your Tuition [and] train'd us up." They praised his impartiality, honor, strength, and sincerity. His officers also noted his valor, as had the British officers who had seen him fight next to Braddock. Washington was the first to know that he was courageous under fire. Indeed, he found that when he "heard the bullets whistle," he had discovered "something charming in the sound."[11]

Washington's years in command of the Virginia Regiment also were important in the realization of a personal goal: his military service had given him status as a person. No longer was he compelled to seek his identification through a glamorous older brother or a rich and powerful neighbor. By the time he retired to Mount Vernon in December, 1758, Washington's late adolescent normative crisis had been resolved, for he had, he acknowledged, "acquired [a] reputation." Without exaggeration, he could say that to have been able to command the Virginia Regiment was "the greatest honor of my life," and that the experience "had constitute[d] the greatest happiness of my life."[12]

Washington's pursuit of status reveals to the historian an often forgotten side of his nature. Through an intuitive genius, as well as through his years of observation at Mount Vernon and Belvoir, Washington had learned how to move men. He could be an actor, an obsequious truckler, a flatterer. He could intertwine facile affability, fortitude, and courage. Men were impressed by his sobriety and tenacity, by his vigor and his steely toughness. But no man was permitted to become his intimate friend. It was Washington who threw up the barrier about himself, lest his personal inadequacies be detected.

His behavior was the unmistakable product of his background. It reflected his early years, a time when his shortcomings had seemed so pronounced. The result was an inability to establish warm companionable relationships, save with those superiors who could be benefactors, or with those inferiors who could pose no threat to his ambitions. After long service as a surveyor and a military officer, a protracted time during which he lived apart from conventional society in proximity to other men of similar age and interests, he had no real friends. No one was allowed to become his equal. One could be only a patron, an admirer, or a follower. Otherwise, one could only be a threat.

Washington spent the fifteen years after his retirement from the Virginia Regiment as a gentleman farmer. Two weeks after leaving the army he married Martha Custis, the wealthiest widow in the province. He owned Mount Vernon, and within a few years he purchased thousands of acres contiguous to his handsome estate. Through purchase, as well as from his bounty as a soldier, Washington soon also possessed title to nearly 60,000 acres in the transmontane West. He was a cattleman, and he derived income from lumbering and fishing enterprises. Between 1754 and 1774 his slave properties increased almost tenfold, until his chattel totaled nearly 100 humans. Since the late 1750s he had sat in the Virginia House of Burgesses.[13]

But in his mind no accomplishment equaled his five years of military service. When he hired Charles Willson Peale to paint his family in 1772,

Washington revealingly donned the uniform he had designed two decades before for the army of Virginia. It was his intention, he remarked, that the artist should portray "to the world what manner of man I am."[14] Within two years of sitting for Peale, Washington was presented with an even better opportunity to display his character and his talents, for it was then that Congress selected him to command the Continental army.

Washington drew on his prior military experience when he assumed command of the new army. Immediately upon his arrival in Cambridge, Massachusetts, in July, 1775, he expressed horror at the state of affairs. Unsanitary conditions prevailed, officers fraternized with their men, some soldiers had been browbeaten into toiling on the farms of their dissolute officers, and serious offenses had gone unpunished. Washington's first important step, therefore, was to impose an iron discipline on his army. Next, he sought to create an elect and aloof officer corps. Noticeably incompetent and corrupt officers were cashiered, while those who remained were treated to a crash course in the requirements of command. Be strict but not unreasonable, Washington advised; seek to lead, he added, through a constant display of dignity, diligence, vigilance, and courage. To assess his officers, as well as to heighten their sense of elitism, he soon inaugurated the practice of inviting each day's adjutant, officer of the guard, and officer of the day to dine with him at headquarters. Finally, he designed special insignia for the officers, emblems—he called them "Badges of Distinction"—intended to reinforce the sense that an unbridgeable gap separated the officers from their men.[15]

Washington's ultimate solution, however, was to urge an army of regulars. He expressed his concerns to Congress within a few months of assuming command, and during the next year he and other powerful generals continued to press for "new modeling" the army. Late in 1776 Congress acted, setting at three years the minimum period of service.[16]

While Washington exhorted Congress to make this change, he was careful to avoid a recurrence of the unpleasantness that had characterized his relationship with the civil authorities during the French and Indian War. He certainly was not reticent about approaching the legislators, and during the war hardly a month passed that he did not plead for something, whether additional supplies, a larger army, higher pay for his officers and soldiers, postwar pensions for those in the officer corps, a more draconian disciplinary code, or still more aides to assist with his work. However, Washington had learned from experience when to push the legislators and when it was expedient to let matters lie. He wisely refrained from siding with one faction in Congress, and he understood that it would be foolhardy to appeal over Congress to the general public. He refused to allow himself to be drawn into the labyrinth of congressional fights over the ranking of various officers, and he carefully avoided the folly of pushing for anything that could possibly be construed as narrowly self-serving. Above all, he knew better than to revert to the whining, plaintive manner that had so tarnished his rapport with Dinwiddie.

Washington also was careful to pursue a course that was unlikely to arouse the ire of Congress or the public. Above all else, his service appeared to be the essence of personal sacrifice for the common good, the very embodiment of republican virtue as understood by the patriots at the outset of the Anglo-American war. Washington refused to accept a salary. Moreover, unlike many congressmen and other officers who shortly departed public service for more lucrative private endeavors, General Washington remained at his post through good and bad, and, if he is to be believed, he suffered financially for his efforts. Washington did not see his home for more than six years, and he saw his wife but infrequently, usually only for a few weeks each year. The general was a man of business, one who rarely escaped the cares of his post. During the first three years or more of the war he left his army only once, and that at the request of Congress which had called him to Philadelphia for consultation.

If Washington did not quite experience the spartan life-style of the common soldier, neither did he enjoy a grand or sumptuous manner. Headquarters usually was established in the capacious dwelling of a local patriot, though at Morristown in 1777 he took over a tavern and at Valley Forge the following winter he resided in a comfortable country farmhouse. During the campaign season he often occupied only one room at headquarters.

Washington ordinarily put in a long work day. Rising about 5:00 A.M., he worked in the solitude of his chambers for three or four hours. Thereafter, he broke away briefly, daily riding for about forty-five minutes, then returning for a hurried, light breakfast. An additional four or five hours of work followed, this often in the form of meetings with his staff or various officers and dignitaries. At about 3:00 P.M. all work stopped for the day's principal meal, an affair that customarily lasted two hours or more. Washington always was joined at this mess by numerous others, including foreign guests, other army officers, visiting national and local politicians, the wives of those at headquarters, his military aides, and the young officer of the day. Even while his men struggled with hunger at Valley Forge and Middlebrook, Washington appears to have enjoyed an adequate, if unspectacular, cuisine. At other times his table was laden with eight to ten separate dishes of meat and poultry, and a plethora of vegetables and pastries. Work resumed following this lengthy repast, and continued until nearly 8:00 P.M. when Washington returned to the dining room for a light meal of wine and fruit, and two or three hours of relaxation in the company of close acquaintances.

Washington not only appears to have worked hard, he eschewed the pleasures he had enjoyed as a civilian. As a Virginia planter he often had taken his pleasure in taverns, where he played cards and shot billiards. He shunned such recreation during the war, and, save for one instance in the last months of his service, he also disdained fox hunting, his favorite sport at Mount Vernon. On rare occasions he attended dances, and from time to time he emerged in the late evening to toss a ball or play wickets with the younger officers. Now and then he attended the theater or visited a local landmark, and from time to time he and his associates relaxed over a picnic lunch. Principally, however, Washington adhered to a rigid and strenuous schedule, living in what, for a man of his station, could only be described as a simple and unaffected manner.[17]

General Washington's deportment was of vital importance for a people in the midst of a great revolution that sought nothing less than a moral reformation of society and politics. In Washington's character there appeared to be none of the luxury and corruption that allegedly had caused Great Britain to succumb to despotism. In the public mind he was the citizen who had laid aside his plow in order to meet the national crisis, and it was his apparent selfless, sacrificial service—what his fellow activists alluded to as the noblest virtue a leader could evince—that came to be seen as the embodiment of the moral dimension that the revolutionaries believed essential for the success of their new republican polity.[18]

Washington's most often described attributes were his "virtue," his "integrity," and his "honest" and "noble" manner. He was thought by some to be "the last stage of perfection to which human nature is capable of attaining," and by 1777, while Washington's cold and hungry army suffered at Valley Forge, some already called him the father of the country. Others suggested that his presence was indispensable for an American victory. Such talk worried John Adams. Excessive adulation of any leader could "endanger our Liberties," he feared. Few shared his concern. The president of congress thought Washington "the first of the Age"; a Pennsylvania congressman described him as the "first Man in this World." "I love him to a Degree of Adoration," a member of the Board of War remarked. The loss of the general would mean "the ruin of our Cause," said South Carolina's Henry Laurens, while the Marquis de Lafayette feared that if ever Washington was "lost for America, there is nobody who could keep the army and Revolution [intact] for six months."[19]

But was General Washington's presence indispensable for the success of the American cause? It was a considerable claim, especially considering that by the time of that terrible winter at Valley Forge, about thirty months after he had taken command, Washington had suffered two ignominious thrashings at the hands of his adversaries, and that through his indecision he had very nearly met with two other potentially devastating defeats. Moreover, before Washington took command a battle of great significance already had occurred, and by the end of 1777 America's most important victory had been won by another general, in command of another army.

Washington took command two weeks after the Battle of Bunker Hill. Led by General William Howe, the British had driven the colonists from the Charlestown heights that overlooked Boston, but their success came at a frightful cost. Nearly 1,000 British soldiers were killed or wounded during the engagement. After that "unhappy day," as he thereafter referred to Bunker Hill, Howe seemed to change. Once the daring, eager warrior, he grew cautious and reluctant to act. Within a few weeks of the battle he also succeeded Thomas Gage as commander of the British forces in America. Thus, at perhaps the only time Britain could have won the war, the years between 1775 and 1777, the British forces passed under the guidance of an irresolute and overly cautious commander.

Washington assumed command of a conventional army engaged in a siege of British-occupied Boston. Almost from the beginning he chafed at his enforced inactivity. In part, he suspected that he might forfeit the "esteem of mankind" if he remained inert. He spoke of his desire to assault the British lines, even though he acknowledged that an attack might be imprudent. He felt political pressure to act, but his itch to fight also was imbedded in his character. Gilbert Stuart, the painter, understood this side of Washington, and he once remarked that the general's features were redolent of the "most ungovernable passions." Had Washington "been born in the forests," he added, "he would have been the fiercest man among the savage tribes."[20] It was a dark side of Washington's character, not bloodlust, yet some animal passion, something almost feral and barbarous that at times seemed to course through his veins. All his life Washington was aware of these black emotions, and all his life he struggled to keep them within bounds.

Twice Washington's officers rejected his call for an attack on Boston, but in March, armed with artillery that Colonel Henry Knox had returned from Fort Ticonderoga, Washington's men took Dorchester Heights, overlooking Boston harbor. When Howe learned of his adversary's accomplishment, he considered an attack. Then he thought better of it. Soon the British army was gone from Boston. Bunker Hill had paid a dividend. So, too, had Washington's leadership. Always an extraordinary judge of character, he had understood Howe. During the previous autumn Washington had concluded that his counterpart was "afraid of us," and would not strike. He was correct. "I resolved to take possession of Dorchester," he boasted, and soon "the Flower of the British army" withdrew "in a shameful and precipitate manner."[21]

Washington did not have long to wait before the British returned. By summer's end the redcoats and their Hessian allies had landed on Staten Island, and the Battle of New York had begun. During the next eighteen months the British had their best opportunity to suppress the American rebellion. America was without foreign assistance in 1776, and the next year it received only modest and clandestine French aid. The Continental army was untested, its officers inexperienced, and the colonists had no naval arm at the outset of the war. The British did not succeed, of course, but

Washington suffered his worst battlefield disasters during this period, two of which very nearly resulted in a cataclysmic American defeat.

Washington's brush with catastrophe in 1776 was due in large measure to his inexperience. He chose to defend two islands—Long Island and Manhattan—against an assailant possesed with total naval superiority. That Washington faced political pressures to defend these islands is beyond question. However, he also naively believed that the defensive installations he and Charles Lee had prepared were virtually impregnable, and he was certain that "an agreeable Spirit and willingness for Action" within the breasts of his callow men would enable him to repulse his professional adversary.[22]

The blow fell first on Long Island, and it soon was obvious that Washington had committed several errors. First, he had divided his army in the face of his huge adversary, placing one-half his men on Manhattan, the remainder on Long Island. In addition, Washington seemed confused as the battle neared. Not only did he change commanders on the very eve of the engagement, but key highways were left unprotected. The result was worse than the snare that Braddock and young Washington had walked into twenty years before, for in this battle Howe's army of 10,000 men succeeded in getting behind the Continental army and launching a surprise attack. The result was a debacle. In one morning more than three hundred Americans perished and three times that many were captured. Those who survived were in a box, trapped with their backs against the East River.

Of course, Washington escaped. He utilized a sudden storm and the resulting thick fog that descended about his Brooklyn redoubt to convey his men to Manhattan. But Manhattan was another island, and soon, said one of Washington's aides, the army again was "cooped up . . . between hawk and buzzard."[23]

Although his entire army once again faced the likelihood of entrapment, Washington seemed unconvinced of the scope of his predicament. Not even a successful landing by the British at Kip's Bay on the eastern side of Manhattan seemed to awaken him to his danger. He appeared to believe that Howe had little choice but to attack his entrenched army in Harlem Heights, and that another Bunker Hill inevitably would result. Instead, Howe planned to envelop the Continental army by invading the mainland above Manhattan. Not until Howe moved did Washington at last seem to comprehend the peril he was in, but once again luck was with the American commander. Howe's initial landing site on the mainland proved inexpedient, and he was compelled to withdraw and stage a second landing six days later. The danger now was too apparent to ignore. Washington made the decision to abandon Manhattan, save for Fort Washington and its 2,800 men.

It soon was apparent that Washington's decision to hold that garrison on Manhattan was still another blunder, his worst, it turned out, in 1776. Although certain to be encircled, the post obviously was incapable of withstanding a protracted siege. For one thing, the fortress had no well! Yet, in mid-November, with a British assault imminent, Washington could not decide whether to fight for the fort or to abandon it. He vacillated indecisively until it was too late. Howe attacked Fort Washington before the American commander could make up his mind, and on the very day of the assault the bastion fell, its entire army of defenders taken captive.

One aspect of the August-November campaign for New York stands out. When General Howe pushed his army into battle, he succeeded. On Long Island, at Manhattan, at Fort Washington, he had struck, taking territory, inflicting a heavy casualty rate, capturing huge numbers of prisoners, eviscerating morale within the green American army. Too often, however, Howe acted with caution, pausing, hesitating, moving with exasperating languor, until Washington had succeeded in escaping the traps into which he had so ineptly blundered. That Washington survived these months was due as much to his adversary's foolish ineptitude as to his own good fortune.

After the fall of New York, Washington's diminutive army reeled across New Jersey, one step ahead of its British pursuers. The chase ended in December. Washington was across the Delaware River, and with freezing weather setting in, Howe retired to winter quarters, posting his men in seven cantonments across New Jersey. Injudiciously, he placed a Hessian brigade of 1,500 men in Trenton, just across from Washington.

Since mid-December Washington had vaguely alluded to a design for striking out at his adversary. Practical factors urged some act. A bold move might arrest the collapse of civilian morale; a victory might serve as a spur for the recruitment of the army of 1777.

But there was more to Washington's thirst for action. A proud, vain man, Washington was distressed and frustrated by events since late in the summer, and he was grieved to learn that some had begun to question his ability. He was no less mortified by the evasive, retreating tactics that he had been compelled to follow, fearing that such a course would stain his character. He even referred to his own conduct as an instance of "fatal supiness." Always he had most admired men of "Activity and Spirit," always he had longed for the "honor of making a brave defense," that is, of having the opportunity to stand and resolutely fight his adversary.[24] Always he longed for the brilliant stroke, for the audacious act. To imagine Washington thinking any other way is to fail to understand the man, for the personality style that shaped his inescapable quest for esteem also structured the decisions he made in this war.

Even "a Failure cannot be more fatal" than inaction, Joseph Reed, once an aide to Washington, counseled just prior to the attack on Trenton.[25] But Washington's strike was not a failure. He surprised the Hessians, and after a brief clash two-thirds of the garrison, about 950 men, were killed or captured. Nor was that the end of Washington's audacity. He soon marched into New Jersey, penetrating the lion's den where a large enemy force lay slumbering, and struck his foe at Princeton.

Because Washington spoke of the necessity of a "war of posts," this unflinchingly daring side of his character often has been overlooked.[26] Lurking within Washington was the instinct and temper of a gambler. He was not given to impetuous action, but his militant, activist, venturesome character at times led him to chancey undertakings. He had yearned to strike at occupied Boston in 1775, and his wagers at Trenton and Princeton sprang from the same instinct. So, too, did his assault on the British at Germantown a year later, and the surprise attacks on the British-held Hudson River forts, Stony Point and Paulus Hook, in 1779.

If Washington's instinct for the audacious was rooted in his character, the nature of his interpersonal relationships was no less tied to his personality. Washington appeared to be a man who felt a deep need to surmount a haunting sense of inadequacy, a trait that he had exhibited at least since his awkward days in the presence of genteel fops at Mount Vernon and Belvoir. Beset by uncertainties, Washington sought to screen himself from others; the most common characterizations of his manner left by persons who spent time in his presence were descriptions of a noble, grave, stately, formal, cold, and aloof man. Few got close to Washington, and no one ever seriously believed that he had become the general's close friend. Only with certain company did Washington drop his guard, and then but slightly. Several women left behind flattering portraits of Washington, finding him to be friendly and relaxed. Similarly, foreign observers were more likely than American acquaintances to describe him as "amiable." Many of the general's young aides, moreover, believed they had achieved a warm, affectionate relationship with Washington, ties that grew from those times when the commander, following a long day of work, relaxed over wine and nuts, listening to their conversation and, on occasion, baring some of his inner self.[27] Persons in these three groups shared one common element. None could possibly be a threat to George Washington.

Upon his arrival at headquarters in 1777, the Marquis de Lafayette noticed immediately that Washington's inner circle consisted largely of flatterers and trucklers.[28] The needs that compelled Washington to surround himself with sycophants also colored his relationship with his principal subordinates. Of the thirteen general officers which Congress named in June, 1775, to serve under Washington, four died early in the conflict. His relations with the remaining general officers, as well as with those who emerged as the war progressed, bore the stamp of his personality.

Three of the original officers soon fell out of favor with Washington. The three shared two attributes: each had command experience, and each had important supporters among public officials. In short, each posed a potential threat to Washington. Almost immediately upon assuming command, Washington began to denigrate General Artemas Ward, his predecessor. Ward, he charged, was a fat and lazy incompetent, a man too inert to remove himself "from the smoke of his own chimney." Ward soon was shifted to posts of little importance, and after two years he left the service. Historians have tended to accept Washington's characterization of Ward, but there is little evidence to support such a view. A graduate of Harvard College, Ward had served for years in a militia unit, and, like Washington, he had been an officer in the French and Indian War. His neighbors in New England were sufficiently impressed to send him to the colonial assembly, and in 1774 Massachusetts, the colony with perhaps the most men of military experience, chose Ward to command its army.[29]

Although Washington had beseeched Congress to tender commission to Charles Lee and Horatio Gates, he ultimately grew to distrust and dislike both men. Both were veteran British officers, skilled, trained professionals with credible prior records. Lee's English birth had disqualified him from consideration for the commander's post in 1775, but following his successful defense of Charleston, South Carolina, a campaign that coincided with the dreadful American defeats at New York, Washington learned that some now looked upon Lee as the best hope for the provincial cause. Shortly thereafter Lee was captured by the British and spent nearly eighteen months in captivity. When Lee returned, he found Washington to be proper, but cool, presaging a final break between the two men over Lee's conduct in the Battle of Monmouth.[30] The imbroglio was a complex incident, and Lee, an acerbic sort with an infinite capacity for making enemies, unquestionably brought much of the difficulty on himself. Nevertheless, it is difficult to believe that Washington felt any sensation save relief or exultation at Lee's departure.

At first, Washington's relations with Gates appeared to be satisfactory. However, after Gates's great victory at Saratoga in October, 1777, Washington seemed to change. Even his congratulatory note to Gates seemed forced. Soon, Washington's headquarters buzzed with the tale that Gates had feared to step on the battlefield during that engagement, that he "hug himself at a distance [to] leave [General Benedict] Arnold to win laurels for him."[31] Despite a lack of credible evidence, Washington soon concluded that Gates was part of a conspiracy to secure his removal as commander of the Continental army. Thereafter, Washington grew openly hostile, and he never again urged the appointment of his supposed rival to any command.

The war was not very old before John Adams noted that most congressmen had concluded that three of the original general officers, Joseph Spenser, William Heath, and Israel Putnam were incompetent. Washington quickly reached the same conclusion about Spenser and Heath, but Putnam, "Old Put" to his men, was given every chance to succeed. Fifty-seven when the war commenced, Putnam was thought by many to be too old to withstand the demands of command. Moreover, his demeanor remained so unrefined and rustic that one observer thought him "much fitter to lead a band of sickle-men or ditchers, than musketeers."[32]

No one received more opportunities to command than John Sullivan, the least experienced of the original general officers. With nothing more than militia service before 1775, and precious little of that, he owed his appointment to Congress's desire to grant New Hampshire a general officer. Washington soon deduced that Sullivan's personality was likely to lead "him into some embarrassments" on the battlefield, and he was correct.[33] Sullivan failed egregiously in Canada early in 1776, and at Brooklyn later in the year. Nevertheless, Washington repeatedly turned to him, investing him with an important assignment at Brandywine in 1777, placing him in command of the Rhode Island campaign in 1778, and naming him to lead a crucial expedition into Iroquois territory in western New York in 1779.

Washington was cordial and supportive of Philip Schuyler, the first commander of the Northern army that lay poised on the Canadian frontier. At first glance Schuyler might have seemed, like Lee and Gates, a likely rival to Washington. He was not, however, for he was so unpopular with the New England congressmen and soldiery that his elevation was unthinkable. "The New England soldiers would not enlist to serve under him, and the militia would not turn out" to bear arms under his command, said John Adams, who also became a foe of the New Yorker. Schuyler, thus, never could have been a rival, and in time according to one authority, he came to enjoy "Washington's friendship, high regard, and complete loyalty as did few other generals in the Continental army."[34]

Washington eventually grew to place greater reliance on Nathanael Greene than any of the other original officers. Although almost devoid of military experience before the war, Greene emerged as a bright and good soldier, an officer who could be bold, impetuous even, and who, with the glaring exception of his culpability in the Fort Washington debacle, was a successful commander. But Greene was inclined to be respectful, almost obsequious, to those in authority. His behavior toward Washington was nothing if not approbatory—just as it earlier had been toward Artemas Ward. Dominated by a father who still ordered him about when he was nearly thirty years old, Greene long had been accustomed to deferential conduct. On the eve of the Revolution, in fact, he had helped to organize a volunteer infantry company in his province, but when his candidacy for rank was turned down because of his slight limp, he stayed on as a private.[35] It is unimaginable that Washington—or virtually any other of the principal officers for that matter—would have acquiesced to such an affront. It was equally unimaginable that a person of such temperament ever could have posed a threat to Washington's leadership.

In the course of the war Washington warmly embraced several additional officers, including Henry Knox, Benedict Arnold, Henry Lee, Anthony Wayne, and Lafayette. Most were junior men, some succeeded in attracting legions of political enemies, and some, like Knox, were totally loyal to Washington. None posed a threat to Washington.

The drives that shaped Washington's personality might also have influenced his decisions in other areas. Canada is a case in point, a nettlesome region toward which Washington manifested a curiously ambivalent, even quite cautious attitude after 1776. For a time following the unsuccessful invasion in 1775–76, an American offensive in that theater was out of the question. However, by the winter of 1777–78, the bleak Valley Forge winter, the situation had changed. With the defeat and capture of Burgoyne at Saratoga, Canada was weakly defended. Moreover, French intervention seemed imminent, a factor that was likely to further diminish Britain's ability to hold the region. Some in Congress and the army soon found the conquest of Canada to be an alluring goal. Acquisition of the region would close the door to any future British invasion of the United States through that portal. In addition, an American triumph in that sector might be the quickest way to end the war; Lord North's government in London would find it difficult to withstand such a catastrophe. Postwar factors were of concern, too, for if Canada was not won on the battlefield, it likely would not be won at all. Given these factors, Congress, in January, 1778, endorsed an "irruption ... into Canada."[36] The author of the planned invasion was Horatio Gates.

Normally inclined to "run all risques," Washington unexpectedly balked at the proposed campaign. He derided the notion that Britain ever again would seek to attack the United States from Canada, and he predicted that the American invasion army would meet the same fate as its predecessor. An invasion of Canada, he said, would be "folly" and "not practicable." Washington's objections, together with recruitment problems, ultimately led to the cancellation of the operation.[37]

However, late in the summer of 1778 the notion of an "irruption" into Canada resurfaced in Congress. Once again Gates and his New England allies were the principal proponents of such a campaign. To the reasons given earlier for such an operation, new justifications were cited. There now was talk of seizing Canada's fisheries and fur trade. Control the St. Lawrence River, some added, and Britain would be unable to supply its native American allies, thus pacifying the frontier. Finally, it was argued that an invasion of Canada would divert British troops from United States soil, for the redcoats would be compelled to defend their northern domain.[38]

Once again, however, Washington counseled inaction. The Commander's arguments were deserving, but not without a hollow ring. So long as Britain held New York and Rhode Island, he said, America would lack the manpower for the operation. While the acquisition of Canada was desirable, he went on, it was not crucial to the war effort, and a military setback in that region could decimate American morale. Moreover, the very factors that had stymied American efforts in Canada in 1775 and 1776—manpower and material shortages, the lack of an American fleet, the vastness of the country—would auger against success this time as well. Finally, he added, he did not quite trust the French, who, he feared, might seek to use American men to regain their old imperial possession. Washington carried the issue. Congress mulled over his thoughts, then vetoed the project.[39]

But Canada would not die. In the spring of 1779 Washington learned from the Spanish minister to the United States that the French High Command was considering a naval assault on Halifax and on bases on the Newfoundland coast. Once these installations were secured, the French wondered, could the United States be trusted to hold them? Canada again! And once again Washington did his best to thwart such an operation. He lacked the manpower for garrisoning those bases, he said, and, instead, he urged France to consider a joint attack on the British forces in New York. France acceded to his wishes.[40]

In the fall of 1780 Washington inexplicably reversed himself on Canada. Having journeyed to Hartford to meet with his French ally, General Washington suddenly proposed a joint Franco-American invasion of Canada. Strangely, not one of the objections to such a venture that he first had raised thirty months earlier had been remediated, nor had the misgivings he had uttered in mid–1779 been corrected. The only change, in fact, was in the altered status of General Gates. A month earlier, at Camden in South Carolina, Gates had sustained a terrible defeat. Soon he was removed from command.[41] At least for the time being Gates no longer was a force with which Washington would have to reckon. For the first time since 1775 Washington saw Canada as an alluring target.

After 1778, the period when the question of Canada continued to surface, Washington evinced a cautious aura that previously had been absent from his generalship. Secure as never before, he had acquired the complete control that his disposition required. His self-enhancement fulfilled, the inner needs that had driven him to feats of daring before 1778 now were assuaged. Thereafter, his very tone seemed different, and even when he contemplated an action a note of hesitancy appeared to hover in his thoughts. Now he would fight, he said, only when there was "a moral certainty of victory."[42]

Only the prospect of a Franco-American siege of New York seemed to reawaken the adventurer within Washington. Indeed, he embraced this notion until it seemed to become a fixed idea. Historian John Shy even has charged that Washington was so mesmerized by the possibility of scoring a decisive victory in New York that he displayed "little grasp" of the dangers posed by the new strategy Britain implemented in 1779, its "Southern strategy," that included assaults on Savannah and Charleston, and forays into Virginia, all aimed at the pacification of those colonies below Pennsylvania. Thomas Jefferson, the governor of beleagured Virginia, might have agreed with Shy's judgment. Ultimately, he, too, criticized Washington's obsession with New York, likening the probable futility of a joint siege to the failure of France and Spain to regain Gibraltar.[43] Jefferson's cynicism was well founded. The size of the siege armies was not likely to be substantively greater than that of the British defenders, nor was the French navy likely to be any better than the equal of the British fleet.

While most contemporary observers lauded Washington, some perceived a dark side to his character, and a few understood how it affected the decisions he had to make. Alexander Hamilton, who spent nearly six years at the general's side, found Washington to be extraordinarily vain and "neither remarkable for delicacy nor good temper." Charles Lee called Washington a "puffed up charlatan...extremely prodigal of other men's blood and a great oeconomist of his own." Some discerned a hard, violent, and insensitive edge about him, and others thought him vindictive and petty, at least in his dealings with General Lee. The brother of one of his aides found him to be coarse, "better endowed by nature in habit for an Eastern monarch, than a republican general." One visitor was struck by his "repulsive coldness...under a courteous demeanor."[44]

Washington was not an evil man, but he was a man. More people saw positive qualities in his character than remarked on the flaws in his make-up, yet there is sufficient evidence to suggest that the insecurities that colored his personality, as well as his malignant ambition and his penchant for the grandiose, were factors in his decision-making process, and not always with salutary results.

But there also was much to praise in Washington's performance, and much that was laudable also grew from the striking nature of his character and temperament. He intuitively understood the American mind, and through his behavior he came to be seen as the embodiment of the republican soldier. He understood what was required to maintain a pleasant and productive relationship with Congress. He succeeded in maintaining the esteem of most political leaders, as well as of those who served under him. He showed no inclination to misuse the power of the army for political reasons, nor did he abuse his position for personal profit. After 1778 he worked well with the French, establishing a proper, and in some instances an amiable, relationship with the allied commanders. It was impossible to charge that Washington shirked his duties, and no one ever suggested that he lacked courage, for when he threw his army into battle he was present on the field, exposed to the very dangers faced by his men.

Washington made many mistakes as commander of the American army, but the worst were committed during 1776–77, the early, most amateurish years of his tenure. It also was a time when his principal subordinates often were even less experienced, and when the army's ranks consisted of an untrained citizen-soldiery. Indeed, so desperate was the situation in these years that it is difficult not to believe that an aggressive, daring, and resourceful British command could have used its numerical superiority, professional soldiery, and unchallenged naval predominance to inflict debilitating defeats on the American army, perhaps even resulting in the restructuring of the Continental army's command.

That did not happen, and, instead, Washington came to be seen as the "indispensable man" of the Revolution. John Adams once remarked that the Revolution was too great an event to hang on the performance of one man, and he probably was correct.[45] That said, it also probably was correct that Congress would not likely have found a better general than Washington. Ward was old, Schuyler indolent, Putnam rustic, Lee temperamental and acerbic, and Gates overly ambitious, political, vain, and manipulative, though no one can say how any of these men, or others, like Nathanael Greene, for instance, might have responded to the challenge of command. What is clear is that Washington coupled many exemplary qualities with a generalship that was mostly laudatory, if not brilliant.

The American triumph, Washington once said, was due to the "patronage of Heaven." He added that his victories at Trenton and Princeton also contributed to winning independence, as did the French entrance into the war.[46] In short, luck, daring, and foreign assistance won the war. But Washington contributed to or seized upon each of these ingredients of victory. He understood his adversary; he boldly grasped opportunities; he could and did act with resolution; his behavior could be bafflingly unpredictable, even audacious; he kept the army intact and introduced reforms that strengthened it as a fighting force; he was a sound and capable administrator; and he comprehended what was required to gain the victory. His character— whatever its defects—was his greatest contribution to the American triumph, however. His public morality, his apparent selflessness, his unwillingness to abuse the power that his fellow men had bestowed upon him ultimately came to symbolize the preservation of the army and the Revolution, until, in time, General Washington was acknowledged as the unbending guardian of the Revolutionary credo.

5

Washington's Lieutenants and the American Victory

Hugh F. Rankin

England's defeat in the American Revolution may be attributed to many things: America's aid from France; the American geography; the distance between Britain and America; and the fact that there was no real capital whose capture would signal the end of the war. And, of course, there was the American army, even with its lack of discipline and chronic shortage of supplies, commanded by George Washington and his generals. This essay is concerned with some of those general officers and their contribution to the American victory. Of the twenty-eight Continental generals, the five who had the greatest impact—either positively or negatively—upon Washington's actions and feelings have been selected for scrutiny. These are Charles Lee, Horatio Gates, Nathanael Greene, Marquis de Lafayette, and Henry Knox.

Other generals also played crucial roles in this war. John Sullivan, Philip Schuyler, Benjamin Lincoln, Anthony Wayne, and Daniel Morgan exercised command at pivotal moments, as did Benedict Arnold, whose treachery weighed heavily on Washington. Nor was Baron von Steuben, who trained and instilled discipline in the army, unimportant. Yet none of these officers touched General Washington as did the five who will be examined.

Charles Lee, forty-three years old in 1775, had an impressive military record. He had served with distinction in Europe and America, having been wounded in the French and Indian War. After his regiment had been disbanded during the long peace that followed the war, Lee retired to America and purchased an estate in Berkeley County in western Virginia.[1] When the war with Britain began he sought rank in the new Continental army, and with Washington's assistance he was the third general officer—after the commander-in-chief and Artemas Ward—appointed by Congress.

On his first tour of duty with Washington at Boston, Lee, as did the commanding general, realized that the initial task before them was the construction of proper fortifications. He seemed appalled by the lack of engineering experience among the officers, remarking that "not a single man of them is capable of constructing an oven." He added that "our miserable defeat of engineers imposes upon me eternal work in a department to which I am a stranger."[2]

The second task was to make—and preserve—an army out of the citizen-soldiers who rushed to volunteer in 1775. Lee's conduct in this enterprise indicated that the name given him by the Indians among whom he had lived (with whom he had "married," in fact) while serving in the French and Indian War was apt. They had called him "Boiling Water," and, indeed, Lee's behavior toward the amateur soldiery under his command in 1775 was characterized by explosive outbursts. For example, "Stephen Stanwood for saucy talk to Gen. Lee had his head broke," a young lieutenant observed. "The General gave him a dollar and sent for the doctor."[3] Nor did Lee have any use for the undisciplined frontier riflemen who arrived in camp in the summer of 1775. Although some politicians believed they would be the secret weapon with which the Americans could win the war, Lee supported Washington's efforts to be rid of them.[4] But when men in the Connecticut regiments threatened to return home upon the expiration of their enlistments in December, 1775, Lee really did reach the boiling point. He addressed them in no uncertain terms. "Men, I do not know what to call you, [but you] are the worst of all creatures." After cursing them, he threatened to dispatch them to Bunker Hill where he would order the riflemen to fire upon them. He grabbed one soldier's musket and struck him over the head with it.[5]

By 1776 Lee, because of his own boasting and his past reputation, and perhaps too because of his sympathy both for republicanism and American independence, was considered by many members of Congress to be, next to the commander-in-chief, the most competent general in the army.[6] In fact, some had come to consider him superior to Washington. Thus, when reports circulated of an imminent British strike to the south, the Continental Congress appointed Lee to the command of the Southern Department.

Leaving unpaid bills behind him in New York, Lee hurried south, accompanied, as always, by his pack of dogs, for whom he demanded the best bacon when they were fed. Reaching Williamsburg, Virginia, he set himself up in the governor's palace and sought to fathom his adversary's intentions. As North Carolina had no center of importance, Lee concluded that the expected British attack would come against either Virginia or South Carolina, and when it was learned from an intercepted letter that the British fleet was headed for the North Carolina coast, he thought himself to be in a "damned whimsical situation.... I know not where to turn.... I am like a dog in a dancing school." He remained at Williamsburg until he was certain of his adversary's destination, and when, at least, the British fleet was sighted off Cape Fear he marched for Charleston, in command of 2,000 green Virginians and North Carolinians.[7]

Arriving on June 6, Lee unhappily inspected the defenses of the city as constructed by the natives. They had placed their greatest reliance upon the partially completed fort on Sullivan's Island in the harbor, an installation that was likely to be a "slaughter pen," in his estimation. To make matters worse, the fortification was under the command of Colonel William Moultrie, whose slow and deliberate manner led Lee to compare him to General Artemas Ward, a man he once had characterized as better suited for a church warden than a general.[8] Lee's solutions were to abandon the citadel and to remove Moultrie from command, but local political pressures and the rush of events prevented such actions.[9]

It was just as well. Late in June, 1776, enemy warships were spotted loosening their sails and beginning to work their way across the bar at the mouth of the harbor. Soon, the fleet lined up opposite Sullivan's Island and began to bombard the fort. During the battle Lee emerged from the fort, laid a couple of guns himself, and then departed, telling Moultrie: "Colonel, I see you are doing very well here. You have no occasion for me. I will go to town again." From the mainland he watched the fleet deliver "the most furrious fire I ever heard or saw."[10]

After an all-day bombardment, Lee received word that the fleet not only had failed to knock the fort out of action, but the fort had just about finished the flotilla. The light of the following day brought confirmation, revealing the shambles of the British fleet, now undertaking repairs and making preparations to sail back to New York. Ecstatically, Lee visited the fort and thanked the troops for their gallant conduct. He also sent the British general, Sir Henry Clinton, a present of fresh food for which, in turn, he received some porter and cheese.

Lee remained in South Carolina until early August, when he was recalled to Washington's army in New York. He arrived in mid-October, after the British had driven the rebels from Long Island and following the landing at Kip's Bay. Upon his arrival, Lee was given the command of the troops north of King's Bridge, the key position in the defense of Manhattan Island. Because of Washington's defeats during the past few weeks, and because of his own victory at Charleston, many officers had begun to look to Lee as a savior.

The next few weeks were the gloomiest that Washington faced during the war. In October he was forced off Manhattan Island and driven back at White Plains, and during the following month his indecision largely was responsible for the pernicious defeat at Fort Washington. By December, General Washington was reeling south across New Jersey, pursued by a British army under the Earl of Cornwallis.

Lee, meanwhile, had fought capably both in a delaying action that helped Washington escape Manhattan and again in the retreat above New York. In late October, when Washington began his withdrawal to the south, Lee was left in command of some 7,500 New Yorkers and New Englanders and charged with the task of defending the provinces east of the Hudson River.

Soon, however, Washington, outnumbered by his foes and watching helplessly as resistance in New Jersey apparently crumbled to nothing, was compelled to order Lee to join him. Lee responded slowly to his chief's orders, his move delayed by his army's shortages of shoes and blankets. Nevertheless, within five days of receiving Washington's order Lee's army was marching south, although it advanced with such exasperating leisureliness that Washington soon grew aggravated. Lee, on the other hand, announced bombastically that he was "going into . . . Jersey for the salvation of America."[11]

On December 12, his army still languorously moving toward a rendezvous with Washington, Lee accepted an invitation to stay the night at an inn near Baskinridge, some three miles from his command. That night, he wrote Horatio Gates, criticizing Washington with the words, "*entre nous,* a certain great man is most damnably deficient—He has thrown me into a situation where I have my choice of difficulties—if I stay in this Province I risk myself and the Army and if I do not stay the Province is lost forever." The following morning he was surprised and taken prisoner by a British cavalry patrol. Even as exasperated as he was by Lee's behavior, Washington felt that the cause had received a "severe blow" with the capture of the general.[12]

Lee was ordered home for trial as a deserter, but General William Howe, commander of the British army, did not comply because he felt that Lee had resigned his half-pay pension from the British army. Some historians have felt that Lee was guilty of treason while a prisoner, for in March, 1777, he had submitted a plan to the British commander for ending the rebellion, a scheme that would "unhinge the organization of American resistance" by gaining control of the middle colonies, Maryland, Pennsylvania, and Virginia. The British apparently paid no heed to his advice.[13]

Washington still believed in Lee and missed him so ᴴ that he prevailed upon Elias Boudinot, Commissary of Prisoners, to work for an exchange of the captured general. In April, 1778, after Lee's release had been effected, a grand reception was staged for the returning general. He was given a room at Washington's headquarters, only to appear the next morning dirty and dishevelled. It soon was discovered by Boudinot that "he had brought a miserable dirty hussy with him from Philadelphia (a British sergeant's wife) and had actually taken her into his room by a backdoor, and she had slept with him that night."[14]

Lee had only a short wait before he faced another kind of action. In June the British abandoned Philadelphia and under General Henry Clinton headed overland for New York City. Washington shadowed the British army, thirsting for action, but most of his generals wanted only a partial attack; all agreed that a "general action" should be avoided. Lee was among those who urged caution. After two councils of war debated the issue, a compromise was reached. A detachment of 1,000 men was to harass the British flank and rear. Lee was offered, and at first declined, command of this detachment. Lafayette then was given the post, but when Washington subsequently augmented the attack force to more than 5,000 men, Lee asserted his rights as senior major general and claimed the right of command. Washington agreed.

The battle that soon followed—the famous engagement at Monmouth in New Jersey—was one of the most confusing encounters in this war. Early in the fray Lee's troops became disoriented in the confusion of battle, and when one of his units was threatened with being cut off, Lee ordered a general retreat. Washington came up about this time and the commander-in-chief and the weary Lee engaged in an angry exchange of words. Lee was relieved of his command on the spot. Washington rallied the retreating troops and finished the battle in good order.

Now in disgrace, Lee wrote to Washington demanding an apology for the treatment he had received. An exchange of letters followed, with Lee demanding a court-martial, a request that soon was granted.[15] Lee was tried on three charges: disobedience of orders by not attacking the British at Monmouth; ordering "an unnecessary, disorderly and shameful retreat"; and disrespect toward the commander-in-chief. Lee blamed the incidents of the day on General Wayne, while Wayne testified that Lee was dilatory both in his decisions and his actions upon the battlefield. Although a careful examination of the first two charges would have found Lee not guilty, he most certainly had behaved impudently toward Washington. Nevertheless, as a sop to Washington, he was found guilty on all three counts and was suspended from command for one year.[16]

Lee retired to his Virginia farm and eventually was dismissed from the army for disrespectful letters to Congress. He also was forced to fight a duel with Colonel John Laurens for his attacks on General Washington. When he died in 1782 he was drawing up plans for a model settlement in the west.

Charles Lee was arrogant, overbearing, and outspoken, a combination of qualities that has led most historians to cast him in the role of villain in his relationship with Washington. Certainly, he considered himself superior in military matters to Washington, a view shared by some congressmen. Washington must have known of Lee's boastings, for he certainly had enough supporters in Congress to have passed the word on to him. Washington also was aware that Lee favored the use of irregular tactics, hit and run operations along the lines of what now is called guerrilla warfare, rather than the conventional methods of European campaigning upon which he relied. Yet Washington held Lee's military abilities in high regard, so much so that he sought to arrange an exchange when Lee was a prisoner of the British. Sometime between the exchange and the battle of Monmouth, however, Washington seems to have become disenchanted with Lee, and it appears that he may have used Lee's behavior during the battle as a means of getting rid of him. Indeed, Lee appears to have been found guilty of the court-martial charges brought against him after the engagement at Monmouth solely as a favor to the commanding general. Perhaps Lee's abrasive personality simply had become too burdensome for Washington any longer to bear. Without question, Lee's abrupt, acerbic manner made him his own worst enemy, overshadowing even his considerable military abilities.

Horatio Gates was an enigma in the history of the American Revolution. His victory over John Burgoyne at Saratoga is considered by many to be the turning point of the war, but others have held him in a bad light because of his supposed involvement in an alleged plot to replace Washington as commanding general of the American army. Gates's defeat at Camden gave his enemies additional coals to heap upon his head.

Born in humble surroundings in Maldon, England, Gates was commissioned in the British army about 1749, and served two tours in America before retiring from active service in the mid–1760s. Shortly thereafter he grew frustrated with the lack of opportunity in English society, and, like Lee, moved to Virginia. At the outbreak of the revolutionary war Gates, again like Lee, utilized Washington's influence to secure an appointment in the new American army. He was appointed brigadier general and adjutant general of the Continental army.

Almost fifty when the war erupted, Gates did not look like a soldier. He was stoop shouldered, his cheeks were ruddy, and his grey hair was thinning. His spectacles perched on the end of his nose gave his men another reason for referring to him as "Granny Gates."

Caution was the key word in Gates's ideas on strategy. During the siege of Boston he urged Washington to stand firm and let the British wear themselves out by expending money and men in trying to root him out. In September he opposed Washington's scheme for attacking the British positions in Boston, and early in 1776 he disapproved of the commander's plan to seize and fortify Dorchester Heights. Washington persisted in the latter instance, however, and his plan succeeded in driving the British out of Boston in March, 1776.[17]

In May, 1776, Gates was promoted to major general and a month later was given the command of the northern army, then retreating from Canada into New York. He not only found that morale was low in the disease-ridden army, but there also was a dispute over command. Major General

Philip Schuyler claimed that Congress had appointed him commander of the northern army, and there was no little justification for his claim.

While Congress sought to resolve the command imbroglio, Gates was busy. Aware that Sir Guy Carleton, the commander of Britain's Canadian army, was busily constructing a fleet that could secure Lake Champlain, he, too, engaged in a shipbuilding operation. Moreover, Gates sought to whip his army into shape. He largely succeeded in restoring the sagging morale of the northern army, primarily by seeing to the comfort and physical health of the soldiers. He reduced smallpox in the ranks by isolating those men with the disease, and soon he was reporting that the "army here are in good spirits and think only of victory." By then, however, Schuyler had been confirmed by Congress as commander of the northern army. Gates gracefully acquiesced in the decision and served faithfully under him for the remainder of the campaign, accepting appointment of the forces below Lake Champlain.

The initial engagement was waged on the lake. Gates selected Benedict Arnold to command America's motley little fleet, ordering him to remain near the American army. Arnold did not heed these instructions, however; he brought on an engagement with the British vessels at Valcour Island in mid-October, 1776, and was soundly defeated. Nevertheless, after securing the lake and occupying Crown Point, Carleton, not ready for a winter's campaign so far from his primary source of supply, pulled back to Canada.[18] Gates deserves much of the credit for forcing the British retreat, for his actions forced delays upon the British that ultimately caused their commander to abandon his hopes for an offensive until the following year.

In December, 1776, Gates was ordered south with troops to reinforce Washington, but after a winter in command of troops in Philadelphia, he was ordered back to Ticonderoga and into the lingering dispute with Schuyler over the command of the northern army. Indeed, while in Philadelphia Gates had lobbied his cause with Congress. Initially, his politicking had failed. Not only had he hurt his chances by his display of temper, but by showing himself to be petty and vindictive where matters of rank and authority were concerned, he had alienated some congressmen. Nevertheless, when the British invasion of New York—led by General John Burgoyne—commenced in 1777, Schuyler quickly lost Fort Ticonderoga, and Congress removed him in favor of Gates.[19]

The return of Gates had a dramatic effect upon the demoralized northern army, now faced with the British invasion that Carleton had contemplated in 1776. Schuyler had been heartily disliked by the New England men in his army. They held Gates in high regard however, and he had won the respect of his other men by sharing with them the discomforts of camp life. Much of the army's effectiveness, moreover, was restored when he instilled strong discipline among the soldiers.

By the time Gates assumed command of the northern army, Burgoyne

already had suffered two devastating defeats. In the west, the force under
Barry St. Leger had sustained a defeat at Oriskany and had turned back.
To the east, two Hessian forces raiding for supplies near Bennington, Ver-
mont, were beaten by a force of New England militiamen under General
John Stark. Despite these setbacks, the British general continued his thrust
toward Albany.

Gates, meanwhile, was not inactive. He used shrewd propaganda to discredit Burgoyne. Learning of the death of Jane McCrae, a young frontier
maiden who had been killed by Indians supposedly loyal to the British,
Gates wrote to Burgoyne denouncing the atrocity and describing the victim
as a "young lady lovely to the sight." He pictured her as dressed in her
bridal gown. He did not mention that she was a British sympathizer. Made
public, his letter aroused the locals, inducing many militiamen to join his
army.

Gates was at this best in using the militia. He had great confidence in
these occasional soldiers and was well aware of their strengths and shortcomings. They trusted him, too. He had a reputation for not calling them
out until almost time for action, then, when their duty was over, for expressing his appreciation for their efforts and sending them back home.
During this campaign, moreover, he was aided by the fact that most of the
farmers had already harvested their crops and were more inclined to serve.

Gates's rejuvenated army at last clashed with the British in mid-September, 1777, the beginning of the Saratoga campaign. As Burgoyne approached, Gates took up a position on Bemis Heights, across the British
road to Albany. His right wing rested on the Hudson River, with his left
ending at the high ground to the west. On September 19 Burgoyne's army
pushed forward in three rather widely separated columns. Two American
groups of special troops under Colonel Daniel Morgan and Major Henry
Dearborn met the enemy head on. After an all day battle, the British suffered
losses nearly twice those of the Americans. The following day the British
went on the defensive and began throwing up a line of fortifications. Thereafter, Gates steadily pressured his foe by sending out raiding parties, and
early in October he repulsed Burgoyne's final attempt to retake the offensive.
When the British army fell back to the north, Gates began his pursuit. By
mid-October Burgoyne's army was nearly surrounded, and after several
days of negotiations the British army laid down their arms near the village
of Saratoga. Gates had not been able to persuade Burgoyne to sign a surrender. Instead, the British general had convinced Gates to accept a "Convention" that would allow the British troops to return to England on their
guarantee that they would not fight again in America. Congress refused to
accept this agreement and placed Burgoyne's troops in prison camps.[20]

Benedict Arnold, who fought magnificently in rebuffing Burgoyne early
in October, deserves some credit for the victory. But Gates, who developed
a strategy that allowed him to remain snug behind his fortifications while

Burgoyne wore himself out with repeated and ineffectual thrusts, was responsible for the victory. It was a case of Burgoyne's recklessness versus Gates's caution, and the latter prevailed.

Shortly after the victory at Saratoga, relations began to deteriorate between Gates and Washington. For one thing, Gates wrote directly to Congress reporting his success, rather than to the commander-in-chief as courtesy demanded. Washington also complained that Gates was lax in returning troops detached to him for the northern campaign. And, one suspects, Washington knew that people were comparing Gates's victory with his own defeat at Germantown.

None of these strains made matters any easier when the so-called "Conway Cabal" broke. General Thomas Conway, a French officer serving with the American army, wrote Gates criticizing Washington as a "weak general." Word of this letter reached Washington, who immediately convinced himself that Gates was a member of a "junto," or conspiracy, formed with the idea of replacing him—probably with Gates—as commander-in-chief. There is little evidence to support the idea of a cabal. Although Washington had his critics, there had never been a proposal in Congress to replace him.[21] Yet the damage was done, for Washington thought there was a cabal.

In November, 1777, Congress appointed Gates to the presidency of the Board of War, where he took the opportunity to be both petty and rude to the commander-in-chief. Without consultation with Washington he drew up plans for an invasion of Canada, and although that did not materialize, he engaged in a silly quarrel with the commanding general over expenses that had been incurred while drawing up the plans.[22]

During the next two years Gates had several commands, and once during this period he turned down an opportunity to lead an expedition against the Indians in the Mohawk Valley, pleading the infirmities of age. Toward the end of 1779 he requested and was granted a furlough to his home in Virginia. But when the situation in the Carolinas became desperate in 1780, Congress, without communication with Washington, appointed Gates to command the southern army. Gates might have heeded a statement supposedly made by Charles Lee: "Take care lest your Northern laurels turn to Southern willows." At any rate, Gates assumed command of a decimated legion, the tattered remnants of the southern army that recently had surrendered Charleston to an invading British force.

He joined his new command at Hillsborough, North Carolina, and soon discovered that he faced myriad problems. Not only was his diminutive army poorly supplied, but the southern militia were well nigh ungovernable.[23] Nevertheless, within a few days of his arrival, Gates started his army marching for the small British outpost at Camden, South Carolina, taking a direct route through the pine barrens and areas controlled by loyalists. His plan was to travel the quickest route in the hope that he would arrive before the British could receive reinforcements. It was a dreadful march.

Undertaken in the broiling southern summer, Gates and his men were forced to undergo hunger, dysentery, and the threat of mutiny. And it was pointless, for Lord Cornwallis had arrived at Camden with reinforcements for the garrison. When he reached Camden, Gates felt compelled to strike a blow as quickly as possible. Otherwise, his soldiery, already near mutiny because of their meager supplies, might simply have vanished. Moving ahead, he stumbled into a sortie led by Cornwallis. Gates's position was good and he had the consent of his generals to give battle. Therein lay the seeds of disaster.

The battle began in the early morning hours of August 16, 1780. Gates ordered the Virginia militia on the right to attack, but as they stepped forward Cornwallis ordered his men to fire a volley, to be followed by a bayonet charge. In sheer terror the Virginia militia, soon to be joined by the North Carolina militia, fled. Unable to rally them, Gates also took flight, pursued by a British cavalryman. He covered the 180 miles from Camden to Hillsborough in three days.[24]

The defeat at Camden was a disaster for Horatio Gates. At a cost of only 320 casualties, Cornwallis inflicted nearly 650 losses on Gates's army. The militia were scattered, some never to return to active service.[25] For Cornwallis, the road to North Carolina and Virginia lay open. Gates's great faith in the militia had led to his downfall.

Gates's reputation was ruined. Not only was there the shame of the loss of the battle, but he was accused of cowardice for having left the battlefield. And he was not believed when he said that he hurried to Hillsborough in order to regroup his men. Congress removed him from command in October and ordered a court of inquiry into his conduct at Camden.

Gates retired to Traveller's Rest, his home in Virginia, there to grieve over the recent death of his son and to besiege Congress with calls to initiate the court of inquiry. His pleas were unavailing until 1782, however, when, at last, he was reinstated into the army. He rejoined Washington and became the second ranking officer in the American army, but by then the fighting in this war had come to an end.[26]

In retrospect, Gates had the military talent, but he also had shortcomings, the greatest of which was his inability to get along with his colleagues, especially General Washington. Yet his virtues outweighed his vices. For one thing, he played an influential role in winning one of the most decisive battles of the war, and he had been a major figure in blocking British moves from the north. He was an able organizer and administrator, although his greatest talent perhaps lay in his leadership. He was a firm disciplinarian, but he treated the common soldiers with kindness, and was able to inspire their confidence and to rouse their spirits to a fighting pitch.

These talents deserted him in the South, however. Given little support by General Washington—the commander had too few men to spare—Gates was compelled to rely on the southern militiamen. It proved a fatal mistake. The southern militia were of a different character from their counterparts in New York and New England. They were more casual in their comings and goings, and, unlike their northern brethren, they had not known Gates long enough to like and trust him. Gates committed another blunder, too. He started marching for Camden before his army was ready, and by a route that promised few or no supplies. Following his defeat, his enemies within Congress, assisted by some of Washington's aides, including Alexander Hamilton, forced his recall, effectively nullifying any future contributions from this man who had talked too much and who sometimes had acted too impetuously, but who must still be remembered as a force in winning the American Revolution.

Nathanael Greene was a self-taught military man. Almost alone of the revolutionary war generals, he had no military experience. He also had little formal education. The son of a wealthy anchor smith in Coventry, Rhode Island, Greene was brought up a Quaker, although his support of the colonial resistance movement led to his expulsion from the Society of Friends. As a young man, he worked for his father, sat in the Rhode Island Assembly, and on the eve of the war joined a local militia company, the Kentish Guards. Some of his fellow militiamen intimated that his stiff leg would be a blemish on their marching. He offered to resign, but was persuaded to stay—at the rank of private.

Greene long had been an avid reader of things military, and he had served as a member of a legislative committee planning Rhode Island defensive measures in 1775. Consequently, when the assembly voted to support an "Army of Observation" to join the New England force then besieging the British in Boston, Greene was chosen to command the troops. He was elevated from a private in the Kentish Guards to brigadier general. Why? His military talents, though undeveloped, were recognized. General Greene knew how to handle men and to conserve resources. He was able, it was thought, to exercise great patience and intelligent caution. Finally, it was apparent that he was a great believer in firm discipline.[27]

When Greene presented himself to Washington he was not a polished soldier, but he learned fast. Henry Knox was to note later that Greene "came to us, the rawest, the most untutored being" he had ever seen, but in less than a year he was the equal in military acumen of "any General Officer in the army, and very superior to most of them."[28] Indeed, upon the British evacuation of Boston in March, 1776, Washington made Greene responsible for the defense of Brooklyn Heights, the next most likely target of the redcoat army.

Greene fell seriously ill during the summer of 1776, however, and did not participate in the Battle of Long Island. Upon his recovery he was placed in command of the troops guarding the shores of New Jersey. Under his command was Fort Washington, on Manhattan, past whose walls British warships defiantly sailed. Greene reinforced the fortress, and he was con-

vinced that if General Howe attacked the position the Americans, snug
behind their fortifications, would inflict a disastrous defeat upon the enemy.
Possession of Fort Washington, Greene argued, would prevent the British
from driving into New Jersey or threatening General Charles Lee's command
in Westchester County. A number of other generals were in agreement with
Greene, and General Washington agreed to hold the position.[29] On November 17, Howe appeared before Fort Washington with 10,000 men and
on the following day attacked the fortification. The 3,000-man garrison
gallantly defended their position, but were forced that same day to surrender.

Greene's reputation plummeted. Some questioned his ability, and Washington briefly wondered if he had not overestimated his subordinate. Yet
the commander-in-chief bestowed upon Greene the command of one wing
of the American army that attacked Trenton on December 26. Following
the victory Greene was among those officers who attempted to persuade
Washington to push on and attack the Hessian garrison at Burlington. The
commanding general refused, but later admitted he had made a mistake.

After he went into winter quarters at Morristown, Washington, in March
1777, dispatched Greene to Congress to lobby on his behalf. Among the
things the general wanted was the creation of three new major generals, of
which Greene would be one. When Congress did not act on any of Washington's suggestions, Greene left Philadelphia feeling that Congress was little
more than a debating society. Upon his return to the army he was assigned
the task of inspecting the defensive work along the Hudson Highlands. Then
he was sent to Middlebrook, New Jersey, to select a spot from which the
army might launch a campaign.[30]

General Howe made the decision for Washington. He decided to strike
at Philadelphia, landing his army at the head of Chesapeake Bay, then
marching overland to the city. Washington stationed the main part of his
army at Chad's Ford, the most likely site, he believed, for Howe to attempt
a crossing of the Brandywine Creek. But he was outwitted by Howe, who
made a feint at Chad's Ford while marching the greater part of his army
in a wide sweep to outflank the Americans under General John Sullivan.
Greene was ordered to support Sullivan, and in less than fifty minutes he
had marched his men four miles. He succeeded in establishing defensive
positions that allowed the American army to retreat without further losses.

In early October, after Howe had taken Philadelphia, Washington decided
to make a surprise attack upon that portion of the British army then in
camp at Germantown. Greene commanded the left wing of the attack, but
arrived at Germantown forty-five minutes late after becoming lost in the
darkness and the fog. Before he could suffer defeat, Washington pulled out
his force.

After these two defeats, both Washington and Greene were subjected to
heavy criticism. Greene was blamed for influencing the commander-in-chief,
as he was generally considered to be the officer closest to Washington.

Washington came to Greene's defense by stating that should anything happen to him it was his desire that Greene should be his successor.[31]

During the winter at Valley Forge Washington, against Greene's wishes, appointed the Rhode Islander as quartermaster general. Although unhappy with the job, Greene's efforts were almost superhuman, and he managed to get at least a minimum of supplies to the army. He did come under criticism for making money out of his position, although the law allowed a commission of 1 percent on all funds spent by his department, which he split with his assistants. He also practiced a form of nepotism by awarding contracts to his relatives in Rhode Island, but he felt that he had done nothing improper as the supplies were in good condition and were purchased at the current prices.

Greene still yearned for a field command, but the opportunity did not arise—save for brief moments—until Gates's disaster at Camden. When that unfortunate general was removed, Congress left the choice of a commander of the Southern Department to Washington. He selected Greene, and he also gave him the services of Baron von Steuben and the Legion of Henry "Light Horse Harry" Lee.

When he joined his army in Charlotte, North Carolina, Greene found that he commanded a ragged force of 2,000 men. "This is really making bricks without straw." he wrote.[32] Yet there was one bit of encouraging news. Cornwallis had planned to invade North Carolina and had ordered Major Patrick Ferguson to protect his left flank with loyalist militia. In October, 1780, a group of mountain men had defeated Ferguson at King's Mountain. Cornwallis had fallen back to Winnsboro, South Carolina, to await reinforcements from Virginia.

Learning of these developments, Greene made a decision that was to shape his destiny. He split his army. Daniel Morgan, in command of light troops and cavalry, was ordered to take a position to the north of Cornwallis. Greene marched his force to Cheraw Hill, South Carolina, seventy-five miles from Cornwallis. Small mounted detachments under Francis Marion and Henry Lee were harassing loyalists and blocking British supply lines.

As reinforcements under General Alexander Leslie neared Winnsboro, Cornwallis decided that it was time to do something about Morgan. He sent Colonel Banastre Tarleton, with approximately 1,150 men to attack him. On January 17, 1781, in a little gem of a battle, Morgan defeated Tarleton at the Cowpens. Morgan started moving northward with his prisoners the day after the battle.

Cornwallis also started northward, seeking to intercept Morgan. Greene, too, moved to the north, hoping to join Morgan and direct his retreat. It was Greene's intention, however, to stand and fight only if the North Carolina militia turned out in substantial numbers. That did not occur. In fact, he lost troops when the Virginia militia, declaring their time was up, went home. Even Daniel Morgan, complaining of "sciatica," went home.

Thus weakened, Greene was compelled to dance away from Cornwallis in a race across North Carolina. So quickly did he move that the British general burned his baggage in a vain effort to pursue faster. At Guilford Court House Greene was joined by the main army, but because so few militia had responded to his call, he decided to continue his retreat across the Dan River and into Virginia. Late in February, 1781, however, Greene, reinforced by Virginia militia, recrossed the Dan. Cornwallis fell back slowly. As the American force swelled to 4,200 contrasted to about 2,000 under Cornwallis, Greene decided to make a stand at Guilford Court House. On a slowly rising hill he stationed his men in three rows.

As the British line fired a volley and charged, the first American line, the North Carolina militia, broke and ran after firing one round. The Virginia militia, making up the second line, held for a while and then were slowly pushed back. The third line, composed of Maryland and Delaware Continentals held firm. After two hours of fighting, Greene's ammunition was running low and the Maryland line had been breached. Greene ordered a withdrawal from the field. Cornwallis, too weak to pursue, marched down to Wilmington where he could be supplied by sea.[33]

Cornwallis guessed wrong as to Greene's next move. Deciding to march into Virginia and make a junction with the British forces in that state, Cornwallis was certain that Greene would follow. Instead, Greene turned back into South Carolina. Over the next few months, Greene fought a series of inconclusive, even unsuccessful, engagements. Yet he was not dismayed. "We fight, get beat, rise, and fight again," he wrote, and by late summer all of South Carolina, except the area near the seacoast, was free of British occupation.[34]

The British forces in South Carolina remained strong, however, and Greene sought to destroy them in the battle of Eutaw Springs on September 8, 1781. Prior to the engagement he had been joined by the militia under Francis Marion and Andrew Pickens. In the bloody battle that followed, the British claimed a victory because Greene had left the field. But the British losses were so considerable that they thereafter were compelled to evacuate all of South Carolina except the Charleston area.

After the surrender of Cornwallis at Yorktown fighting continued in the south, although Greene was not strong enough to do anything but lay siege to Charleston. Not until December, 1782, did the enemy evacuate the city, and it was not until the peace treaty was ratified that Greene disbanded the remnants of his army. Thereafter, Greene retired to Mulberry Grove, the plantation given him by the state of Georgia, where he died in 1786.[35]

In retrospect, Nathanael Greene was perhaps the best general officer of the American Revolution. He had begun the war as an inexperienced political appointee, but he grew in stature as the war progressed, until he was recognized as unsurpassed in the realm of military knowledge. His sound judgment, as well as his ability to learn, drew Washington to him. Not only was the commander inclined to overlook the Fort Washington disaster, but when Washington was given the opportunity to appoint a commanding general in the south, he immediately chose Greene. It was a splendid choice. Greene made greater use of the region's partisan leaders, men like Francis Marion, Thomas Sumter, and Andrew Pickens than had his predecessors. He also made judicious use of a military tactic that he had learned from Washington, that of pulling his troops from battle if there was any doubt of complete victory. By that means he was able to keep a force in the field to pose a constant threat to the enemy. Technically, Greene never won a battle in the south, yet after every battle his opponent was so weakened that he always retreated, freeing the area from enemy occupation. And it was his spirited opposition that led Lord Cornwallis to abandon the Carolinas, a move that so weakened the British general that it played a role in his eventual surrender at Yorktown. Despite his lack of military experience before 1775, Greene learned well all the basic rules of warfare. He eventually became Washington's most trusted subordinate, a general who deserves to be remembered as the greatest strategist of the Revolution.

The Marquis de Lafayette became the epitome of the American Revolution. This young French aristocrat, only nineteen years old in the year of America's independence, spoke with Silas Deane, America's envoy in Paris, about the possibility of joining the American army. Although Lafayette was but a reserve captain in the French army, a brash youth who never before had been in combat, he demanded a major general's commission. He agreed to serve without pay, however, and Deane accepted his terms.

When the French government prevented the departure of French officers recruited by Deane, Lafayette bought a merchant ship and he and fifteen other officers secretly sailed for America. Upon his arrival Lafayette learned that Congress had had enough of foreign officers. But the young Frenchman persuaded Congress to grant him a major general's commission, without pay, and on the promise that he would not exercise his right to command a division.

Lafayette reached Washington's headquarters in August, 1777, and the American commander seems to have been immediately impressed by the young general's eagerness and charm. Washington assured him that he would be happy to be regarded as a "father and a friend."[36]

Lafayette did not have long to wait for his first military action. In the battle of Brandywine in September he played a prominent role. He also displayed exceptional bravery, continuing to fight long after he sustained a serious wound. Nursed back to health by the gentle Moravians in Bethlehem, Pennsylvania, Lafayette rejoined the army around the middle of October, finding himself to be something of a hero. That, and his valorous service in engagements during the next few weeks, demonstrated to Washington's satisfaction that Lafayette was ready to command a division. Nor was his attitude a hindrance. "I read, I study, I examine, I listen, I think, and out of all that I try to form an idea into which I can put as much common sense as I can," he once said of his philosophy. "I shall not speak much for fear of saying foolish things," he added. "I will risk still less for fear of doing them, for I am not disposed to abuse the confidence which they have deigned to show me. Such is the conduct which until now I have followed and will follow."[37]

In 1778, when the Board of War proposed an expedition into Canada, Lafayette was selected to command the invading army. It was felt that he would impress the French Canadians. But when he arrived at Albany, he found things in such disarray that he wrote the Board requesting a new command. He rejoined Washington at Valley Forge in April, 1778, and was given a force of 2,000 men and sent off on a probing march toward Philadelphia. Half-way to the city he established a camp on Barren Hill. He managed to evade the three columns sent out by the enemy to trap him and returned to the army unscathed.[38]

Early that fall the young general requested permission to return to France for a visit. Detained there because of his participation in the abortive Franco-Spanish invasion of England, he did not come back to America until the spring of 1780. He desperately hoped to return as the commander of the expeditionary force that his king was dispatching to America, but he was forced to conceal his disappointment when the veteran Comte de Rochambeau was selected.

After Lafayette rejoined the American army, he served briefly as something of a liaison between Washington and Rochambeau. However, when Benedict Arnold, now a British brigadier-general, invaded Virginia early in 1781, Lafayette was sent south with 1,200 Continentals. He hoped to bag Arnold in Portsmouth by a combined land and naval effort, although he was compelled to abandon the project when, after an engagement with a British fleet, the French naval vessels were forced to return to the northward. Fearing that he might miss out on more important Franco-American endeavors in the North, Lafayette was not anxious to tarry in Virginia until he learned that the British reinforcement for Arnold was commanded by Major General William Phillips, who had commanded the artillery unit that had fired the shot that killed his father in 1751. Lafayette also soon discovered that he would find quite enough action in Virginia to keep him busy, for the Earl of Cornwallis and his army of 7,700 men promptly invaded the state. Lafayette, half of whose command was militia, could muster no more than 2,500 men to defend against the redcoats. To Washington, he complained, "I am not strong enough to get beaten."

As Cornwallis approached Richmond, Lafayette moved north, putting his force between the British and the American supply depots. In early June he was joined by Anthony Wayne and 900 Continentals, and shortly thereafter Colonel William Campbell, who had fought at King's Mountain, rode in with 600 mounted militia.

After failing to catch "the boy," as Cornwallis called Lafayette, the British general raided deep into Virginia, sending the legion of Banastre Tarleton to Charlottesville in a vain attempt to capture Governor Thomas Jefferson. But as Lafayette was reinforced, Cornwallis fell back toward Williamsburg in expectation of receiving new orders. Following closely on his heels was the young Marquis.

At Williamsburg, Cornwallis found dispatches from Sir Henry Clinton ordering him to take up a defensive position on the coast and to detach a part of his force to the north, as the British command anticipated an American-French attack on New York. Cornwallis, on his way to Portsmouth, started to cross the James River.[39]

On July 6, in the evening, while the British were crossing the river at Jamestown, Wayne came upon and charged what he thought was the enemy rear guard. He did not realize that the main British army lay just beyond them, a trap adeptly laid by Cornwallis. When the British charged out of concealment, Wayne recognizing that a retreat would bring on a rout, pulled a bluff by ordering a charge. Lafayette came up with troops and saved the day, with Wayne's men falling back. Lafayette pitched camp above Williamsburg on Malvern Hill, but as he watched Cornwallis settle in at Yorktown, he began to plead with General Thomas Nelson, the new governor of Virginia, for men and supplies that might enable him to strike his foe. His entreaties were unavailing, yet late in August he received word that the French fleet of Admiral François de Grasse and the combined armies of Washington and Rochambeau were on their way to entrap Cornwallis. During the siege that followed in September and October, Lafayette's division played a key role, especially in the seizure of British redoubts outside the Yorktown fortifications.[40]

He had come to America with almost no previous military experience, and he probably was given his high rank by Congress for diplomatic reasons. An ambitious person, he realized that Washington was susceptible to flattery, and he seems to have used that technique to the fullest to win the favor of the commander-in-chief. Nevertheless, while he blundered in several early military engagements, Lafayette did seem to learn from his mistakes, for he performed well when he was given the command in Virginia. He took good care of the men under his command, and was something of a genius in scraping up food and supplies, even if he had to spend his own money for the good of his troops. He was idealistic and deeply committed to the principle of self-government. He was devoted to Washington, and with good reason the commander apparently came to love him as the son he never had.

Henry Knox, a Boston bookseller of humble origins, had educated himself on military matters through extensive reading. He well may have known more about the use of artillery than any other colonist in 1775; at any rate, no one with greater knowledge in these matters presented themselves to

General Washington that first summer of the war. This corpulent young man—he was barely twenty-five years old—so impressed Washington that the commander acquiesced quickly when John Adams proposed that Knox be made a colonel and chief of artillery.

If Washington had few cannon, there were captured artillery at Fort Ticonderoga, only recently taken from the enemy by Ethan Allen and Benedict Arnold. Knox proposed that he be appointed to bring back the guns, and when Washington consented he made the long journey to northern New York to retrieve the weapons. At Ticonderoga Knox selected some sixty cannon, then he faced the problem of their return, for the artillery not only weighed over 120,000 pounds, it had to be transported some 300 miles, much of that distance a forbidding mountainous wilderness.

For the trek back to Boston, Knox loaded fifty-nine artillery pieces on forty-two sleds to be drawn by horses and oxen. Over the snow and frozen streams and lakes they trudged. Some of the sleds broke through the ice, but in almost every instance the cannon were recovered. In early February, after a journey of six weeks through inhospitable terrain, Knox arrived in camp with his "noble train of artillery." Soon the weapons were placed on Dorchester Heights overlooking Boston, the move that led to the evacuation of the city by the British.[41]

When the Continental army moved to New York, Knox played an important part in the fortification of that city, but in the battle that raged in August and September his units played an ineffectual role, partly because many of his cannon were defective, partly because his men were inexperienced or poorly disciplined, or both. At year's end, however, the artillery regiments made a better showing. On Christmas night, Knox first supervised the ferrying of the artillery across the Delaware River, then he directed their placement so that they commanded the village of Trenton. The fire of his guns played a significant role in the victory. A few days later at Princeton the Continental army appeared to be on the edge of defeat until Knox's artillery came up, allowing Washington's troops to rally and win a substantial victory.[42] It was a fitting triumph for Knox, too, for Congress, unaware of his contribution in the Trenton victory, already had promoted him to the rank of brigadier general.

Knox had little time to bask in glory before he became involved in an ugly situation. Among the foreign officers sent from Paris was one Philippe du Coudray, an arrogant Frenchman who claimed to have been commissioned by Silas Deane as a major general and "commander-in-chief of Continental Artillery." Moreover, he had the documents to prove it. Knox, Greene, and John Sullivan each wrote letters requesting that they be retired if Coudray was given the command. After some debate, Knox was left in command, and Coudray solved the problem by falling off a ferry and drowning. Coudray's misfortune seemed almost providential when at the battle of Brandywine that September the artillerymen under Knox once again gave good accounts of themselves. Indeed, Knox was led to boast: "My corps did me great honor."

Knox's military star, clearly in the ascendancy, nearly was shattered during the battle of Germantown in October, 1777. Early in the engagement, after a surprise attack, the Americans had the British on the run until the advancing Continentals came upon the large stone mansion of Pennsylvania Chief Justice Benjamin Chew, a residence stuffed with redcoats. The American attack stalled because of the hail of lead that poured from its windows. Baffled, Washington called a council of war on the battlefield. Some of the generals advised that he leave a small force to entertain the defenders of the abode while the main army continued the pursuit of the fleeing enemy. Knox objected, urging instead that a summons to surrender be sent to the defenders. "It would be unmilitary to leave a castle in our rear," he added.[43] Unfortunately, Washington listened to Knox. The artillery commander brought up his guns and began to pound the building, but the balls ricocheted off the thick stone walls. Saved by the delay that resulted from the Americans' misguided strategy, the British regrouped and repulsed the subsequent attack. The possible victory at Germantown became a defeat.

After the Battle of Monmouth, the last major battle in the north, Knox spent much time training his men. During the winter of 1779, for instance, he established at Pluckemin, New Jersey what he termed "the academy," a "school" in which gave instructions on gunnery, tactics, and other military subjects.[44] This training paid off at Yorktown in 1781 when Washington and Rochambeau laid siege to Cornwallis's army. Knox put forth precise orders as to the firing of his guns, and in the afternoon of October 6 they opened up on the British position. It is said that one of the first shots tore through the house in which Cornwallis's staff officers were meeting, killing the British Commissary General and wounding three others. When Washington opened a second siege line Knox brought his artillery pieces forward and their accurate fire prevented an answering fire from the British guns. The highest accolade for Knox's work was perhaps penned by Washington in his subsequent report to Congress. "His genius supplied the deficit of means," he wrote of Knox, and he also recommended that his loyal artillery chief be promoted to major general. Among Washington's last official acts as commander-in-chief was to name Knox as his successor.[45] That gesture, more than any words could convey, indicated what Knox meant to General Washington.

Henry Knox, like Greene, had no military experience prior to the revolutionary war, but he, too, was well read in military matters. A tenacious and courageous man, Knox demonstrated great loyalty and affection for Washington, and taken together, these traits may explain why the commander overlooked his inadequate performances at New York and Germantown. That, and the fact that he trained the artillery under his command to a near degree of perfection.

It was with considerable irony, therefore, that in the course of this long, often agonizing war, George Washington, who labored tirelessly to construct a regular army along the lines of the English model, ultimately was drawn to depend most upon the talents and advice of Generals Greene, Knox, and Lafayette—two callow amateurs and a green youth from abroad—while he turned his back on Generals Gates and Lee, the two professional soldiers whose services he had sought at the outset of the conflict.

To the general public of our day, the names of Lafayette and Knox are perhaps the most recognizable of Washington's chief lieutenants, although, the details of their contributions very likely are not well known. Yet each of the five men scrutinized in this essay aided the American victory. In the dark early days of the conflict Lee assisted Washington in molding the army, and before his capture late in the autumn of 1776 he had played an important role in military operations in Boston, New York, and Charleston. Gates led the northern army to the decisive victory in 1777 that resulted in the Franco-American Treaty of Alliance. Greene presided over the provisioning of the Continental army during one of the most desperate periods of the war, and later he took command of the ragtag southern army and guided it to successes that no one could have imagined. Lafayette fought with valor and distinction in the South, helping to keep Virginia open and assuring that the flow of supplies to Greene in the Carolinas could continue unabated. Knox fashioned a capable artillery arm for the Continentals, and in crucial moments—at Boston and on the Brandywine, and still later at Yorktown—his presence was critical to Washington's success.

Had General Washington not been served—well served, in fact— by each of these officers, the War of Independence might have been fought to a very different conclusion.

6

Logistics
and the American Victory

Mark Edward Lender

Few historians have had anything good to say about rebel efforts to pay, clothe, feed, and equip their armed forces. Rather, the usual story has been one of good intentions gone wrong, of incompetence, and of the limited resources of the young nation squandered or broken under the stresses of war. Most early studies saw efforts to provision the army as virtually doomed, the result of inherently flawed organizational and administrative arrangements in the Quartermaster and Commissary Departments, and of congressional policies that divided logistical responsibilities between Continental and state authorities.[1] On the other hand, students of revolutionary finances have observed that even if logistics administration had been sound the young nation's fiscal problems alone were enough to make procuring the sinews of war a nightmare; and worse, some of the essential sinews—including food and forage—became dangerously scarce as the war dragged on.[2] More recent scholarship has suggested that the army went without because local authorities, infused with a republican jealousy of the military, often cooperated only warily with quartermaster and commissary personnel, thus impeding the establishment of a firm logistical structure or financial base.[3]

Whatever the viewpoint, no historian has offered a case for logistical efforts making a major direct contribution to the American victory. If it is true, to paraphrase Napoleon, that armies travel on their stomachs, one can wonder how the Continental army ever traveled those long years to Yorktown. But the result of the war remains: the rebels won it, or at least held on until the British quit. Indeed, throughout the conflict patriot forces not only received enough provisions and equipment—and had sufficient support services—to remain operational (albeit sometimes at reduced levels), but never in the long war did the British conclude that the American army was not a credible threat. If the logistical picture was often bleak, wrote Congressman William Whipple in 1779, "I do not quite dispair."[4] Poor by European standards, the Continental army had enough to get the job done, if only barely.

This might suggest the possibility of a more positive view of the American logistical effort than previous scholarship was allowed. At any rate, the role of logistics in securing the patriot victory merits a reconsideration. Much of the early scholarship, preoccupied as it was with supply-related deficiencies that dogged the rebel military—no matter how justified—may have obscured other equally important questions. How well, for instance, did patriot quartermasters and commanders manage the resources that were available to them? How did they compensate for the materials they lacked? And to what extent did they take these matters into account when planning operations?

"Logistics" is a broadly defined term. Traditionally, it has encompassed all aspects of the production, acquisition, transportation, distribution, supply, finance, and support of military personnel and their food, equipment, and related material. It often includes such activities as recruiting and medical support. This essay, however, will restrict the meaning of logistics to the actual gathering of supplies and the mechanisms, formal and informal, that brought them to the armies.[5] In general, these were the concerns of the Quartermaster and Commissary Departments, as well as of General Washington and other senior commanders. This is an operational approach to logistics, and it admittedly recalls the "old" military history with its emphasis on events in the field, but it has the virtue of focusing on those elements that contributed most directly to maintaining the Continental line as an army in being.

Whigs launched their revolution with more enthusiasm than gunpowder, or, for that matter, stores of any sort. The First Continental Congress in 1774 had taken few steps to prepare for war, and the efforts of most provinces to procure arms during that autumn proved to be ineffectual. It is true that some of the larger provinces, notably Massachusetts, Virginia, and Pennsylvania pulled together munitions and material to equip respectable militia forces, and even in New Jersey, which was anything but a hot bed of radicalism, Whigs began setting up local magazines.[6] Overall, however, there was too little of everything. The rebels lacked domestic sources for most provisions except food and forage, military transport was nonexistent, and there was no central control of logistics, either within colonies or between them. In short, the Americans were utterly unprepared to fight a war.

Any effort to move and supply troops in eighteenth-century America was a formidable undertaking. In June of 1775, however, when Congress assumed control of the Continental Army, it also took on logistical responsibilities that dwarfed those faced in any of the individual states. Continental forces quickly expanded into the thousands, and early on contingents operated across vast distances. During the first year of the conflict alone, Washington conducted a protracted siege at Boston, General Richard Montgomery and Colonel Benedict Arnold assaulted Canada, and South Carolinians held Charleston against a major sea-borne attack. And as the struggle intensified, there was virtually no logistical base to support sustained operations. The rebellious colonies had to create such a base, a task that constituted one of the most important conditions of victory. Specifically, they needed to procure necessary provisions, to find the means of storing and transporting them, as well as transporting troops, and to devise a system to manage the range of tasks inherent in the entire effort. Moreover, they had to do so in the face of a series of complex and daunting problems.

The new nation lacked the means to produce almost all war material. The American economy was overwhelmingly agricultural, and manufacturing was inadequate to supply large forces with even such basic needs as powder, shot, and clothing, let alone cannon, tents, wagons, picks, shovels, cooking utensils, and the other myriad items necessary for life in the field. By the end of the war, the rebels had stimulated domestic production of cloth, iron, gunpowder, and other military necessities, but these improvements were too little and too late to substantively relieve army shortages.[7] Throughout the conflict, patriots depended most for key supplies on captures, aid from the French, and purchases abroad (usually on credit) by government agents or private merchants. This was risky, as the Royal Navy took a dim view of rebel trade: it blockaded most American ports, and more than once, the interception of key shipments led directly to hardship in the army. Accordingly, Washington always considered imports a "precarious" source of supplies.[8]

The king's men-of-war also impeded America's coastal shipping, a fact that grated on commanders. The British could strike up and down the coast "without our having an hour's previous notice of it," Washington complained. In preparing southern defenses in 1776, General Charles Lee found even the rivers vulnerable. The "circumstances of the country," he informed the commander-in-chief, "intersected by navigable rivers, the uncertainty of the enemy's designs and motions, who can fly in an instant to any spot where they chose with their canvass wings," made it difficult to know where to defend.[9] Clearly, patriot attempts to base logistical operations on water transport, or to establish magazines within range of an enemy sea-borne strike, were tempting fate.

Consequently, most army shipments moved overland. The road network was primitive, and vast areas of back country had no roads at all. To move his supplies in 1779, for example, General John Sullivan had to detail entire infantry companies to hack a new route into Iroquois territory. Established routes were often little better, sometimes no more than wagon tracks which turned into mire in the rain; others were so sandy that wagons sank down to their hubs. Moreover, the British occupation of New York City prevented the use of some of the best intercolonial overland routes, especially those formerly linked to coastal water traffic. Goods moving to and from New England often had to detour through rough terrain in southern New York State and northern New Jersey.[10] Besides the inconvenience, all of this was expensive and kept the army in constant need of teams, wagons, teamsters, repair personnel, and forage. Much of this equipment and staff would have been necessary anyway, but the inability to make wider use of the waterways exacerbated matters. Until the end of the war, the transportation situation was such that it was difficult to distribute even those supplies that were at hand.

The procurement and movement of food and equipment, however, depended to a great extent on the management of the logistics effort—that is, upon the establishment of an administrative structure to supervise the minutiae of quartermaster and commissary operations. In the beginning, there was little that Congress could do. Upon naming Washington commander-in-chief, they appointed a quartermaster general and a commissary general of stores and purchases to assist him. But to name officers was not to create a system. That took time, and despite the presence in ranks of a few veterans of the French and Indian War with supply experience, the colonists generally lacked trained personnel.[11] Most logistics officers had to learn on the job, and the hastily formed support departments spent the war years trying to catch up with the demands of a conflict that had begun before they were established.

It would be difficult to conjure a more perplexing logistical scenario for the new nation. Yet, the Americans were not alone in facing logistical problems. The British had problems of their own.[12] While redcoats and their allies never starved, and while their equipment and supply inventories generally were enough to make rebel counterparts green with envy, they often had to operate under grim conditions. They could use the seas to their advantage, but most of their generals were convinced that their resources were too little to subdue the Americans, and they lamented the fact that they had to conduct operations in a hostile countryside far from their chief garrisons and bases of supply and reinforcement. Patriots frequently moved food and forage out of British range, or made the king's soldiers fight for what they could get. Consequently, British contingents usually had to subsist off whatever they carried with them, which encumbered most enemy forces with large and vulnerable supply trains.[13]

This state of affairs bred caution in most British commanders. While there were exceptions, such as Lord Cornwallis, British leaders preferred to stay within reach of naval resupply. They were, as historian W. B. Wilcox has aptly phrased it, "tethered by their supply lines to the coast," a policy that militated against inclinations to pursue rebels into the interior. Nor was the situation always better in garrison, where, ironically, the very numbers of British troops and pack trains became logistical liabilities. Idle men and animals still needed food, and patriots made it dangerous to forage in the countryside. The British commandant of occupied New York, General James Robertson, became so concerned over forage shortages that he suggested cutting garrison animals to a bare minimum, leaving the army to hire or impress private teams. Sir William Howe faced much the same problem after his conquest of Philadelphia in 1777. Over the winter he was compelled to conduct major foraging operations in order to feed his men and animals, a debilitating task that contributed to his lack of enthusiasm for a winter venture against Washington at Valley Forge.[14] Without control of the hinterlands, then, maintaining an army in any city was a difficult proposition. The salient point, however, was that in garrison or in the field, the British were normally so busy trying to feed and supply themselves that they were impeded from turning their full energies against the patriots.

None of this is to suggest that the British command would have traded its logistical problems for those of Washington. But it should remind us that supply was a constant weak link in both American and British operations. Pressed as they were for the sinews of war, the patriots did not face an enemy that held all of the advantages, and under the circumstances the rebels had more than enough room to use logistics creatively.

Considering the enormity of the task, patriot logistical operations got off to a good start in 1775. The army around Boston received enough equipment to conduct a lengthy siege, and the Massachusetts countryside supplied abundant foodstuffs. There also were enough imported powder and shot on hand (mostly imported on the eve of hostilities), and the rebels acquired a potent addition to their artillery when Henry Knox brought to camp the cannon taken at Fort Ticonderoga.[15] Washington's positions remained relatively stable, which simplified deliveries of food and material; and with the British penned in Boston, patriot transport lines remained fairly secure. There were some problems, including shortages of tents and entrenching tools, but these were irritations rather than major disruptions. The significant point is that for the first year of the war, except for the difficulties in supplying the Arnold and Montgomery sallies into Canada (a tough job even for a mature logisitical system), rebel troops generally had what they needed.[16]

These early successes, of course, were deceptive. Later, with the shift of operations to the middle colonies, patriot logistics proved unequal to the task. Over the campaigns of 1776 and 1777, transport and supply services steadily deteriorated, reaching their nadir during the Valley Forge winter. Not two years after they had forced the British out of Boston, the rebel battalions shivered, nearly starving and on the brink of dissolution, victims, in perhaps equal shares, of British martial prowess and of the mistakes of their own leaders.

The most obvious factor in the near logistical collapse was military defeat. Washington had the wherewithal to fight when he gathered his forces around New York, but keeping his stores intact and his supply lines functioning was another matter. Here the rebel general's problems were of a piece with those of commanders throughout history. Quartermasters in any age have disliked fluid warfare. Troop movements are hard to predict, making it difficult to ship arms and stores efficiently and securely, and even winning combat eats material voraciously and puts a premium on timely resupply. The consequences of supply shortages, or of misdirected, late, or captured supply shipments can be dire even for troops with the initiative; for retreating formations, particularly if their supply efforts fall prey to hostile interdiction, the results can be catastrophic.[17] Such were the circumstances of the patriot army.

Unlike the siege at Boston, the fighting in and around New York and in New Jersey was extremely fluid, and the same was true around Philadelphia the following year. The pace of operations would have tested even a proven logistics command. Indeed, British officers, who had logistical support beyond anything available to their Continental opposites, bemoaned quartermaster difficulties even as they led their men to victory. But in America's case it was not just the tempo of those campaigns that produced problems. Active fighting consumed tons of munitions, food, and animal forage, and tons more were lost when the British overran American positions, especially at Fort Washington and Fort Lee in 1776 and the Delaware River forts below Philadelphia, which fell after a gallant defense in 1777.[18]

Transport was also a casualty. Like men, horses died of wounds and disease, and wagons and gun carriages broke down under hard use and enemy fire. Even with respites in the fighting, such as those before Trenton or the Morristown winter of 1776/77, it took time to refit or replace teams and vehicles. There was seldom enough of either to assure the mobility of supply trains, and even when animals and wagons were sufficient to conduct operations, the system remained fragile. There were too few reserves to replace destroyed or captured equipment, and in some respects the loss of a wagon or caisson hurt as badly as the loss of a cannon.[19] The need to protect vital stores from capture also tied down transportation resources. As the enemy closed on Philadelphia in 1777, for example, Quartermaster General Thomas Mifflin had to divert wagons and teams from other assignments (including the collection of supplies for the coming winter encampment) to haul stockpiled material to safety. The evacuation succeeded in the main, but it was terribly disruptive of other rebel operations.[20] Stretched thin by enemy action, the Continental transport system was tenuous. Pressure from additional quarters would threaten to snap it entirely.

The British army, then, deserves much of the credit (or blame) for initiating the chain of supply difficulties that led ultimately to Valley Forge. Howe's command forced the Continentals to expend vital munitions and supplies in losing efforts, captured tons of other material, interdicted deliveries, and severely taxed Washington's inexperienced commissary and quartermaster capabilities. Given the nature of military operations over 1776 and 1777, major supply problems were inevitable for the patriots no matter what remedies they adopted or how hard those in Congress and behind the lines worked on the army's behalf.

Still, most historians have emphasized that much of the logistical malaise stemmed from self-inflicted wounds, and there is no question that a series of patriot errors in the planning and administration of quartermaster and commissary affairs compounded the damage done by the British. Congress was partly to blame, chiefly for failing to provide effective coordination of logistical services. After the success at Boston, it saw little reason to reform supply operations, and deep into 1776 some congressmen felt that logistics were well in hand, even considering the debacle in Canada. As late as the fall of 1776, for example, supply matters appeared bright to Samuel Adams, who thought the system was functioning excellently. One reason for Congress's optimism was its belief that the states would help equip their Continental troops.[21]

Congress stumbled badly, however, once the magnitude of the disasters in the field became clear. In fact, its responses to the resulting logistical nightmare were less than effective. In June of 1776, Congress had created the Board of War and Ordnance, ostensibly to provide central oversight of the military. But the Board was not an executive department. Composed of congressmen who continued to perform other legislative duties, it had no professional staff and could not act independently. Instead, Congress served as its own executive and looked to the Board only for reports and recommendations. It was an unfortunate arrangement, for the delegates had neither the time nor the expertise to supervise the army effectively. They eventually did realize that they were in over their heads, and early in 1777 the Board was restructured to comprise men from outside of Congress, including military officers. The new Board of War had greater coordinating authority over the military effort, and its writ supposedly ran to the Commissary and Quartermaster Departments.[22] By that time, however, considerable damage had been done, and Congress never relinquished its penchant for intervening directly into military affairs.

One of the most serious manifestations of this lack of central control was in military procurement. At the highest levels, Congress had never issued specific instructions on departmental responsibilities to Commissary General Joseph Trumbull or Quartermaster General Mifflin. Left virtually unassisted to organize their operations, these officers did remarkably well, but they were never able to sort out their precise relationships to each other or to

Congress. Neither man, for example, could appoint his own senior deputies, a prerogative Congress retained. The arrangement did nothing to buttress the authority of the department heads, nor did the fact that Congress also commissioned independent purchasing agents and often made purchasing determinations itself. Agents of Trumbull and Mifflin occasionally competed directly with congressional appointees for the same supplies, and because Congress had no authority over the states, there was competition with state purchasing agents as well. Indeed, pressed to locate food and material of all kinds, departmental agents frequently strayed out of their assigned territories and competed with each other. All of this drove up prices, made procurement planning all but impossible, and exacerbated scarcities of key commodities.[23] Without firm control over their subordinates or clear relationships with Congress, however, Mifflin and Trumbull were powerless to correct the situation.

Muddled lines of authority additionally hindered inventory management. In the case of food, it was the Commissary Department's job to make purchases, while Mifflin's people saw to most of the shipping. But there was little coordination of these functions, thus even rations acquired in advance of immediate army needs frequently arrived late, or not at all. The problem could be worse when Congress made its own purchases. As late as 1779, for example, stores of clothing sat in French and West Indian warehouses because no one could decide whose responsibility it was to ship them. These were extreme cases, but similar episodes, albeit on a smaller scale, continued to plague the rebels. No one ever solved the riddle of warehouse control; inventory records were abysmal and there was virtually no way to quickly ascertain how much of anything was on hand or the status of requisitions or shipments in transit. In June of 1777, Richard Peters, secretary of the Board of War, admitted to Washington that this aspect of the logistics effort had come undone. He had tired repeatedly, he wrote, "to procure exact Accounts of the Receipt & Distribution of Military Stores, arms, &c received" by Continental agents, "but have not yet been able to do it with any Degree of Precision." The situation complicated operational planning and, equally serious, resulted in considerable waste. Food, forage, arms, tools, blankets, and other stocks too frequently rotted, molded, rusted, or fell prey to vermin as they sat in storage through oversight, neglect, or the inability to transport them.[24] Purchasing, warehousing, and distribution, of necessity, generate the minutiae of all logistics operations. They were the kinds of things that departments with clearly drawn responsibilities could learn to manage. However, they were also exactly the sort of things for which congressional delegates had neither the time, the resources, nor the understanding to administer.

Congress was not oblivious to the deteriorating situation, and it undertook a number of reforms over late 1776 and spring of 1777. New officers addressed the procurement of clothing, bread, hides, and forage, while others took up a variety of accounting and management tasks. The delegates also directed the purchase of hundreds of wagons and teams for the army's trains and appointed a wagonmaster, Joseph Thornsbury, to straighten out transport and distribution arrangements. Another step divided the Commissary Department in half, one department to look after purchases, the other to handle issues.[25] Still, even these attempts at reform betrayed crucial weaknesses.

The new appointments brought a number of troublesome matters to a head. In the case of commissary operations, the reforms quickly went awry. Congress had wanted Joseph Trumbull to stay on as commissary general of purchases. But the delegates (in his view) had ignored his advice on departmental financing and reorganization, and there is no doubt that they had politicized the process of departmental appointments. Keeping Trumbull in the dark, congressional factions maneuvered for the selection of friends. "We had a delicate Card to play and which required much Address," James Duane wrote upon securing the selection of a deputy commissary for New York State. The new deputy would influence the regional market for provisions, Duane told Philip Schuyler, which in his view justified the fight to control appointment.[26] After the fact, however, when Trumbull learned that Congress already had named his deputies, it was too much. He resigned effective August 20, and his successor, William Buchanan, proved ineffective, although the situation was probably beyond the control of any one man. Thus the department drifted without firm direction into the critical months of the 1777 campaign. By December, Congress was having grave second thoughts. "Buchanan is as incapable as a Child," James Lovell of Massachusetts wrote meanly, "and knows not how he can feed the army three weeks from any parts, or how to feed them from day to day with what he has on hand." Trumbull, he added, "would be deified if he was on the spot." He never hinted at the congressional role in fashioning the crisis.[27]

The Quartermaster Department did little better. Despite prodigious efforts over the summer and fall, Commissary General of Forage Clement Biddle found it impossible to secure forage enough for the projected winter needs of the army. Among other impediments, he faced too much competition from other purchasing agents whom, to his chagrin, he found that neither he nor his superior, Mifflin, could control. In fact, Mifflin all but gave up trying to direct the department. He spent his time in Philadelphia lobbying for quartermaster reforms, assisting with recruiting operations, and supervising the removal of stores from the path of the British. His absence, no matter how justified, left Biddle and other subordinates virtually without instructions. Finally, on October 8, Mifflin quit, pleading ill health. It may have been more a matter of disillusionment, for he was well enough to retain his major general's rank and join the Board of War. Congress asked him to hold the departmental reins until they found a replacement, but Mifflin demurred, delegating matters to a deputy.[28] In one of the real lapses of the war, Congress did not name a new quartermaster general until February 1778. Thus, during the trying times that saw the invasion of Pennsylvania and the beginning of the Valley Forge encampment, both of the support services labored without experienced leadership and without resolution of the administrative problems that had dogged their operations.

The most serious deficiencies, however, lay in transportation and distribution. Despite the congressional appropriation of June, the army never acquired enough teams and wagons. By fall of 1777, even trying to get them was too much for Wagon Master Thornsbury. Never energetic, he quit in October and Congress, again allowing a crucial post to remain vacant, named a replacement only in December. It may not have mattered. By this time, Continental finances were in such disarray that the army could little afford a major baggage train. Instead, it depended on contracting for private teams, which became difficult as owners feared for the loss of their property and resented congressional aversion to paying enough to overcome their anxieties. As the 1777 campaign closed, Continental forces found it impossible to replace losses to its transportation system and could barely find enough private transport to haul supplies to camp. The sad irony was that as transport services, along with inventory control and supervision of the logistics departments, collapsed over the autumn, stores generally remained adequate. In late December, Henry Laurens, the president of Congress, plaintively observed that the army at Valley Forge was "on the very verge of bankruptcy," wasting away through want of clothing and food, and "that we are Starving in the midst of plenty—perishing by Cold, & surrounded by Clothing Sufficient for two armies, but uncollected."[29] At least temporarily, then, the strain on patriot transport had reached the breaking point.

The grim logistical situation, of which Valley Forge was the grimmest example, reduced the patriots to embittered finger pointing. Before his resignation, Trumbull had accused Congress of allowing commissary affairs to run out of control. Washington, usually the soul of discretion, agreed in pointed terms. In reviewing 1777, the commander-in-chief noted that want of provisions had disrupted most of his operations; and in December he warned that the army faced disaster for the same reason. In a chilling account of the condition of his men, he held out the possibility that they would have to disperse in order to feed themselves. Others joined the lament. "An officer of merit," reported Pennsylvania Congressman Daniel Roberdeau, wrote "that he could shed Tears of blood for the opportunities lost through want of provisions," shortages which had negated "cutting off the flower of the British Army." And it was all the fault of Congress Roberdeau concluded bitterly.[30]

Other congressional voices, however, maintained that all of the problems were not of their making. In fact, some delegates were bewildered at the amount of material lost to enemy action. John Adams saw the loss of Fort

Ticonderoga in 1777 as a case in point: "Don't you pity me to be wasting away my Life," he wrote to Abigail Adams, "in Laborious Exertions, to procure Cannon, Ammunition, Stores, Baggage, Clothing &c. &c. &c. &c., for Armies, who give them all away to the Enemy, without firing a gun." Congress also wondered at Washington's reticence about impressing what he needed. As early as November, both the Board of War and Congress, which had voted approval of the policy, urged him vigorously to this course. Yet Washington, as well as a number of his lieutenants, feared that such levies upon the public would erode the army's popular support and quickly become counterproductive. Congress never conceded this point and questioned why Washington did not at least confiscate goods from Tories.[31]

There was blame enough to go around, but there seems little doubt, as most students have agreed, that the greatest patriot failing was the congressional inability to create effective administrative machinery to run the war effort. Even a charitable interpretation of logistical developments, especially over 1777, must hold that Congress aggravated the damage suffered at the hands of the British; a more severe view would hold that if the redcoats staggered the Continental line, congressional mismanagement almost finished it off.

The desperation of the Continental line in late 1777 was quite real, and no amount of hindsight about later victory can mitigate the plight of the men who suffered through that awful winter. But the fact remains that they got through it, and even before that, while logistical support services crumbled around them, they had fought creditably. The army that encamped at Valley Forge was, at least early on, still a force to reckon with, and Howe never considered that he could attack it successfully. While they suffered at the hands of the enemy and the bungling of friends, the Continentals survived, and the experience revealed a great deal about the practical—rather than officially prescribed—workings of maintaining the army in being.

Whatever other problems the rebels faced, they usually were able to maintain stocks of essential supplies. This is not to say that important commodities often were not scarce or, as we have seen, that patriots always were able to ship supplies when and where they were needed. Yet, when Washington's army entered Valley Forge in December, 1777, New England had an abundance of cattle, and sizeable herds awaited opportunities for shipment south. In addition, while intensive foraging for two years had picked sections of New Jersey fairly clean by that winter, harvests in the middle Atlantic states through 1777 had been good; and if food and forage reserves were nowhere near enough to last the winter, the army had acquired at least some small stockpiles of produce and salted meat. Indeed, commands detached from the main army usually had an easier time over the winter, especially if they were close to stored rations or in areas not overforaged. Early in 1778, when the commander-in-chief reported that his men were "literally reduced to a starving condition," he chafed over the fact that a post some miles way under General Israel Putnam had an abundance of fresh and salted beef.[32] At Valley Forge itself, once emergency measures broke transport logjams, the crisis in food and forage passed. What is clear, therefore, is that the rebels never ran out of food or forage. Their problem was getting it to the army.

The story was much the same with war material. Despite the best efforts of the Royal Navy, supplies slipped through to the beleaguered patriots. Over the Valley Forge winter, important shipments of French arms and munitions reached the army. Considering the modest size of the Continental line, even a single delivery could have a major impact. In December alone, a French transport tied up at Portsmouth, New Hampshire, with 48 brass cannon, 19 mortars, some 4,100 stand of arms, powder and shot to go with them, and much-needed entrenching tools. It took some time to get this to Washington, but it got there. So did other shipments of tools, ordnance, cavalry equipment, and other martial supplies. Clothing was a bigger problem than guns, and Washington pressed supply officers, Congress, and the states to forward dry goods, shoes, hats, and the like to camp. But imports helped here as well, and so did captures. In fact, throughout the war the Whigs managed to get a good deal of what they needed in all supply categories from the enemy. If the British frequently took American stores in battle, patriots often returned the compliment, mostly at sea. Rebel ships, generally privateers, tallied impressive scores against royal transports. In June of 1777, for example, patriots lost substantial stores, especially salted meat and rum, to a British raid into Connecticut. But shortly thereafter, a privateer redressed the balance of bringing in prizes that virtually replaced the plundered goods. Later in the year, another action took two ships that yielded uniforms for four regiments, a thousand weapons, and a large amount of foodstuffs.[33] There is no way to determine precisely how many supplies fell into American hands through the fortunes of war, but such victories were anything but rare, and Congress and Washington followed them with keen interest.[34]

Given the general availability of provisions, however, the key to patriot logistics remained the survival of at least a semblance of transportation and distribution capabilities. And they did survive, although it is important to stress that frequently they did so outside of authorized channels, or at least outside of what should have been normal Commissary and Quartermaster Department procedures. Over late 1777 and early 1778, only extraordinary exertions on the parts of congressional delegates, the Board of War, and the army itself managed to keep supplies moving. In fact, the Board probably never did more on behalf of the army than it did during these months. Recognizing that the supply departments lacked effective leadership, Board members moved directly into the business of commissary and quartermaster operations, focusing their efforts on the actual shipping of material. Had they not, Henry Laurens noted, "we should not now be tottering, we should be flat down."[35]

To its credit, there was also an awakening in Congress. This new attitude stemmed in great measure from the reports of the congressional Committee at Camp, appointed in early January 1778 (and reorganized before the month was out) and charged with investigating Washington's dire reports on the organizational and supply status of the army. Committee members worked with the commander-in-chief until March, and their letters graphically depicted the miseries of the troops. They fixed the blame squarely on the mismanagement of supply operations, especially the inability to establish reliable transport; implicitly, they blamed Congress as well. The committee's messages to governors, Congress, military officers, businessmen—anyone who might provide teams, wagons, supplies—spurred relief efforts over the winter and impressed Congress with the need for longer-range improvements in logistics.[36] Few legislative committees have served their country better than this one.

Washington also moved decisively and, in effect, became his own quartermaster. He had shown genuine skill in marshaling resources to rebuild the army after the 1776 campaign, and the experience served him well at Valley Forge. He prodded supply officers, Congress, and the states to press shipments; made innumerable inquiries on inventories, the locations of stores, and the availability of teams; and took pains to assure that supplies reaching camp received proper distribution and care.[37] It was a tedious and almost continuous labor, but the patriot commander performed it with distinction.

The frantic efforts to keep supply shipments moving also brought Washington around on the question of impressment of civilian properties. The commander-in-chief never lost his aversion to the practice, but he could not deny that other procurement measures had failed to avert a logistical crisis. Cautiously, over December and the early months of 1778, he incorporated impressment into his provisioning operations; as he directed his own quartermaster affairs, he was at least in a position to control the process and, he hoped, to limit excesses. Washington issued careful instructions to his foragers, specifying what they were to collect and insisting that property owners receive appropriate receipts in order to file later claims for their losses. Although he ordered special attention to impressments from the "disaffected," he never allowed the process to become a full-scale foraging campaign against suspected Tories. A heavy-handed approach might have produced more provisions, but only at the cost of civilian ire. As it was, Washington's more judicious policy was still quite successful in gathering supplies and clearly did help alleviate distribution problems; the fact that military personnel and wagons were directly involved in the impressments generally assured that collected food and material reached camp quickly. The need to impress goods abated with the end of the supply crisis of late

1777 and early 1778, but the practice briefly provided one of the army's chief sources of provisions.[38]

No single measure, however, rescued army logistics over the Valley Forge winter. Rather, it was the combination of emergency efforts that brought results and, at the same time, indicated that patriots still commanded the resources necessary to assure their own military salvation. If the established logistics system—embodied in the Commissary and Quartermaster Departments—often proved inadequate, experience demonstrated that good men in key places could still get the job done (or at least muddle through). Trumbull and Mifflin, despite their later troubles, were very good at times, and members of the Board of War and of the Committee at Camp also performed well during late 1777 and early 1778, although Washington was perhaps the best of all in pulling the logistics effort together. Of course this was not the way that things were supposed to work. An army devoted to feeding itself had little time to spend on the enemy, just as a commander-in-chief running his own logistics spent proportionately less time on other matters. For all of that, the Continental line remained a force in being, which in itself was ample testimony to the achievements of rebel logistics.

Of equal importance was the fact that patriots did more than simply labor to survive. Even as they struggled to keep the Continentals in the field, key individuals sought to use logistics against the enemy. Perhaps no one knew better than Washington what it meant to command an army short of food and supplies, and he did his best to place his opponents in the same circumstances. Indeed, over 1777 he became an experienced hand at the game. In the spring, before Howe had evacuated New Jersey, he struck hard at enemy foraging parties, waging a small-unit campaign to deny the enemy access to the countryside. The British were compelled to provide heavy escorts for supply sallies, and they frequently paid in blood for any crops or stores they collected. Late in the year, after the fall of Philadelphia, Washington thought along the same lines. He renewed his assaults on foraging columns and, in an attempt to prevent the Royal Navy from shipping supplies up the Delaware, he ordered a stubborn defense of the river forts below the city. Even his resort to impressment was, in part, a calculated blow at the British. The general concluded that he had to confiscate supplies in some areas if only to keep them away from Howe's foragers.[39] This aspect of the war favored the Americans. While the British got a good deal of what they needed, the risks inherent in foraging operations were such as to keep them off balance and concerned about their own logistical situation, and thus less able to go after the rebels. In fostering those concerns, Washington displayed a clear understanding of how to weight the logistics equation in his favor, and he won a victory as important as any he ever won in the field.

This sort of fighting also helped set off the unquestioned fact that Continental supply problems had reduced Washington's offensive capabilities.

In late 1777, for example, despite the wishes of many in Congress and the government of Pennsylvania, Washington ruled out any attempt to retake Philadelphia. He simply lacked the supplies to mount the assault.[40] If crippled, however, it is well to recall that the army faced genuine paralysis only during the darkest period at Valley Forge. Otherwise, Washington, albeit with difficulty, could maneuver and fight defensive and harassing engagements. If he had the time to pick a target and to collect men and material, he could still strike hard. Trenton, Princeton, and—although a losing effort—even Germantown were all examples. In fact, once a Continental army operation was actually under way, Washington never broke contact solely because of logistical problems.

There is a final point, perhaps more difficult to assess, but still significant. By early 1778 the Continental line was a seasoned outfit. The ranks were too thin, but the officer corps was experienced and the regiments had a core of veterans. As armies went, it was lean and it mounted operations knowing that it had to endure supply problems that no European regular force would tolerate. The regiments learned to make do with less of everything and gradually found ways to get more out of what they had. This took time and experience, but coping with privation became part of army routine, a fact reflected in any number of small but cumulatively telling ways. Over time, for instance, the army established regulations discouraging militia from walking off with arms and equipment when their tours of duty ended. Other orders made individual soldiers responsible for the care of their weapons and made them accountable for any issued tools. These rules extended even to items as small as tin canisters used in the distribution of liquor rations.[41] To the extent that it could, the army also tried to make certain key skills organic. By late 1777, for example, it could bake some of its own bread in field ovens, artificers could fabricate a range of gun and vehicle parts, and military tailors could turn fabrics into better clothing than their civilian counterparts.[42] The Continentals were never self-sufficient, but they learned to do a great deal to help themselves, an ability that marked the passage to veteran status and that proved a continuing benefit to the logistics effort.

Without question, then, the audit of the three years after 1775 found patriot logistics a troubled business. Yet it also found an inherent resilience and a sense of enterprise. Experience from the siege of Boston to the winter at Valley Forge demonstrated that the Continental line could fight, even on short supplies, and that it would take a great deal of punishment—in fact, a veritable combination of calamities—to bring rebel logistical operations, and thus the army, to a full stop. That combination never quite occurred. If American blunders contributed to logistical problems, American initiatives helped to set them right. It is well to remember that after barely surviving the campaign of 1776, Washington assembled the food, equipment, and munitions necessary to rebuild his battalions and come out fighting in 1777. In similar fashion, the troops that broke camp at Valley Forge a year later were probably better armed and accoutred than ever. In the worst of times, the flow of provisions gave out only for brief periods and the transport lines, if battered, held together. In the end, as British historian Eric Robson has noted, the crux of the matter was not that the Americans suffered logistical problems, but that, in the face of monumental challenges, they surmounted or learned to live with them so well.[43]

The outlook for patriot logistics improved considerably in 1778. Even as the army endured the most serious phase of the Valley Forge crisis, a chastened Congress acted to put military support services on a more solid footing. Responding to the entreaties of the Committee at Camp, the delegates took up consideration of candidates for quartermaster and commissary general. The committee urged the appointment of strong department heads, with authority to select their own deputies, and with adequate fiscal resources behind them. That Congress agreed was a sign of how deep an impression the Valley Forge experience had made. After lengthy and often acrimonious debate (mostly over the quartermaster's position), Congress had new department heads in place by April. The post of quartermaster general went to Major General Nathanael Greene of Rhode Island, who took up his duties on March 2. Greene had emerged as one of Washington's more able lieutenants, and it was only with the urging of the commander-in-chief that he gave up his line command. "No body ever heard of a quarter Master in History," he lamented at one point. In early April, Jeremiah Wadsworth, a Connecticut man, accepted the post of commissary general of purchases. A former deputy of Trumbull and without aspirations to military glory, he never asked where commissaries stood in history.[44] Neither man, as events subsequently proved, had anything to fear from the verdicts of posterity.

Greene and Wadsworth wasted no time grasping departmental reins, and soon the formal channels of the logistics system began to function better at all levels than ever before. Deliveries to the army became more regular, and by 1780 even clothing was in generally good supply. Significantly, the Quartermaster Department, with considerable effort, was able to establish regional magazines that made troop movements easier throughout the middle states and the upper South. Logistical suport for operations also improved. After Valley Forge, for example, the army, backed by an adequate baggage train, fought well at Monmouth, and the following winter Washington was able to keep his largest army in three years under arms. In 1779 the department heads simultaneously supported a build up of southern forces while assisting General John Sullivan in provisioning his expedition into the Iroquois territory.[45] Greene and Wadsworth had considerable help and good fortune. French aid was generous, the winter of 1778/79 was mild, the army itself was more efficient, and the pace of combat had slowed after the Battle of Monmouth. The two department heads, however, were diligent and competent, and to them belonged much of the credit for the improved state of logistics.

Washington was pleased with both of his logistics chiefs, but he was especially close to Greene and, with good measure, he believed in his subordinate's administrative abilities. Management was one of Greene's real talents. His voluminous correspondence reveals an analytical approach to supply needs and transport capabilities, keen assessments of operational possibilities, and careful attention to how the Continentals might derive the most from what was at hand. He distilled all of this into thoughtful reports to his chief, of which his advice on the 1778/79 encampment at Middlebrook was a classic example. Drawing on a range of data on available forage, possible enemy intentions, clothing supplies, transportation requirements, distances to various sources of food, and related considerations, the quartermaster concluded, and Washington agreed, that the central New Jersey site offered the best place for the army simultaneously to subsist, react to British movements, protect the countryside, and maintain communications with the rest of the states.[46] This kind of planning, together with Greene's and Wadsworth's efforts to get the machinery of the supply services turning, was of enormous benefit to Washington. A century and a half later, the German general Erwin Rommel would write that before anyone had fired a shot, the quartermasters already had decided the battle. One can guess that it was quartermasters like Greene that he had in mind.

Even in success, however, Greene's personal role pointed to what remained an inherent flaw in the logistics system. When it recommended the appointment of Greene in the first place, the Committee at Camp noted "that it is upon the Characters of Men principally, & not upon Paper Systems that our Success must depend." And despite the improvements in the Quartermaster and Commissary Departments, logistics administration remained an extremely personal business, dependent on men in key places and private connections, men with "Knowledge of the Country & of Business," as the committee put it. In fact, even at their best, formal departmental mechanisms failed too often, and Greene found that almost every aspect of the department required his personal attention. Problems ascended the chain of command. Local agents had little authority to interpret regulations to suit special circumstances or to deal with recalcitrant state officials. Thus any unusual questions or thorny issues ended up on Greene's desk.[47] So did matters requiring shipments across local jurisdictions, which regional deputies often lacked the resources to handle, or situations touching on relations with senior Continental officers. More than once, Greene had to tactfully ask brother generals not to intercept supplies meant for other commands, or to issue special instructions to a local agent to pay bills arising from another general's procurements "not in the regular channels of business." He was perplexed at such things, and never reconciled to the fact that his time should be consumed this way. "My Time is so taken up upon matters of business," he wrote his wife, "that I can hardly spare a moment to write a friend."[48] All this was illustrative of Greene's command of logistics minutiae while under enormous pressure, but not to the workings of a smoothly functioning department. Indeed, there was a dangerous side to trusting to men rather than systems. Among those in touch with the situation, there was a feeling that without Greene or Wadsworth at the helm, there would be no system at all.[49]

As much as personal leadership, however, better logistics depended on money. Expenses spiraled upward over 1778 and 1779, reflecting increased costs in virtually all aspects of supply operations. In the Quartermaster Department, where Greene had added substantially to the staff, the payroll alone was staggering. By 1780, he employed some 3,000 agents, regional deputies and their assistants, clerks, accountants, teamsters, artificers, boatmen, and other workers. Salaries and wages came to over $407,000 a month. Market forces also played a critical role. As inflation overwhelmed rebel currencies, prices for goods and services—notably transportation—soared to record levels and, with poor harvests after 1778, the scarcity of some crops made the situation even more acute. In war-worn New Jersey, for example, forage was at a premium, with military needs competing directly with those of the farming economy. Necessities were still available, but quartermasters had to ship them farther and to pay dearly for them. Competition between purchasing agents remained an issue as well, which also pushed prices higher. As a result, Greene's agents were perpetually short of money. Throughout his more than two years on the job, Greene devoted a large part of his time to keeping his purchasing and transportation personnel fiscally solvent. It was money, he knew, that drove logistics, and while he and Wadsworth took pains to keep accurate accounts and assure that public funds were well spent, they refused to pinch pennies.[50]

Ever cost-conscious, Congress eventually balked at the rising expenditures. Greene and Wadsworth explained at length that they could do little about inflation or crop failures, and that supplies were reaching the army precisely because they were spending a great deal of money. Yet their explanations did little to stem the chorus of alarm, and the department chiefs were vulnerable to criticism on at least one important count. Both were better paid than their predecessors, and both insisted that their subordinates also receive adequate compensation. This was no minor point, as the rebels had lost some of their best support personnel—Trumbull, for instance—in part over pay disputes. Rather than accept a fixed salary, Greene urged that supply officials receive commissions on all purchases. This was standard practice in eighteenth-century armies, an incentive for quartermaster and commissary agents to pursue their duties aggressively. Congress disliked the idea, fearing it would only encourage higher prices. They foresaw agents willingly paying top dollar in order to line their own pockets with commissions. But Congress relented after the Committee at Camp reluctantly endorsed the notion and after Greene made it clear that he would not serve otherwise. The arrangement allowed Greene and his two chief deputies to divide 1 percent of all purchases made through his department, while other subordinates received smaller commissions. Wadsworth worked out a similar settlement for the Commissary Department.[51]

Throughout the tenures of Greene and Wadsworth, the commission payments generated considerable resentment. In fact, the department heads and their principal lieutenants derived comfortable incomes from military business, and, despite their best efforts, there were some abuses. Critics made the most of the situation, insisting that widespread fraud and the pursuit of commissions lay at the bottom of runaway costs. The reputations of supply personnel suffered badly, and Greene and Wadsworth were furious at insinuations that they either took part in or winked at peculation themselves. Indeed, by late 1779 their resentments were such that only a congressional endorsement of their integrity prevented both men from resigning. Nor did they change their positions. Throughout the controversy, they held that critics were missing the point. At a time when the sinews of war were increasingly hard to find at any price, the commission payments, no matter how high they seemed to partisan observers, at least brought results. All previous arrangements, Greene frequently pointed out, had left the army without adequate transport, close to starvation, and short of equipment.[52]

Finally, the disputes became too much for the department heads to endure. While arguments over commission payments continued to rankle, the really insurmountable problem was inflation. Aware that its paper emissions had contributed to soaring prices, Congress drastically curtailed its currency issues in late 1779. Theoretically a sound anti-inflationary move, this step had the immediate effect of drying up most of the funds on which procurement and transport depended. As a result, Greene and Wadsworth, who argued that inflated money was better than none at all, gradually found it increasingly difficult to sustain logistics operations. This, in turn, generated additional criticisms of the support departments. It was the last straw. Wadsworth left on January 1, 1780, and, after defending his performance in a bitter exchange of correspondence with Congress, Greene followed on August 5.[53]

As some had feared, the departures of Wadsworth and Greene marked the rapid demise of the logistics system per se. There were still supply departments—the new quartermaster general was Timothy Pickering, while Ephraim Blaine took over as commissary general of purchases—and there were still agents in the field, but the formal channels of the support services never again operated as effectively as they had in 1778 and 1779. Indeed, in a major effort to reduce operating costs, Pickering, with the endorsement of Congress, ordered deep cuts in departmental personnel and shed all responsibilities not directly related to procurement and distribution. He never assumed Greene's planning role, nor did he concern himself with such matters as route reconnaissance.[54] These duties reverted to the commander-in-chief and his immediate staff.

The grave financial situation led Congress to one of its most desperate departures of the war. Without adequate credit or hard money, and unwilling to print more inflated currency, Congress lacked the means to support logistics. As an alternative, the delegates voted an arrangement of "specific supplies," under which the states were to furnish Continental agents with specific quotas of goods. In theory, these contributions would feed and provision the army and spare the virtually bankrupt Congress the expense. In practice, the scheme failed almost from the start. Many of the states were hard-pressed themselves and could not meet their quotas, or could not meet them on time. Others met them all at once, and the army found itself with tons of meat or foodstuffs that it could neither store nor distribute properly.[55] Reliance on specific supplies only aggravated the old problems inherent in late or uncoordinated deliveries, poor warehousing operations, and shortages of key commodities. By late 1780, the formal mechanisms of patriot logistics were approaching their lowest ebb.

Congress has come in for considerable criticism over the specific supplies system. Without sound currency or credit, or the taxing power to establish either, however, what else was possible? There was little choice but to turn to the states and hope for the best, at least until the government put its financial house in order. The financial crisis, moreover, was exacerbated by bad luck. Poor harvests made crops dear after 1778, and the brutal winter of 1779/80 was the worst of the war.[56] It is hardly surprising that mutinies exploded among the Pennsylvania and New Jersey lines in January of 1781.

During this period army operations suffered along with the men. Indeed, the army simply sought to stay in the field. Lacking the strength to close with the British, Washington husbanded his resources and renewed appeals on behalf of the supply services. Over 1780 and 1781 he was able to disperse elements of the main army to subsist them closer to regional stores and provisions, and he even sent some troops on furlough for want of food. At one point, the general had to leave the bulk of his artillery parked at Morristown, having sent the gun teams into the countryside to find adequate forage. The army survived, of course, but the logistics dilemma once more had robbed patriots of their offensive capabilities.[57]

Yet privation never bred paralysis. Indeed, in some important respects, the picture was not entirely gloomy. As in 1777–78, the support lines never gave out entirely. Inaction on the part of Sir Henry Clinton, the British commander, not only allowed Washington to conserve resources, but generally left the vulnerable rebel transport network unmolested. In the emergency army personnel once again moved to supply their regiments directly. In the spring of 1781, for instance, General William Heath skillfully organized the collection and shipment of New England provisions to the main army. Staff officers and local officials had scoured the region for supplies, and a number of merchants had extended credit to add to the total. Thus the success of Heath's mission reflected the combined efforts of the military, quartermaster agents, state authorities, and private businessmen in bringing much needed relief to the Continentals, and it also demonstrated anew that rebels could keep their regiments operational.[58]

Grave as was the situation, the army never lost the ability to fight stiffly on the defensive. Militia units continued to give enemy reconnaissance forces a very hard time, but it was Greene's southern campaign that offered the most convincing example. The former quartermaster took command of the southern army in December 1780 and quickly grasped that logistics would determine the fate of his mission. Appealing to southern governors to forward emergency supplies, Greene divided his forces to facilitate foraging operations and then fell back through North Carolina as Cornwallis came on. Collecting troops and supplies as he went, Greene kept a step ahead of the aggressive British commander. He impressed provisions and transport with a free hand, and managed to keep his men fed, equipped, and organized as he moved.[59] Greene's strong right arm was the southern army's quartermaster, Edward Carrington, who became to Greene what Greene had been to Washington. He ranged in front of the army, handling route reconnaissance, establishing supply dumps along the line of march, and personally rounding up boats to assure Greene's ability to pass the difficult southern rivers. Carrington's men generally had food and material ready when and where Greene needed it, sparing the commander the need to stop and forage for himself. Each step of the way Greene and Carrington effectively integrated supply functions into their planning, and by the time the patriots reached the relative safety of Virginia the southern army was on the mend. On the other hand, the campaign had vastly complicated British logistics, and Cornwallis, low on supplies after his unsuccessful chase, turned south again to pursue a frustrating campaign that ultimately led to Yorktown.[60] The patriot campaign was stunning, a true masterpiece of skilled logistics. The fact that the rebel officers had done so well when their government was nearly bankrupt only placed their achievement in bolder relief.

As the rebel armies struggled to remain operational, however, dismay over the state of army supply and national finances continued unabated. Congress linked the two problems—money and logistics—recognizing a solution to the former eventually would solve the latter. As patriots groped for a way out of their financial morass, they set in motion the last great effort to put military logistics on a workable footing. The process began on May 14, 1781, when Philadelphia merchant and congressman Robert Morris accepted the new post of superintendent of finance. Morris looked toward the restoration of public credit through drastic cost cutting in all areas of Continental expenditures, stabilization of the currency, and taxation. He also wanted to continue floating loans in France until America could meet its needs with domestic revenues. Morris understood, too, that only an infusion of sound money or credit could reanimate the supply services, which he sensed held the key to victory. If the country could mobilize enough funds or credit to keep the Continental line in the field, he argued, the British eventually would quit.[61] Thus Morris committed himself to provisioning the army and, in short order, became the central figure in logistics operations.

The emergence of Morris epitomized the personal nature of revolutionary logistics, once again demonstrating how dependent army supply had become on the intervention of individuals from outside of the Commissary and Quartermaster Departments. The superintendent was no stranger to military supply. His firm, Morris, Willing, and Company, had long traded in war material. He became personally involved in the matter, however, as he took up his financial duties. In May, 1781, to forestall impending impressment actions, he pledged his personal credit to arrange flour shipments to the army. In June, Pennsylvania contracted with him to raise that state's quotas of specific supplies, and the financier did fairly well. Calling on business contacts, Morris induced interested suppliers to submit bids on rations, and arranged to have them privately shipped.[62]

In effect, Morris had convinced Congress to privatize key elements of patriot logistics. His first step relieved the states of forwarding specific supplies to Continental agents. Instead, he asked the states to sell collected supplies and to send the proceeds to the Congressional treasury; Morris then intended using the funds to let contracts for army supplies and transport services. The Quartermaster and Commissary Departments had a much reduced role in all of this. Indeed, Morris, with Pickering's cooperation, radically trimmed the number of quartermaster deputies and agents—an action aimed at cutting public costs as private enterprise assumed a larger role in logistics operations. Pickering's staff continued to handle inventories and distribution, but Morris sought to put most procurement and shipping responsibilities securely in private hands.[63]

Events overtook Morris's plans, however. In August, in the midst of discussions with Washington over reducing logistics expenditures, the commander learned of the intended arrival of a French fleet off the Virginia Capes in October. Seizing the moment, Washington convinced Morris to forego economies in favor of a crash effort to trap Cornwallis at Yorktown.[64] Morris, of course, complied, launching an intensive effort to assure the general the means to fight. What followed was an almost flawless demonstration of logistics planning and execution.

Head of Elk, Maryland, where Washington planned to rendezvous his troops before the final trip to Yorktown, became the campaign's logistical center. Morris had commissary personnel establish magazines and bring in supplies from Maryland and Delaware. Simultaneously, using business connections and pledging his personal credit to expedite matters, he had Baltimore merchants forward supplies and vessels, which quartermaster personnel fitted out to transport the army. Morris followed every aspect of the work. Firing off communiques to local officials, the army, and business associates, he exhorted everyone to their duty. He pressed the gathering of provisions and equipment, followed transport arrangements, and managed the finances that paid for it all.[65] When Washington arrived at Head of Elk in mid-September, everything was in place to carry his battalions—and those of the allied French—to Virginia. Unquestionably, Morris had done yeoman service, and many of the laurels of the final victory properly accrued to him.

In the meantime, Washington had been just as busy. He impressed teams, wagons, forage, food, whatever he needed, with abandon; working closely with Rochambeau, he planned a route of march that brought the allied forces to Maryland well equipped and fully organized, a major feat in itself. Eleven days later, the first units appeared in front of British lines, and Cornwallis was doomed.[66] From a logistics perspective, the operation was almost perfect. No other campaign, American or British, matched York-town in its coordination of material, financial, transport, and administrative resources.

After Yorktown, supply problems resurfaced and American logistics ended the war as it began—searching for a reliable means of keeping the rebel military in the field. There were some difficulties the patriots never solved, including money woes, unreliable transportation, and a dependence on imports. Complicated at various times by military defeat, hard winters, parochial politics, and poor harvests, these burdens periodically over-whelmed the capabilities of the Quartermaster and Commissary Depart-ments. Neither a formal system nor tinkering with logistics mechanisms ever prevented cyclical supply crises or the suffering they caused. Certainly, as historian James Huston had argued, supply shortages helped deprive Wash-ington of the large regular army he wanted—the country could not have fed it—and just as certainly blunted the offensive capacities of the one he did have. The commander-in-chief never had the resources he needed to assault New York for example, and similar concerns, in part, prevented a renewed drive against Canada.[67] Frustration, it often seemed, was the only thing not in short supply.

A revolutionary government with only limited political authority and marginal fiscal resources, and under enemy assault, was unlikely to produce logistics operations that functioned like a Swiss watch. As it was, the rebels managed a great deal. Despite all difficulties, procurement and distribution operations never ceased, transportation lines ultimately remained open, enough key imports got through, and every supply crisis passed. Indeed, the truly dangerous periods—the months spent rebuilding the army at Mor-ristown over 1776–77, the Valley Forge winter and its successor, and the discouraging experience with specific supplies in 1780 and 1781—had some-thing of a self-correcting element in them. In every case, the dire circum-stances prompted responses in which patriots rallied to pull their resources together. All concerned knew that this was not the best way to run the war, but at least it ran. The work of the Committee at Camp, Washington, Greene, and Morris were all of a piece. With or without a formal system, and often confronting dismal prospects, the rebels could still make arrangements to keep logistical support functioning, which was always the salient point.

Yet did the effort maintain the army as a force in being? To this, the answer must be yes. The Continental regiments were never strong enough to destroy the British in the field, but neither were they so weak that the redcoats could finish them. And the rebels were always dangerous. At their weakest, the logistics base was adequate for a defensive posture in which they could avoid major engagements and still make it costly for the enemy to move in the countryside. At their peak, of course, given an opening by the British and the chance to accumulate sufficient supplies, the Continental army could hit hard, as it did brilliantly at Trenton, as it did decisively at Yorktown.

Viewed from this perspective, American logistical problems may have been less debilitating, in relative terms, than British supply difficulties, and, to push the point, one can credit the rebels with coping better with logistics affairs generally. The patriots, after all, accomplished their mission, while the British did not. The British army, with all of its comparative material advantages, always found logistics its Achilles' heel—a fact which owed much to American design. While British soldiers never suffered the privation endemic among Continental troops, the king's army broke neither the rebel military nor the rebel government. Indeed, there was something symbolic in the fact that at Yorktown when the British marched out to surrender to the tune of "The World Turned Upside Down," Cornwallis's men wore fresh red uniforms, while along their route of march were the American veterans, ragged even in victory. Yet there was an impressive "soldierly bearing" about the Continentals, an attitude that said more of their character than a new uniform ever could.[68] Like the logistics effort that supported them, they were not elegant, but they proved up to the job.

7

Frontier Warfare
and the American Victory

James H. O'Donnell III

Two prominent historians of the American Revolution—ironically, a mentor and his student—have suggested rather different interpretations of the roles played by the frontier in the War for American Independence. John Richard Alden writes of the West as critical to our understanding of the outcome of the revolutionary struggle. Don Higginbotham, on the other hand, refers to the incidents in the West as merely a side show, peripheral and incidental to the larger struggle.[1] As is the case with most disagreements, the answer may be more nearly a blending of the two positions.

To understand the role of the West, the frontier, in the American Revolution, one must perceive the war as a struggle fought on many fronts. People were dying in military engagements from the Atlantic to the Mississippi and from the St. Lawrence to the Gulf, all in inexorably intertwined conflicts that stemmed from what had begun as a colonial war of rebellion. In the broadest sense, moreover, the struggle became a world war after 1778 when the French signed a treaty of friendship with the United States, a commitment that brought Spain into the struggle in 1779. In the following year, Dutch trade with the fledgling United States dragged that small nation into a naval war with Great Britain. In sum, then, one cannot envision the revolution as having to do only with the clash of armies led by General Washington against the British army and its several commanders-in-chief.

If historians have quibbled over the significance of the West, contemporaries certainly did not ignore the frontier. As the long intercolonial wars with France still were fresh in the minds of British military leaders, it was logical that planning for any new conflict inevitably would take into account the western territories acquired through the Peace of 1763. No strategic planners had ignored the frontier in over 150 years of warfare. None could now, and after 1763 the British ministry sought to implement policies both to control the flow of population into the West and to provide for frontier government. Nor could any imperial planner ignore the Indians who inhabited the West. While no one applauded the savagery of Indian warfare, the presence of these people and their potential allegiance could not be overlooked. Especially was this true at a time when the British army was relatively small, given the empire's global commitments. In effect, the Indians were regarded in the same light as the loyalists, as useful allies who could be counted upon to fight for the preservation of the empire.

The leaders in America could no more brush aside or disregard the frontier than could their counterparts in London. When their brethren who lived on the New York frontier, or in Virginia's Kentucky region, suffered, the officials in the capital soon knew of it and tried to offer aid. Once the war with Britain began in 1775, moreover, eastern magistrates viewed the western citizenry as a buffer in the way of British invasion via the back country. If the frontier folk held the British partisans and Indians at bay, the patriot armies in the East could more freely carry on the struggle against the British forces bent on crushing the rebellion. In addition, some officials hoped to recruit the militia from "over the mountains," the "wild and fierce inhabitants" of Kentucky who were thought to possess special qualities as hearty soldiers and riflemen.

It is these frontier soldiers and their contribution to the American victory that this essay will consider. Frontier warfare was not the hinge upon which an American victory turned, but without the contribution of the fighting men from "over the mountains," the ultimate American success might have come at a much later time and at a far greater cost.

From the very eve of the war British military thinkers foresaw the need to consider the "lawless banditti" of the frontiers. Early in 1775, when General Thomas Gage, the commander of the British army in America, conceived an overall British plan for crushing the colonial rebellion, he was prepared to use the Indians against the inhabitants on the frontiers.[2]

The commander's larger motive surely was to harass the frontiers, a strategy that might keep the militia at home in defense of their loved ones, rather than in the service of the Continental army. General Gage's plans were not unanticipated by the newly formed American government. During the first summer of the war, Congress adopted a plan for the management of the Indians. Since the legislators were familiar with Britain's prewar system of Indian departments for North America, the Continental scheme was modeled roughly after the imperial precedent, but with three administrative divisions rather than two. The boundaries for the three divisions coincided roughly with the territories of certain powerful tribes: the Northern Department would include the lands of the Six Nations and their allies; the Southern Department would be responsible for the areas claimed by the Cherokees and the other tribes living to their south and southwest (east of the Mississippi); and the Middle Department included any tribes not administered by the other two.[3] Because none of these arrangements accounted for the New England tribes, Congress later appointed a superintendent with responsibility for those native groups.[4] The commissioners were to seek to neutralize the Indians.[5]

To assist the commissioners Congress drew up a model Indian "talk" for delivery to any tribe. According to this presentation, the happy state of relations between the colonies and the mother country had been disturbed when the king's evil ministers attempted to steal the colonists' livelihood through taxation. When the colonists objected, the monarch's advisers urged that their protest be met by force. The war which resulted, however, was a matter between the colonies and the mother country. The Indians should remain neutral. "BROTHERS AND FRIENDS," the discourse began. The settlers' war was "a family quarrel between us and Old England. You Indians are not concerned in it." Remain at home, the natives were told, and "keep the hatchet buried deep."[6]

Naming the commissioners was not an easy task, for Congress had to balance political considerations with recognition of experience in Indian affairs. As a result, Pennsylvania and Virginia had representation in two departments, while South Carolina was given the privilege of naming three of the five appointees in the South. Accordingly, Congress appointed General Philip Schuyler (New York), Major Joseph Hawley (Massachusetts), Turbot Francis (Pennsylvania), Oliver Wolcott (Connecticut), and Volkert P. Douw (New York) to the Northern Department. The commissioners for the Middle Department were to be Benjamin Franklin and James Wilson (Pennsylvania) and Patrick Henry (Virginia). At first Congress named only two men to the Southern Department, John Walker (Virginia) and Willie Jones (North Carolina).[7] Later George Galphin and Edward Wilkinson, both of South Carolina, and Robert Rae of Georgia were added.[8]

By and large the activities of these commissioners would be restricted to what Galphin called "rum and good words." Because Congress could not provide the much needed trade goods that the Indians so much desired, the commissioners had to settle for occasional meetings where they met a few native leaders, repeated the story of Great Britain's injustices, assured the Indians of American intentions—Galphin's "good words"—and then distributed limited quantities of rum. In rare instances this bottle diplomacy actually attracted a few followers to the patriot cause. More often, however, the Continental initiatives proved ineffectual.[9]

Hostilities first erupted on the southern frontier. Many months of pressure by the western inhabitants of Virginia, the Carolinas, and Georgia pushed the Cherokee to the breaking point. Convinced that no one would listen to their pleas about incursions by settlers onto their lands west of the mountains, the Cherokee decided that only force could remove the invading frontiersmen. Consequently, by early summer of 1776 bands of warriors filed through the mountain valleys to destroy the cabins and stockades of the encroaching settlers.

At about the same time, coincidentally, Britain launched an invasion of Charleston led by Sir Henry Clinton and Admiral Peter Parker. The rumor quickly spread that the British and the native Americans had conspired in planning a joint venture to crush the rebellion, the redcoats assaulting the coast, the Indians marauding on the frontier. Although there was no evidence that the British and the Indians were acting in concert, and, indeed, the communication capacity and logistical possibilities of the eighteenth century augered against such a complicated venture, the patriots often put faith in the chimera of conspiracy.

The rumors of Anglo-Indian intrigue may have helped to excite feverish countermeasures among the westerners, but, in reality, the frontiersmen already had sufficient motives to act. Confronted with the possibility that they might lose their homes, their lives, and their loved ones, the militia of the western counties always responded swiftly. Such was the case in 1776.

No officials belittled the threat from the West, most certainly not Virginia and North Carolina which acted defensively to protect both its citizens and the flow of essential raw materials. Virginia dispatched Colonel William Russell with six companies of frontier militia to patrol the southwestern frontier of the state, while North Carolina, hoping that the Cherokee would be given no excuse for attacking, instructed its western militia not to cross the Indian boundary line unless the tribal warriors attacked first. In the meantime, General Charles Lee, commander of the Continental forces in the South, urged the southern colonies to jointly launch a powerful punitive expedition into the Cherokee towns. Such a destructive thrust into the Indian country not only would counter the Cherokee raids, it would discourage parties of Creeks who might be tempted to join the attacks against the much-despised frontier settlers. In addition, if the Carolinas, Virginia, and Georgia cooperated in a crushing invasion of the Cherokee settlements, the bitterness of the defeat might deter the Southern tribes from ever considering extending support to the British. Although General Lee was too short of men to assign any troops to such an expedition, he drafted a comprehensive plan: from the north a Virginia force was to level the Cherokee Overhill villages; combined armies from the Carolinas would march westward carrying fire and sword into the Cherokee Middle and Valley settlements; and South Carolina alone would support the invasion of the Cherokee Lower Towns. The sharply divided loyalties of the Georgia frontier inhabitants made it impossible for the southernmost state to join the venture.

South Carolina was the first to act. Indeed, the colony's dangerously explosive mixture of frontier political tensions had driven it to action within a matter of days after the first Cherokee raiders struck. Six hundred South Carolina militia volunteered for service under Colonel Andrew Williamson. In addition, a battalion of Continentals was added to his command, and, wise in the ways of forest warfare, Williamson also secured the services of twenty scouts from the domesticated Catawba who lived within South Carolina. At the head of more than 1,100 troops, he marched northwest into the heartland of the Lower Cherokee. Brandishing the torch, Williamson's forces reported that they destroyed all the villages and corn "from the [South Carolina] Cherokee line to the Middle settlement."

Williamson's tactics were not unique. Most frontier expeditions, whether launched from South Carolina or Pennsylvania, sought to destroy the Indians' supply of corn. This did not mean simply the dried grain cached in the villages, but new corn standing in the fields. Without the harvest of this staple, the warriors and their families faced a bleak winter. The August timing of the raid was perfect, for the year's crop had ripened and could not be replanted successfully before the first frost.

In September, General Griffith Rutherford, in command of a 2,000-man militia force from North Carolina, joined with Williamson's army at the Hiwassie River. The two commanders led a two-week sweep that left a wide path of destruction through the Cherokee towns.

As the Carolinians marched homeward in early October, the third phase of the joint expeditions got underway. The Virginia militia volunteers commanded by Colonel William Christian marched through the mountain passes and into the villages of the Cherokee Overhill towns. Thousands of bushels of corn and potatoes were destroyed, livestock was scattered, and towns were leveled.

Thus in the space of four months more than 4,000 troops had been mustered, organized, and marched into the Cherokee villages. The success of these missions was unmistakable. Not only were the defeated Cherokee forced to sue for terms, the other southern tribes now had the image of the humiliated Cherokee before them should they ever be tempted to join the British.[10]

At this early point in the war, the troops from the frontier had effectively suppressed Britain's potential native American allies in the South. The various campaigns had been waged adroitly and with stunning swiftness. In an age when traditional military campaigns usually were reckoned in terms of the seasonal year—operations from April to October, winter camp from October to April—the frontier forces had demonstrated their ability to mobilize, strike, and withdraw at almost any time. Indeed, this capacity was so well understood that their opponents often were intimidated into inactivity.

These abilities of the frontier forces so intrigued George Washington that he explored the possibility of transferring their swift-strike capacity from the frontier to the eastern battle front. He commissioned Nathaniel Gist, the son of an old companion, frontiersman Christopher Gist, to recruit a company of frontier riflemen from Virginia's western counties, and by August, 1775, they had arrived at Washington's headquarters outside Boston, together with several other frontier rifle companies raised in Pennsylvania and Maryland. The experiment did not succeed, however. Washington soon found them to be too undisciplined to be incorporated into a conventional army. In addition, Gist already had discovered that the frontiersmen were difficult to recruit for such duty, for they were reluctant to leave home for the extended period which service with Washington's army would require.[11] It was not a question of loyalty or courage, but one of survival. If the family breadwinner was absent for an entire season, the family was likely to starve; during his absence, moreover, hostile neighbors with loyalist leanings, or Indian raiders, might destroy his home and family.

The frontiersman was a better soldier, therefore, when his service was a matter of passion. He was likely to volunteer for a campaign against nearby enemies, as he understood that his service was in defense of loved ones, home, and livelihood. A passion for land that might be acquired from the Indians was another motivating factor. One common method for spying-out new land was to take part in an expedition into the Indian country, for the standard settlement following any Indian war, regardless of how the conflict started, was for the tribe involved to grant a land cession, either as a punishment for past transgressions or as evidence of their future good faith.

The world which these western soldiers knew was a simplistic one, a place in which they were on the side of good, their opponents on the side of evil. Thus in the American Revolution, it was assumed that no Indian raid occurred anywhere on the frontier, from New York to Georgia, without the prior knowledge and planning of British officials. That had been the assumption about the Cherokee assaults of 1776 against the southeastern frontiers. When attacks occurred against western Pennsylvania, northwestern Virginia, and the badly exposed western Virginia frontier known as the Kentucky settlements, frontiersmen reached a similar conclusion. In this western world view the Prince of Darkness was the British commandant at Detroit, the evil manipulator who gleefully ordered Indian scalping parties to bring trophies back to Detroit for rewards. That official was Lieutenant Governor Henry Hamilton.[12]

Given this view, Virginia laid plans for an expedition aimed at capturing Hamilton and punishing the Indians who had been raiding the frontiers. There was some truth to their belief about Hamilton, for in the summer of 1777 he had parleyed with several tribes at Detroit, telling them that the king wanted his rebellious subjects struck until they came to their senses. Hamilton emphasized his point by singing the war song before the assembled tribal delegations. The Indians needed little more encouragement.

Throughout the summer of 1777—the summer of the three sevens, the frontiersmen called it—native American raiding bands moved east from Detroit and other sites in the western country. At least thirty-two war parties comprised of 429 warriors went out from Detroit, while another 436 braves departed from other places in the West. In the month of July alone, 290 men divided into twenty-one parties left from Detroit and returned with thirteen prisoners and twenty scalps. Apparently, some of these raiders carried proclamations from Governor Hamilton offering equal pay and rank, plus a western land bounty, to anyone who would leave the American cause and join the British. These handbills were left at cabins as the raiders departed.[13]

Governor Patrick Henry of Virginia was convinced that a successful expedition could be made into the Indian country, a view that was endorsed by General Edward Hand, the commander at Fort Pitt, who believed many frontiersmen would volunteer for such campaigns since they "liked chastising Indians."[14] Aside from shortages of men and supplies, Hand fretted only over the difficulty of selecting the proper target in the Indian country. While the Virginians, both in the frontier settlements and at the state capital, were convinced that the bands of warriors assaulting the western counties were all Shawnee, Hand thought otherwise. Although he agreed with the Virginians that some of the warriors from Pluggy's Town were culpable, he also knew that by far the majority of the attackers against the frontier were Wyandots; the Shawnees and Delawares, he believed, were so badly divided over the question of allegiance that it would be hard for them to organize a raiding party.[15]

Virginia's choice of a plan and a leader was daring. Under commission from the governor, Colonel George Rogers Clark, just twenty-five years old, was selected to recruit 350 men in the frontier counties. Because the western area had suffered so heavily at the hands of the Indian raiders, Clark was convinced that he could persuade a sufficient number of men to go on the mission. He would assemble them south of Fort Pitt, from whence they would proceed to the falls of the Ohio (present day Louisville) and construct a stockade for defensive purposes. That outpost would become their departure point for a dangerous raid deep into the country of the western Indians. Clark's ultimate mission was Kaskaskias in the Illinois country, formerly a French post, now an Indian settlement with a small garrison of British regulars.[16]

While an effort to seize Kaskaskias might seem puzzling, it certainly was in keeping with the philosophy of the frontier Indian fighter who sought to terrorize as many tribes as possible. Frontier warriors understood that this would be especially frightening and intimidating for the tribes of the Ohio country, for they long had dreaded the day when settlers crossed into the transmontane West. The alarm at last had gone out through the Ohio country in 1775 when scouts from two Seneca villages visited Kentucky and returned with word that cabins and forts were being constructed south of the Ohio. So alarmed were the Shawnee that they burned the abandoned stockade fort at the mouth of the Great Kanawha River and posted watch parties at the entrances to the Great and Little Kanawha, Hockhocking, and Muskingum Rivers.[17] Already fearful that the settlers in Kentucky might attack at any time, the tribes of the Ohio Country now realized that if the Americans held a post at Kaskaskias, they would be almost completely encircled, then systematically eliminated.

In order both to protect himself and to allay the fears of the native peoples in the Ohio country, Governor Hamilton, meanwhile, had gathered an army consisting of regulars, volunteers, and Indian warriors, which he led from Detroit southward along the Maumee-Au Glaize-Wabash water route into the Illinois lands. Late in 1778 he occupied the post of Vincennes (St. Vincent's) and then settled down to wait for spring weather before moving against Colonel Clark's frontier army.[18]

Hamilton acted too late to save Kaskaskias, which fell to Clark in July, 1778, but by early in 1779 the Virginian realized he was in trouble. Although Hamilton's army was smaller than the diminutive Virginia force, Clark had received no reinforcements or supplies from home. Moreover, if Hamilton succeeded that spring in recruiting additional Indian allies, Clark would face certain defeat. In January, however, Clark learned from Creole inhabitants in Vincennes that the British commander was terribly exposed, with only about ninety troops plus a few Indians and some villagers. The Virginia leader was now confronted with the kind of situation in which he functioned best—a critical juncture that called for bold action.

Clark knew that in late January the native people either were absent on their winter hunt or resting in their villages; they would not be moving to Governor Hamilton's assistance. The British commander, on the other hand, assumed that no man in his right mind would attempt military operations during the heart of a western winter. Indeed, rain and snow had forced streams out of their banks across the bottom lands, so that travel by the usual paths near the rivers was supposedly impossible. Clark, however, believed that "great things have been effected by a few men well conducted." Deciding to strike, Clark and his men set off through what one described as the "rain, mud, and mire" of the Wabash bottom lands. For three weeks in February they slogged along, driven by hunger, cold, and the charismatic Clark to cover 180 miles in 19 days.[19]

With hunger gnawing at them, the Americans attacked on the night they arrived, surrounding the village and stockade completely. During the brief siege, a band of pro-British Indians returned from a scouting mission on the Ohio. Clark's men seized the band and began to tomahawk the natives on the spot, the American commander allegedly leading the way.[20] Only one Ottawa warrior was rescued; his life was spared through the intervention of Captain Richard McCarty, who had been rescued from the stake in the French and Indian War by this young brave, a son of the great Pontiac. The rest were bludgeoned senseless and thrown into the river. Clark's immersion in this activity reportedly was so complete that he was still trying to wash the blood off his hands, arms, and clothing when Governor Hamilton was brought to him for a parley about the terms of capitulation.

Under less than propitious circumstances, Governor Hamilton was forced to surrender the town and the stockade, including not only his men but all supplies for the post and the Indian trade. The soldiers were paroled, but Clark made a prize of Hamilton and some of the officials who were with him, men who were particularly hated by the Virginia frontiersmen as the officials responsible for the recent Indian raids. The western settlers accused the British officer of encouraging the attacks by paying rewards for scalps. Consequently, Hamilton had to be guarded carefully during the long journey from the Illinois country to Virginia, not so much out of fear of his escape, but from the possibility that some vengeance-seeking westerner might assume the moral responsibility of killing him.[21]

Late that same year Indian problems in another sector provoked an even larger American response. Since the summer of 1778, when Iroquois warriors had struck deep into Pennsylvania, frontier residents had pleaded for assistance from the Continental army. General Washington immediately gathered information about the country of the Six Nations and all the neighboring Indian territories as far west as Detroit.[22] From Nathanael Greene, Philip Schuyler, and other knowledgeable officers, Washington sought specific answers to such questions as the location of the native villages, their population, and the easiest routes to reach them.[23]

One of the general's informants suggested the efficacy of a winter campaign on snowshoes, but Greene offered the soundest advice. He proposed a powerful expedition when the corn was half-grown, thereby simultaneously dispersing the population and destroying its food supply for the coming winter. Furthermore, Greene and others argued that Iroquois pride had to be broken. Some of the commander-in-chief's respondents even suggested that all the Six Nations be exterminated. Unwilling to go that far, Washington concluded that the Iroquois towns should be "overrun [and] . . . destroyed."[24]

While the Americans planned an invasion of the Six Nations, bands of loyalist partisans and Iroquois warriors continued to harass the frontiers of New York and Pennsylvania. Striking near the Wyoming settlements in Pennsylvania early in 1779, the attackers destroyed numerous farms and confiscated 110 cattle and thirty horses.[25] Meanwhile, the capture of dispatches that revealed the intention and the tactics of the Americans led the Senecas and their Iroquois kinsmen to resolve to defend their country against the impending invasion.[26]

By that time Washington had completed his plans. He contemplated dispatching an expedition from Easton, Pennsylvania, directing the army to drive northwest into the very heart of the Iroquois country, burning and destroying as it advanced. Washington first offered the command of the expedition to General Horatio Gates, the popular hero of Saratoga. When he declined, Washington placed the operation under General John Sullivan, who was given an army of more than 4,000 Continentals. According to Washington's intelligence estimates, there were some 3,000 Iroquois and loyalist partisans ready to resist the invaders. Sullivan's instructions were blunt. He was to destroy all towns without exception, take as many prisoners as possible, and grant no peace until all settlements were destroyed.[27]

The American troops soon forced open the eastern door of the symbolic Iroquois longhouse, beginning at Canojoharie Creek on June 27. By late August, Sullivan and his men had reached Tioga, near the Pennsylvania–New York border. En route every Indian town was leveled, every cornfield sickled and burned. At Great Genesse, for example, over one hundred houses were put to the torch. So extensive were the grain fields in that town that eight hours were required to destroy over 15,000 bushels of immature corn. In addition, all visible inhabitants were killed, captured, or dispersed.[28]

Both General Washington and Nathanael Greene had worried about Sullivan's tendency to procrastinate, and he did seem to delay the start of the expedition for an interminable period, earning the sobriquet "the Duke de Sully" for his exasperating stalling. But once the expedition commenced, it proceeded with ruthless efficiency, pausing only to commemorate the Declaration of Independence. The officers celebrated the third anniversary of the break with Great Britian with thirteen toasts, the most appropriate and prophetic being: "Civilization or Death to all the American Savages."[29]

While Sullivan's army moved through the eastern end of the Iroquois country, the western end of the territory was invaded by troops from Fort Pitt under Daniel Brodhead. His force attacked the Seneca towns located along the lower Allegheny River, destroying ten villages and all their provisions. This expedition, however, failed to reach the more numerous Seneca towns located along the so-called oxbow of the Allegheny.[30]

It cannot be argued that the Sullivan expedition totally crushed the Indians, but the campaign did resolve several matters of great concern to Washington and his staff. Washington had known that while the Iroquois warriors and their loyalist allies operated unchallenged from these western sanctuaries, there could be no peace; nor could any troops be recruited for the Continental army from the immediately adjacent areas of the New York or Pennsylvania frontiers. The Iroquois towns had been places of refuge where the partisans could find shelter, supplies, and support. The leveling of the towns meant there was no place to hide and no food to supply immediate needs or long-term winter necessities. For a time, at least, the success of this American frontier campaign had driven the enemy back to the protection of the British fort at Niagara.

A much more profound effect of the Iroquois expedition, however, came in the peace that followed. The Continentals now could claim Iroquois lands as the spoils of war. The president of Congress was exacting in his expectations for a treaty with the Iroquois. The United States, explained Samuel Huntington, would overlook the serious injuries done by the Indians. Out of the goodness of its heart, America would grant peace, provided that the Indians begged for a settlement, surrendered all American prisoners, expelled all British agents, buried the hatchet forever (on penalty of being exiled), and gave "hostages for their strict adherence to the promises to be by them made."[31]

Despite the blow dealt the Iroquois, as well as the assumptions made by the United States on the basis of the successful expedition, the power of the Iroquois was not broken. Nor were the frontiers free from the threat of Indian attack. This was especially true in the Fort Pitt sector, where Daniel Brodhead found himself so short of provisions and troops in the days after his Seneca campaign that he could not protect the frontier. The settlers, furthermore, would neither volunteer for Continental service nor provide supplies, even when Brodhead sent out impressment parties. His agents reported that farmers drove their cattle into the mountains at the first report of approaching impressment parties. Fort Pitt was an empty shell, its garrison so impotent that raiding parties from Niagara could operate on the frontiers with impunity. Brodhead's frequent promises to invade the Ohio country and capture Detroit were as empty as his larder.[32]

That neither Fort Pitt nor any other western post offered protection to the western frontier was revealed by western military occurrences in the summer of 1780. For example, Virginia's leaders, still convinced that the Shawnees were the personification of the Devil, encouraged George Rogers Clark to lead a party of Kentucky militia into the Shawnee towns of Chillicothe and Pickaway. Since Clark had limited supplies, however, his only accomplishment was the destruction of the two villages and their fields of corn. When Governor Thomas Jefferson congratulated Clark and his men, he apologized that he could not offer provisions sufficient to support Clark's troops in the destruction of additional Shawnee towns and the long-desired advance against Detroit.[33]

The Shawnees, meanwhile, reciprocated the hostile feelings of the Virginians. To the Shawnees the Virginia "Long Knives" possessed all the worst features of the white frontiersmen. Not the least of the depradations of the Long Knives was the treacherous murder of Cornstalk, the Shawnee leader, killed in cold blood while he was held hostage against a peace treaty with Virginia. Moreover, every day it seemed that more and more of these despised Long Knives ventured into Kentucky, occupying the rolling lands once prized as Indian hunting preserves. Such incursions into native territories had prompted Henry Hamilton's observation that while Indian raids were a "deplorable sort of war . . . the arrogance, disloyalty and impudence of the Virginians had justly drawn [the attacks] upon them."[34]

In the spring of 1780, therefore, the Shawnees consulted Alexander McKee, the British Indian agent living in northern Ohio, who agreed to

commit a small detachment of British troops to assist a substantial party
of warriors from the Ohio country in an incursion into the Kentucky country. In the troop detachment would be an artillery officer who would direct
the use of a small field cannon. Given the extraordinary nature of this
mission, the warriors were carefully instructed to "act with spirit" from the
beginning to the end of the campaign, or the British soldiers would return
home immediately. This unusual party of regulars, partisans, and Indians
swiftly dropped below the Ohio River, where they were able to destroy
three frontier stockades and capture 400 prisoners. The party was back in
Detroit by mid-summer, but the pace and the demands of the campaign had
left the regulars and partisans with feet so badly blistered that they barely
were able to walk.[35]

At about the same time that the British force terrified the Kentucky country, the backcountry of the Carolinas was becoming alarmed by the British
invasion approaching from the coast. The rout of General Gates and his
force at Camden seemed to bare the interior to incursions, some of which
might threaten frontier settlements. Even more worrisome, however, was
the fear that British successes in South Carolina would encourage the southern Indians to once again take up arms in support of the king's cause. If
such attacks did take place, the people of the frontier knew they would
have to defend themselves on every front, for the collapse of the American
army in South Carolina had left no significant number of American troops
available for any purposes.

The alarm over British activity and Indian assistance came sharply into
focus late in the summer of 1780. Colonel Elijah Clarke of Georgia had
attempted to nip the bud of British machinations among the Indians on the
southern frontier by capturing Augusta, Georgia, the new headquarters for
Colonel Thomas Brown, the recently appointed superintendent for the Atlantic Division of the British Southern Indian Department. Clarke led 600
men in a siege of Brown's loyalist partisans and Indian allies, but the campaign was foiled by the arrival of a relief column from the British post at
Ninety-Six, South Carolina. In fact, not only was the siege broken, but the
American attackers had to retreat in haste. Colonel Clarke explained that
"the Circumstances of the Times Suited me to Retreat from thence, and
through much Difficulty Got through the Mountains to Nolechucky [sic]."[36]

In referring to "Nolichucky," Clarke meant the settlements on the Watauga
River in present day eastern Tennessee. It must have been alarming indeed for
the western settlers to shelter troops fleeing a conflict that was coming all too
close. Something had to be done to keep the war at a distance. That something
was to volunteer to serve with the groups gathering in opposition to the Earl of
Cornwallis's movement toward Charlotte, North Carolina, and especially the
operations of the partisan band under Patrick Ferguson.

The flamboyant Colonel Ferguson was leading several hundred loyalist
troops westward from Cornwallis's main army, terrorizing the settlements

and intimidating those who might be inclined to volunteer for service with
the newly forming Continental army in the South. Whether Ferguson actually sought to overtake Elijah Clarke's band retreating from Augusta is
open to question, but that he aroused the ire of the settlers—whom he called
"backwater men"—is certain.[37]

A thrill of alarm swept through the transmontane settlements as word
spread that Colonel Ferguson was marching west through South Carolina
toward the North Carolina mountains. The likes of Colonels Isaac Shelby,
John Sevier, Arthur Campbell, William Cleveland, and Joseph McDowell,
together with several border captains from the frontier regions of North
Carolina, Virginia, and Tennessee, sounded the call to arms.[38] Soon there
were more than 900 mounted frontier soldiers—the hated Long Knives—
clattering southward toward a confrontation with Ferguson's band.
Through the dust of the advance unit, company after company of frontier
militia marched in support of this heroic effort to protect their homelands.

As Ferguson and his troops neared Gilbertown, North Carolina, the rising
numbers of patriots threading through the countryside made it apparent
that he could not stand and fight. Ordering his men about, the British leader
began to withdraw toward Cornwallis's army, but when it became clear
that the main body of the British army was not within reach, Ferguson
turned and took position on a woodland shrouded shoulder of land near
King's Mountain, South Carolina.

Seasoned by countless campaigns against the Indians, the frontier soldiers
were unequalled, save perhaps by native Americans, at fighting in the woods.
The clash that soon ensued at King's Mountain was typical of forest warfare.
There was little open ground and no place for lines of soldiers to advance
upon one another; terrain became both liability and asset as the attackers
used hills, trees, and rocks to hide themselves, fire at the enemy, and advance
at every opportunity. Ferguson's forces in part were defeated because they
could not adjust to this hide-and-seek warfare. Moreover, patriot feelings
ran high. At King's Mountain the frontier soldiers fought ruthlessly, as they
might have against adversaries whom they regarded as mere savages. Indeed,
in the minds of the frontiersmen there was little difference in engaging
Ferguson's unit or in assailing an Indian village. In a matter of hours the
"mountain men" had triumphed; Ferguson and over 200 of his followers
were dead, while more than 700 others were taken captive.

The hostility pent-up in the mountain riflemen against those whom they
considered "disaffected" exploded in a paroxysm of revenge, not unlike
that when invading bands pillaged Indian villages. Those who survived the
defeat were tried before a drumhead court, and several were executed. In
fact, when it was suggested that some of the prisoners taken at King's
Mountain be marched into the Virginia mountain settlements for safekeep-
ing, some of the mountain militia threatened to kill any prisoners brought
there.[39]

The victory at King's Mountain did not still the frontier violence. By late in 1780 reports circulated that the Cherokee once again planned to strike the frontiers on behalf of the king's cause. Convinced that if the Indians were not immediately subdued, "we must the ensuing Summer be subjected to the depradations of a savage Enemy," western leaders raised still another frontier army, this a collection of volunteers from North Carolina and Virginia under Colonels Sevier and Campbell. The soldiers were subjected to a forced march into the Cherokee country. Sevier and his North Carolinians were so short of supplies that they foraged for "dry grapes, haws, walnuts, and hickory nuts" until Campbell's force arrived with supplies.[40] The combined expedition swept through the Overhill Cherokee towns, including the principal village of Chote, and while the fatigued North Carolinians trudged homeward, Campbell's men swung southward into the Chickamauga towns. Campbell threatened the Cherokee with an occupation force, a warning that was not toothless, since, as he reported to Governor Thomas Jefferson, in this brief invasion "upwards of one thousand Houses, ...not less than fifty thousand Bushels of corn... quantities of... provisions, all of which, after taking sufficient subsistence for the army... were committed to flames, or otherwise destroyed."[41]

In 1781, while Cornwallis triumphed at Guilford Court House, then drove into Virginia, the frontier militia, under Elijah Clarke of South Carolina and Micajah Williamson of South Carolina, resumed the task of attacking Thomas Brown's defenses. Brown grimly held on against increasing odds. In May more South Carolina troops under Andrew Pickens arrived, and they soon were joined by the men of Light Horse Harry Lee's Continental legion.[42]

Surrounded by his enemies, some of them his former neighbors on the Georgia–South Carolina frontier, Lieutenant Colonel Brown urged the southern Indians to come to his aid. Unfortunately for the British commander, the actions of the British in allowing Pensacola to fall into Spanish hands had so disheartened the Creeks that none was willing to run the risk. The Cherokees were engaged in diplomatic conversations with commissioners appointed by General Greene so they, too, were unwilling to take up arms. Actually, it mattered little what any of Brown's Indian allies did, since the frontiers were so closely watched by the patriots that any parties seeking to reach Augusta would have been rebuffed. Thus Brown could hold on for only about a month.[43]

Personally and painfully aware of the violent propensities of the frontier folk toward their enemies, Brown hoped to protect his garrison. Aware of the fate of the loyalists after the King's Mountain disaster, he sought guarantees of safety not only for the men of his provincial corps, but also for the lives of the brave Indian warriors who had come to his defense. He specifically requested that the Indians be permitted to "accompany the King's troops to Savannah, where they will remain prisoners of war, until exchanged for an equal number of prisoners in the Creek or Cherokee nations." Fortunately for Brown, General Greene also realized how the frontier troops might treat both the Indians and the loyalists, and he ordered the entire contingent guarded and escorted via a roundabout route back to Charleston. Without his judicious protective action by the American commander, the aftermath of Augusta might have been far more bloody than the grievous follow-up to King's Mountain.[44]

By the fall of 1781 the frontier troop units in the South were more and more dominant in their struggle with the Indians. In many ways the Indians of the Southeast were no safer in their villages than when they openly sought to aid the British. For instance, at about the same time that Pickens led a mounted unit into the Cherokee towns in order to keep the warriors cowed, General John Twiggs's Georgia militia captured a party of Cherokee and British traders attempting to reach Savannah. The booty amounted to 199 horses, 1,500 beaver pelts, and 15,000 deerskins.[45]

As the southern frontier quieted, the last bloodletting of this war occurred to the north. Lamentably, it was the very kind of blood bath that Colonel Brown had feared following his surrender at Augusta. The unfortunate tragedy occurred among the long-suffering Delawares of the Ohio country, a tribe whose fortunes had become more bitter with each passing year.

During the early years of the war, many Delawares had been sympathetic toward the American cause, especially those loyal to the leader known as Captain White Eyes, and those swayed by David Zeisberger, a Moravian missionary resident among the tribesmen. Zeisberger not only supported the Americans, he forwarded intelligence reports about the Indian country to the commandant at Fort Pitt. White Eyes ultimately paid with his life for his friendship when he was assassinated while he was guiding American troops through the Ohio country. Zeisberger, on the other hand, was forced to lead his Christianized Delaware followers away from their villages on the upper branches of the Muskingum to new homes near the British post at Detroit.[46]

Late in 1781, supply shortages and crop failures reduced these displaced persons to near starvation. Desperate for food, some of Zeisberger's followers retraced their steps to their old homes, hoping that gleanings from their abandoned fields might help them survive the winter. While the Delawares sought these cold ears among the dry stalks, a band of Pennsylvania militia out on an Indian hunting expedition approached the village. One of the Delawares saw them coming, but gave no alarm because he regarded them as fellow Christians. As the young convert went forward to greet the new arrivals, he was shot. The band of frontier soldiers then advanced into the empty village where they took ninety Delawares prisoner.[47]

The captors now confronted a major problem. What were they to do with this large band of captives? How would they provision them or convey them back to Pittsburgh for imprisonment? While the militia leaders debated their choices, the prisoners were locked in one of the abandoned houses. A number of the Pennsylvanians argued that despite their sizeable numbers, the prisoners should be returned to Fort Pitt. By far the most popular idea, however, was that all the prisoners should be killed so the troops would not have to bother with escorting them. When the matter was put to a vote, execution was the unanimous choice.

Accordingly, the executioners stationed themselves in the old Moroavian schoolhouse, to which they brought the prisoners one at a time and struck them in the head. Once the last prisoners had been dispatched, the building was set on fire in an effort to hide the homicides. Unknown to the Americans, however, at least one of the victims had only been stunned by the murderous blow aimed at him. The wounded Delaware lay quietly in the piles of bodies until the Americans were not watching. Somehow he manged to crawl under the building and out into the woods on the side of the building opposite from that watched by the Americans. Within a matter of weeks his gruesome tale would be told at every Indian council and British outpost in the East.

Hardly had reports of the Gnadenhutten Massacre flashed from settlement to settlement when more startling news reached the ears of frontier diplomats. The king was closing down the war in North America! The loss at Yorktown finally had convinced him that the struggle to crush the colonial rebellion no longer was worth the cost in men, money, and material. A cease-fire was to go into effect in the summer of 1782, and diplomatic negotiations were to follow.

The regular armies observed the truce and the diplomatic representatives eventually agreed to terms, but the frontier warfare could not be so easily ended. The murderous feelings between neighbors at war dissipated slowly, if at all, and during the decade following the Peace of Paris, frontier fighting continued off and on over much of the same bloody ground upon which the revolutionary combatants had struggled.

This frontier tension was clearly understood by George Washington, who, as a Virginian sensitive to western affairs, knew from the beginning of his tenure as commander that there were both eastern and western fronts. Acutely aware that Indian attacks drained the recruiting pool for Continentals as well as for state levies, the commander-in-chief never ignored western problems. Indeed Washington realized how fortunate he was that for the most part local citizens defended themselves. Had he been forced year after year to use his army to simultaneously defend the frontiers and the seacoast, his success might never have been achieved.

General Washington's opponents in the British command, on the other hand, initially had anticipated substantial assistance from both forest soldiers and partisans. In the long run this unrealized potential prompted Parliament's sharp criticism of the army's enormous expenses for Indian affairs. Generals Gage, Howe, Clinton, and Carleton complained about expecting much and receiving little, the consequence of which was a dramatic reduction in budgets for the Indian departments after 1779.

In the final analysis, then, what conclusions may be drawn about frontier warfare and the American victory? From the patriot military perspective two powerful Iroquoian tribes had been humbled, a major British frontier official had been captured, the loyalists under Ferguson had been decimated, and everywhere the frontier folk generally had demonstrated their ability to defend themselves. The patriots had shown that they could, if pressed, carry on a two-front war. Most importantly for the future, however, the frontier victory had established the premise that the lands of the West were the spoils of war. As the losers, the native Americans were called upon to capitulate to every whim of the newly independent nation. Without the frontier victory not only would the struggle have been prolonged, but there also would have been less upon which to base the western land claims of the emerging United States.

8

Politics
and the American Victory

Jonathan G. Rossie

The armed struggle to secure American independence was at its inception political in not only its objective, but also in the means chosen to secure that objective. Unlike most modern revolutions whose objective has been the displacement of an oppressive ruling class, the American Revolution was essentially a constitutional struggle to create an independent American nation that could preserve the essential political, social, and economic structures that had evolved in the colonies prior to 1763.

Until the assertion of parliamentary supremacy in the 1760s, the colonies enjoyed considerable autonomy. In the decades preceding the Revolution, the elected colonial assemblies used English constitutional principles to acquire numerous powers, especially in the appropriation and expenditure of public funds. After 1765, when Parliament challenged the assemblies' power, a constitutional crisis arose concerning the structure of the empire. Affirming that allegiance to the Crown, American political leaders developed a defense of colonial rights that assumed in essence a form of imperial federalism. The protesting colonists recognized parliamentary supremacy in external affairs, including the regulation of trade, but they insisted upon provincial autonomy in all matters of internal policy. Parliament, of course, refused to accept any diminution of its sovereign power.[1]

The Anglo-American conflict was not finally resolved until the colonies secured their independence, but long before then the essence of the imperial deadlock was shifted to America, where the newly formed states resisted efforts to create a strong central government after 1776. Having asserted their independence from Great Britain and written new constitutions, the revolutionary leadership should have achieved not only the local autonomy they previously sought, but full sovereignty in internal and external affairs.

In fact, the exigencies created by the military struggle to secure independence forced the states to delegate to a central authority sufficient power to achieve that end. Until the adoption of the Articles of Confederation in 1781, that authority was the Second Continental Congress. Federal in character, with each state possessing one vote, and technically lacking any power of its own, Congress nonetheless exercised real political power. Beginning in the spring of 1775, it assumed the direction of the revolutionary crisis brought on by the outbreak of hostilities in Massachusetts, for only in Congress assembled, could the representatives of the several colonies, and later states, make the necessary political and military responses to the Crown's efforts to subordinate the colonies by force.

War with Great Britain exploded on April 19, 1775, in the bloody engagements at Lexington and Concord. The bloodshed in those small Massachusetts hamlets occurred just three weeks before the Second Continental Cogress convened in Philadelphia. Having resorted to armed resistance, the New England delegates were determined to utilize Congress as the means of transforming the local conflict in Massachusetts into the cause of all America. When the delegates at last assembled in Philadelphia, therefore, New England sought to secure congressional sanction for armed resistance. More importantly, they struggled to have Congress assume resposibility for the direction and support of the New England militia units now gathering before Boston.

Although deeply divided between the numerically superior reconciliationists, led by John Dickinson, and a less numerous but energetic "republican" faction in favor of independence, led by John and Samuel Adams and Richard Henry Lee, events soon forced Congress to recognize that resistance to the British army in Massachusetts required continental support. Further, Congress concluded that organized resistance might be required to counter a British threat to New York. First came news that the British ministry had ordered four regiments, originally intended to reinforce General Thomas Gage in Boston, to proceed instead to New York to secure control of the city and the Hudson River, and "defeat... any attempt to send succor to the New England people from the middle colonies."[2] Hard on the heels of this intelligence came a report that a small force led by Colonels Ethan Allen and Benedict Arnold has seized Fort Ticonderoga in northern New York.

These developments prompted James Duane of New York to propose a policy that was acceptable to both factions in Congress. In essence, Duane recommended that the colonies maintain two armies to confine British troops in Boston and New York. No hostile action was to be initiated by the Americans, but if British troops attempted offensive operations they were to be forcefully resisted.

Ticonderoga, strategically situated athwart the invasion route from Canada, posed a somewhat more complex question. At first a majority in Congress, viewing the seizure of the fort as inconsistent with the newly adopted Duane doctrine of defensive war, favored returning the post to the British. But the fort's potential as a base from which British troops could launch attacks against both New York and New England finally led Congress to accept the fait accompli as a defensive measure. Congress then requested Connecticut to send sufficient force to secure the fort. For the moment, at least, no offensive move toward Canada was sanctioned, and the Duane policy of passive defense remained intact.[3]

Meanwhile, the members of the Massachusetts Congress grew impatient. Their earlier plea for congressional assistance as yet unanswered, they drafted a second letter on May 16. In it they posed two critical questions. Should Massachusetts assume and exercise full powers of civil government? Moreover, would Congress assume responsibility for the support and direction of the provincial army besieging Boston?[4]

For all practical purposes, the provincial congress, an extralegal body, had already assumed the powers of civil government in Massachusetts. What it now requested was congressional approval to transform itself into a "legal" government which would contravene existing parliamentary statutes. Such an act on the part of Massachusetts could be viewed as a de facto declaration of independence, and congressional approval would establish a precedent for other colonies to act in a similar manner. Although such a step might be welcomed by the "republicans", it would seriously undercut the efforts of those who sought reconciliation with Britain.

To lend weight to their new request, the Massachusetts Congress argued that the presence of a growing patriot siege army before Boston necessitated the creation of a strong civil government. Otherwise, the Massachusetts officials warned, the military would be unchecked by civil authority. It was a shrewd ploy. By linking the issues of local autonomy and the creation of a national army, the radicals in Massachusetts had created a dilemma for the conciliation faction in Congress. Without firm civil control, the army gathered around Boston might precipitate an escalation of the war. On the other hand, to accede to Massachusetts's request that its provincial congress be granted full powers of civil government would move Congress dangerously closer to the severance of all political ties to Britain.

The Massachusetts request was referred to a committee consisting of John Rutledge (South Carolina), Thomas Johnson (Maryland), John Jay (New York), Richard Henry Lee (Virginia), and James Wilson (Pennsylvania). The majority, (Rutledge, Johnson, and Jay), favored conciliation, and its recommendation, accepted by Congress in early June, reflected that position. Massachusetts was advised to ignore the Coercive Act, which had sought to alter the province's form of government; instead, Massachusetts was to adhere to the form of government established by their charter of 1691. If Governor Gage refused to cooperate with the constitutional government of Massachusetts, then the duly elected assembly and council should assume full governing powers until he, or "a governor, of his Majesty's appointment, will consent to govern the colony according to its charter."[5] Thus Congress avoided sanctioning the creation of a "new" government in Massachusetts, and would continue to pursue the same course with respect to other colonies until the spring of 1776.

Massachusetts's request that Congress assume responsibility for the siege army—now styled "the New England Army of Observation"—could not as easily be sidestepped. Under constant pressure from New England delegates led by John Adams, Congress gradually adopted the army as its own. On June 9 and 10 it requested both the New York Provincial Congress and the New England colonies to supply the "Continental army" in Massachusetts at the Continental expense.[6] A week later Congress assumed formal responsibility for a Continental army of 20,000 men (15,000 in Massachusetts and 5,000 in New York) and appointed George Washington its commander-in-chief.

Washington's appointment was in part due to his prior military service as a colonel in the French and Indian War (he was also the only delegate present wearing military uniform), but essentially it was an astute political move by certain New Englanders to broaden support for their cause in Congress.[7] Washington was a Virginian, and New England understood that the active support of Virginia, the oldest, largest, and wealthiest of the colonies was necessary if military resistance to Britain was to succeed. So, while appointing Artemas Ward of Massachusetts first major general, Congress also selected two other Virginia planters, Charles Lee and Horatio Gates, as second major general and adjutant general respectively. Ward's appointment was expected, since he was not only from Massachusetts, but also the current commander of the army before Boston. Lee and Gates, on the other hand, had served previously in the British army, and their supporters in Congress argued that it was this, and not the fact that they were from Virginia, that qualified them for command positions.

While Virginia's support for the Continental army was now assured, these earliest appointments created jealousy and disappointment in other quarters. Connecticut, whose contribution in men and material was second only to Massachusetts, was aggrieved that none of its officers had received a major general's commission, and New York, which was to have a Continental force of some 5,000, was similarly chagrined at having been passed over. In the interest of harmony, Congress agreed to increase the number of major generals by two. Philip Schuyler of New York and Israel Putnam of Connecticut were elected to the new posts.

Schuyler's appointment had the strong support of the New York Provincial Congress, which thought him the logical choice to command troops in that province. A man of vast wealth, Schuyler had ties to New York's powerful Livingston family. In addition, he had served with some distinction in the French and Indian War. Like most of the leading men from New

York, he was not an ardent revolutionary and, as member of Congress, a position he retained after his appointment to the army, he strongly supported a reconciliation policy.

If Putnam's election as a major general was designed to soothe embittered feelings, it immediately had an opposite effect. In April, Connecticut had named David Wooster to command its forces, with Joseph Spencer and Putnam appointed first and second brigadiers beneath him. Congress's action, however, meant that Wooster and Spencer were now junior in rank to their former subordinate.[8]

General Washington discovered the problem when he assumed command of the army at Cambridge on July 2. In presenting the commissions for Continental general officers, he found that Congress's disregard for seniority in the provincial establishments threatened to destroy what little command structure existed. Wooster and Spencer, he learned, refused their appointments as subordinates to Putnam. Wooster, in fact, sent his commission to his friend in Congress, Roger Sherman, and asked him to return it to John Hancock with instructions that it not be sent back since he already had a commission from the government of Connecticut.[9] Wooster's attitude is significant, for while he later accepted his commission, he continued to think of himself as first and foremost a major general in the Connecticut service, a belief that soon led to a confrontation with the commander of the Northern Department, General Schuyler. The taciturn Spencer, without informing Washington of his intentions, simply left camp and returned home, although he, too, eventually accepted his commission.

The Connecticut generals were not the only officers who were displeased by the congressional appointments. John Thomas, second only to Artemas Ward in the Massachusetts army, had been appointed a brigadier, junior to two of his former subordinates, Seth Pomeroy and William Heath. To avoid another confrontation with a disappointed general, Washington held on to the remainder of the brigadier commissions, including those for Pomeroy, Heath, and Thomas. He immediately wrote to Congress, informing it that Thomas was respected in the army and that his resignation would be a loss to the service. He also communicated directly with Thomas, assuring him of the high esteem in which he was held, and promising that he would do everything in his power to make his situation "both easy and honorable."[10]

The congressional delegation from Massachusetts had made an error in recommending the appointments of brigadiers, not out of malice, but simply because the Massachusetts government had failed to notify it of the new ranking of generals that had occurred shortly after the engagements at Lexington and Concord. Fortunately, Pomeroy, who was sixty-nine years old, had already resigned his position in the Massachusetts army and now refused the preferment to first brigadier in the Continental service. Congress moved quickly to appoint Thomas to that vacated position. Thomas was satisfied, and Heath made no objection to the alteration, or did Richard Montgomery, who as second brigadier would ordinarily have been promoted to the vacated position.[11]

Acutely aware of the personal jealousies that could disrupt his army, Washington astutely reorganized the army into three divisions, separating potential rivals. Brigadiers Thomas and Spencer were attached to the division commanded by Major General Ward; Brigadiers John Sullivan and Nathanel Greene to that commanded by Charles Lee; and Heath was placed in Putnam's division. On paper, Washington's army now appeared quite formidable. By mid-July, the none too accurate duty rosters showed some 17,000 rank and file with more men arriving every day. If every regiment was brought up to strength, it was estimated that the army would swell to 24,500 men.

As the army grew in size, the creation of an administrative structure to see to its provisioning and supply became esssential. As early as July 10, Washington wrote Congress to urge the immediate appointment of a quartermaster general, commissary general, mustermaster general, and a commissary for artillery. The gross inefficiency of having each province responsible for the provisioning of its troops made the appointment of a commissary general particularly important, he believed. To fill this post, he recommended Joseph Trumbull who had proved himself effective as commissary for the Connecticut regiments. Washington's nomination of Trumbull was unanimously endorsed by Congress, and after some debate it also commissioned James Warren as paymaster general and Jonathan Trumbull, Jr., as his deputy for the army in New York.[12]

It quickly became apparent, however, that the appointment of administrative officers would excite the same interprovincial rivalries as attended the selection of general officers. Unable to reach consensus in filling the remaining posts, Congress instructed Washington to make the appointments himself. This action alarmed some in Congress, including John Adams, who saw it as a potentially dangerous abdication of civilian control over the military. The chief administrative officers, he believed, were a check upon the commander-in-chief, and "ought not to be under any dependence upon him or so great obligations of gratitude as those of a creature to the creator." Principle aside, Adams also feared that Washington would pass over deserving Massachusetts men; a fear that proved well founded when Washington appointed two Philadelphians, Thomas Mifflin and Stephen Moylan to the posts of quartermaster and mustermaster general.[13]

By the end of August, with most of the staff positions filled by Washington's appointees, Congress further distanced itself from control of the emerging Continental army by tacitly relinquishing the power to appoint field-grade officers (regimental colonels, lieutenant colonels, and majors) to the provincial governments in which the regiments were raised. In part, this was a practical decision. Given the difficulties encountered in the selection of a handful of general officers, Congress was understandably hesitant to undertake the direct commissioning of hundreds of field-grade officers. But it also reflected a reluctance on the part of most congressmen to significantly augment the power of the central authority at the expense of the individual colonies. Consequently, Washington was given blank commissions to fill out and issue to the regimental officers already with the army at Cambridge. To deal with the new regiments being raised in New York, Congress asked the New York Provincial Congress to recommend suitable field-grande officers to General Schuyler so that he could issue them commissions in the name of Congress.

Not everyone agreed with the decision to permit the provinces to select high-ranking officers. Washington privately expressed his reservations, for instance, pointing out the ill consequences that would flow from such a practice. First, it gave "that power and weight to an individual colony, which ought of right to belong only to the whole; and, next, it dampens the spirit and ardor of volunteers from all but the four New England governments, as none but their people have the least chance of getting into office." Instead, Washington proposed that the commander-in-chief be given the power to make these appointments on the basis of merit, subject to congressional approval.[14]

From a military point of view, Washington's recommendation was perfectly sound, and would have quickened the transformation of the army from a collection of provincial militias to a regular army responsible only to Congress. However, in 1775 this was viewed as potentially dangerous by many members of Congress. Those favoring reconciliation considered it provocative and a step away from their goal, while radicals looked askance at any proposal that would strengthen the central government at the expense of the individual colonies. Further, many in and out of Congress feared that the creation of a regular army would subvert and ultimately destroy the very liberties that the rebellion was meant to protect.

One of the most fervent attacks on regular, standing armies appeared in a Philadelphia newspaper in August of 1775. The author, who chose the sobriquet "Caractacus" (after the Briton who led resistance to the Roman invasion), warned that throughout history military "officers and soldiers of the best principles and characters have been converted into the instruments of tyranny." All America needed was a trained, vigilant militia in each colony capable of responding at a moment's notice to any threat by the enemy. He even maintained that militiamen should serve without pay.[15] However, political leaders had to consider not only the potential dangers of an American standing army, but the immediate danger posed by the British army. Washington's urgent letters to Congress portrayed an army unfit to oppose any determined effort by a reinforced British army. Discipline was practically impossible with most of the officers and men refusing to sign the Continental Articles of War; in addition, as most enlistments would expire before the new year, there would be no effective force to meet an enemy offensive in the spring. Congress responded in September by asking Washington and his senior officers to determine the most effective way to keep his army together, and to suggest how the various provincial establishments might be reduced into one, unified Continental army. Congress also appointed a committee of three to visit Washington's camp to assist in resolving these delicate matters. No one deluded himself with the belief that change would come easily. As John Hancock, the president of Congress, remarked, alterations—and especially those involving the appointment of officers—"may create great jealousies and uneasiness."[16]

Eventually, acting upon the report of the committee it had sent to Washington's headquarters, Congress authorized a vigorous campaign to encourage men to reenlist for a year's additional service, it made the signing of the Articles of War mandatory, and it placed the appointment of field-grade officers under congressional control. The last measure was vigorously opposed by the New England delegates.

Those who supported congressional control, such as James Duane of New York, argued that since Congress was committed to the foundation of an American army, general regulations had to be established to place the whole army on an equal footing. While Congress itself might not be able to deliberate on the appointment and promotion of every senior officer, it could and should act upon recommendations made by Washington for the main army and Schuyler for the northern army. It was better, Duane added, to trust the judgment of those gentlemen than that of any convention or provincial congress. Duane also asserted that as the burden of supporting the army rested with Congress, this should entitle Congress to appoint its own officers.[17]

George Ross of Pennsylvania was even more vehement on this point, urging that Congress appoint all officers. Until this was done, he said, Congress would have no effective control over its own army, John Jay of New York warmly seconded Ross's position, pointing out that the whole army had recently refused to be mustered by the Continental mustermasters. Jay, moreover, laid bare the real issue at dispute. "The Union," he declared, "depends much upon breaking down provincial conventions."[18]

Not all those advocating congressional appointment of regimental officers were motivated by a desire to strengthen the central government at the expense of the individual colonies. Nor was the reverse necessarily true. Some delegates from the South favored the move simply because it was the only way they could obtain commissions for deserving men in their own colonies. However, in the case of men like Duane, Jay, and Ross it seems clear that they did wish to augment the power of Congress, and in the months and years ahead they consistently pressed for the creation of an effective national government.

The opposition to the congressional appointment of officers can be closely identified with a particular faction, with radicals, or "federalists," as they came increasingly to call themselves. To such men, mostly New Englanders, a strong national government, whether located in London or Philadelphia, represented a direct threat to local self-government and individual rights. Moreover, the creation of an army solely responsible to the central government would increase the dangers associated with a standing army. The wisest and safest policy, they insisted, was to maintain a small Continental army augmented as occasion demanded by the militia. Despite the determined opposition of this faction, however, it was unable to block the extension of congressional authority over the appointment and promotion of all Continental officers above the rank of captain.

While in practice Congress usually appointed men recommended by the colony in which a battalion was raised, it reserved to itself the final authority to grant the commissions. To implement this policy, on December 8, 1775, a standing committee of Congress was appointed consisting of one member from each colony, "to take into consideration the application of . . . persons applying to be officers in the American army, to examine their qualifications, and report to Congress.[19]

When Congress appointed the committee to confer with Washington and his officers at Cambridge, and subsequently appointed a standing committee to review the commissioning and promotion of officers, it established the mode by which it would maintain control and direction of the Continental army throughout the war. Soon, additional standing committees were appointed to deal with specific matters relating to the army, such as the letting of contracts for military supply and the granting of commissions to foreign volunteers. Indeed, in 1777 Congress found itself so overwhelmed by the task of regulating the army, that it was compelled to create a Board of War consisting of men who were not members of Congress. Eventually, with the ratification of the Articles of Confederation, the office of secretary of war replaced the Board of War. However, Congress never relinquished its ultimate authority over the regulation and direction of the army. Thus, while it received advice from the Board of War, and, later, the secretary of war, Congress could, and often did, ignore that advice. Further, it continued to appoint special committees of its own members to provide additional information upon which it based much of its military policy.

By the beginning of 1776, Congress had assumed sufficient authority to regulate and direct the operations of the army. However, it remained dependent upon the individual colonies to supply the manpower and provisions necessary to sustain that army. Congress requested men and supplies from the colonies, and later the states, on the basis of their population. This meant, quite simply, that while each state had but a single vote in Congress, those states which gave more to the war effort not only demanded more consideration in the appointment of new officers, but the promotion of those already serving. Thus, state rivalries continued to frustrate the efforts of Washington and his supporters to fashion an army where proven merit, and not political influence, was the essential requirement for command.

The command disputes that plagued the northern army from 1775 through 1777 offer a good example of how congressional factionalism, based in large part upon provincial jealousies, could seriously impair military operations. The American campaign to secure Canada in 1775 had gone badly. Throughout the early summer of 1775, the reconciliation faction in Congress had resisted the demands of the New England delegates for a decisive invasion before the British had time to reinforce their garrisons in Canada. One tactic they used was to secure congressional instructions forbidding the commander of the army in New York, General Schuyler, from entering Canada unless he was certain that the French Canadians would welcome the American army. The summer was well advanced before these instructions were changed to allow the invasion to proceed as long as the French Canadians did not actively oppose it.

Schuyler was hampered by a lack of both men and supplies, but his greatest problem arose from the fact that the bulk of his army was composed of Connecticut troops commanded by Brigadier David Wooster. Wooster, still smarting from his failure to be appointed a major general by Congress, acted as a major general in the Connecticut service when it suited him. One result was that the Connecticut troops—who refused to sign the Articles of War—would accept orders from Wooster, but not his superiors in the Continental service, including General Schuyler. Thus, it was not until mid-October that Schuyler was able to convince Wooster and the Connecticut troops to go to the assistance of General Montgomery, who was besieging Fort St. Johns at the foot of Lake Champlain. Then, when the fort fell early in November, most of the Connecticut men refused to proceed further into Canada since the season was late, they were poorly clothed, and they wanted to be back in Connecticut when their enlistments expired at the end of December. Even with the promise of warmer clothes, fewer than 200 agreed to reenlist for a longer period; the rest promptly set out for home. As a consequence, Montgomery, together with colonel Benedict Arnold, who had led a small army overland through Maine, were compelled to make a ill-considered and desperate attack on Quebec City on New Year's Eve. Of the 800 men making the attack, 51 were killed, including Montgomery, while Arnold and a further 36 were wounded; a staggering 387 men were captured. The remnants of the American army, little more than 200 at Quebec and perhaps 300 at Montreal, went into winter quarters.[20]

Throughout the late winter and early spring of 1776, Congress directed regiments from New England and the middle colonies northward to strengthen the army in Canada before the arrival of expected British reinforcements. With Schuyler in command of the newly designated Northern Department, Congress also selected a new commander for the army in

Canada, Major General Thomas, and dispatched a special committee to Montreal to investigate the causes of the previous year's failure. In addition, the committee was to determine the present needs of the army, and make one final attempt to secure the active support of the Canadians. However, efforts to reinforce the army were too little and too late. On May 2 a British fleet sailed up the St. Lawrence carrying General John Burgoyne with eight British regiments and 2,000 German mercenaries. Ravaged by smallpox, the American army, reduced to fewer than 1,000 effectives, was forced to retreat to Sorel at the mouth of the Richelieu. There Thomas succumbed in the epidemic that ravaged his tattered army. Early in June he was succeeded by the senior brigadier, John Sullivan. Reinforced by a brigade of some 3,300 New Yorkers, Sullivan chose to attack the British advancing from Quebec. He was bloodily repulsed, and forced to slowly retreat from Canada, reforming the remnants of the army at Crown Point in early July.[21]

Unaware that the army had been driven from Canada, Congress received reports in late May from the special committee it had sent to Montreal. The committee, composed of Benjamin Franklin, Samuel Chase, Charles Carroll of Carrollton, and John Carroll, reported that the previous year's campaign had failed largely because it commenced too late in the season, although it added that a large share of the blame could also be attributed to widespread misconduct on the part of many New England officers and men attached to the northern army. General Wooster in particular was criticized by the committee, which found him "totally unfit" for his command.

The committee's findings came as no surprise to many members of Congress, particularly those from the middle and southern colonies. Reports reaching Congress during the fall and winter from General Schuyler and other officers had amply prepared them to accept the committee's conclusions. Embarrassed and angry, New Englanders struck back, blaming the American failure on Schuyler's poor leadership, and broadly hinting that he was not only a coward, but a secret Tory. The bitterness engendered by attempts to find a scapegoat for the failure of the northern army created deep-seated animosities that profoundly affected the future effectiveness of that army.[22]

While charge and countercharge were hurled by the congressional supporters and detractors of Schuyler, the British army, having secured Canada, prepared to advance and recapture Crown Point and Ticonderoga. Defeated and demoralized, what remained of the northern army was ill-prepared to check the British advance. To make matters worse, New Englanders still constituted the bulk of the army, and with the loss of General Thomas, few in Congress expected officers and men from those colonies to perform well under Schuyler's direct command. Thus, with little dissent, Congress, in mid-June, 1776, appointed Major General Horatio Gates commander of the forces in Canada. Gates was given broad discretionary powers, including the authority to appoint staff and line officers without prior congressional approval.[23]

Gates was a natural choice for the new command. With the death of Thomas, he became the ranking major general in the army, after Lee, Schuyler, and Putnam. His previous experience as major in the British army and, more recently, as Washington's adjutant general, gave confidence in his ability to restore order and discipline to the ranks of the northern army. He also enjoyed the political support of the Lee-Adams faction in Congress, along with that of most of the New England delegation. However, in making the appointment Congress neglected to define the relationship between Gates as the commander of the army in Canada and Schuyler as the commander of the Northern Department, a serious omission since the army that Gates was to command was no longer in Canada, but had retreated into New York. Inevitably, disputes arose between Schuyler and Gates, which soon degenerated into a protracted partisan controversy involving the congressional supporters of the two officers. In the process, the effectiveness of the northern army was seriously impaired and the reputations of both men were tarnished.

The failure of Congress to recognize potential problems concerning the northern command was due in part to its assumption that the Northern army retained a foothold in Canada. In large part, however, it was due to the preoccupation of congressmen with a multitude of pressing business. More than a year after the outbreak of hostilities in Massachusetts, Congress was still attempting to deal with critical issues—from declaring independence to managing the war—through standing and ad hoc committees. The stressful demands that this system placed on individual members often made thoughtful, deliberative assessment of alternative policies impossible, and nowhere was this more evident than in congressional efforts to direct military operations.

By the end of June, 1776, there should have been no reasonable expectation that American fortunes in Canada could be retrieved. The indifferent attitude of the Canadian population, as well as the arrival of more than 8,000 British regulars under General John Burgoyne, doomed to failure any further American efforts to secure Canada. No general, no matter how spirited or talented could have altered the outcome. Yet congressmen found it easier to blame generals—whether Wooster, Schuyler, or Gates—for northern reverses than to reassess their own expectations in light of the changed military and political reality. Thus the practical decision by Schuyler and Gates, supported by Sullivan and Arnold, to abandon Crown Point in July and concentrate the northern army at Ticonderoga was met with a storm of congressional criticism, although the move ultimately was a crucial factor in inhibiting British plans to invade New York in 1776.

Congressional lack of confidence in its military commanders was intensified by the crushing defeats that Washington's army sustained in the course of the New York campaign in 1776. Nor did America's prospects in the North in 1777 appear to be bright as the British army renewed its offensive. General Burgoyne forced the abandonment of Ticonderoga in July and slowly pressed the northern army back toward Albany. Bowing to pressure from the New England delegation, Congress removed Schuyler from his command and appointed Gates in his stead, hoping that by so doing the New England militia, who disliked Schuyler, would now turn out in force.[24]

Gates's eventual victory at Saratoga and the surrender of Burgoyne's army appeared to vindicate the trust placed in his leadership by his congressional supporters. It did not, however, lessen partisan conflict, since Schuyler's supporters insisted that had he not been removed from command, the laurels of victory would have been his. Indeed, factional division became even sharper as a result of the defeats sustained by Washington during the fight for Philadelphia that same fall.

As with past defeats, Congress sought a scapegoat for the army's failures. General Sullivan, who had commanded the American right at the Battle of the Brandywine, was subjected to harsh congressional criticism, but his fellow New Englanders rallied to his defense and prevented his removal from the army. In addition, some congressmen unfavorably compared Washington's lack of success with Gates's momentous victory at Saratoga, and others criticized his decision to put the army in winter quarters rather than prosecute a winter campaign against Howe.[25] Thus, amid rising criticism of Washington's direction of the fall's campaign, rumors spread that a junto of prominent congressional and military leaders intended to make Gates the new commander-in-chief.

The allegations and recriminations that swept Congress and the army during the winter of 1777/78 were more the product of disappointment, combined with the residual factionalism of the Gates-Schuyler controversy, than a serious plot to remove Washington. Largely through the efforts of the president of Congress, Henry Laurens, fears of an anti-Washington cabal were dispelled, factional passions subsided, and members of Congress pledged their unequivocal support for the commander-in-chief and his conduct of the war.[26]

The winter of 1777/78 was the turning point of the Revolution. The American victory at Saratoga brought an alliance with France and a lessening of British military pressure in America. Faced by her ancient enemy France, and soon Spain, Britain could not mount another major campaign in America. In the end, the demands placed on her resources by the spreading international war forced Britian to seek a political settlement that recognized the independence of the United States. That same winter also saw a turning point for the Continental army and civil-military relations.

The confrontation between the supporters of Washington and his congressional critics had a chastening effect on the politicians, and made them receptive to major reforms in the management and direction of the army. The reorganization of the Commissary and Quartermaster departments and the creation of a new, more autonomous Board of War placed a buffer between the army and congressional factionalism. After three years of war, the remaining doctrinaire republicans came to agree with the nationalists that a well-regulated regular army was essential for an American victory. Earlier fears that such an army would lead to a military despotism had proved groundless, and the cherished principle of civilian domination of the military could be maintained without direct congressional involvement in military affairs.

Given the ingrained Anglo-American distrust of the military, the subordination of the army was perhaps not surprising. While there were still occasions, most notably during the winter of 1780/81 and the spring of 1783, when disgruntled elements in the army considered wresting power from Congress, Washington and the army's leadership shunned such a course. Indeed, much of the credit for maintaining the delicate balance between civilian authority and military necessity was due to Washington's restraint in exercising his powers as commander-in-chief and his ability to remain aloof from partisan politics.

Although he was referring specifically to his defusing of the Newburgh conspiracy, Washington might well have been reviewing the often perilous course of civil-military relations during the preceding eight years when he declared: "Had this day been wanting, the world had never seen the last stages of perfection, to which human nature is capable of attaining."[27]

9

The French Alliance
and the American Victory

W. J. Eccles

The first attempt by the French to foment and aid a revolution by England's American colonies occurred not in May, 1776, but in May, 1710. In that year, during the War of the Spanish Succession, the comte de Pontchartrain, minister of marine, received an urgent dispatch from Phillippe Pastour de Costebelle, the governor of Placentia in Newfoundland, informing him that the large British naval force assembled the previous year had been for the purpose of reasserting royal authority in Massachusetts and New York. The minister thus came to believe that the people of both colonies were eager to throw off the authority of their royal governors and govern themselves as republics.

Pontchartrain sent orders to the governor general of New France at Quebec, Philippe de Rigaud, marquis de Vaudreuil, requiring him to inform the Council at Boston of the British plans and to urge it to throw off the British yoke. Vaudreuil was further instructed to discover the Council's intentions and if an American revolt seemed likely, to use every means available to support the English colonials. In addition, he was to be extremely circumspect and employ agents possessed of the greatest discretion to ensure that the plan did not falter or fail.[1]

So there it was: a secretary of state of Louis XIV eager to support the principles of republicanism in order to harm the archfoe, Britain. Pontchartrain had, of course, been sadly misinformed by the governor of Placentia. It was a notion whose time had not yet come. The naval task force assembled in England was intended for an assault on Canada. The eventual operation, which included land forces of New England and New York, was a total disaster. Yet Pontchartrain's reaction was revealing. The French, and others, become convinced that Britain's American colonies would strike out for independence at the first opportunity. The only thing restraining them, it was believed, was their fear of the Canadians, their Indian allies, and the military might of France stretching as it did from Louisbourg on the Atlantic coast to New Orleans.[2]

In 1760 Canada was conquered by a British army and the Royal Navy. The recently appointed French first minister, Étiene-François, duc de Choiseul-Stainville, then adopted the policy long advocated by the marquis de Capellis, a senior official in the ministry of marine, that Canada be abandoned to Britain when peace negotiations were undertaken.[3] Choiseul eventually negotiated the Peace of Paris with the British and insisted that Britain retain Canada. Some of the British had serious misgivings as to the wisdom of this acquisition. Lord Bedford, the British minister plenipotentiary in Paris, wondered "whether the neighborhood of the French to our North American colonies was not the greatest security for their dependence on the mother country, which I feel will be slighted by them when their apprehension of the French is removed."[4] The French were counting on it.

Since Louis XIV's reign, New France had been used as an instrument of French imperial policy, a knight on the maritime powers' chess board, to be sacrificed if necessary. Its role had been to contain England's colonies between the Appalachians and the Atlantic, to prevent their expansion into the heart of the continent. After the acquisition of Canada, Britain found itself forced to adopt that self-same policy to avoid renewed assaults by the Indian nations in defense of their lands, which the Americans were invading.

Choiseul fondly believed that were Britain's American colonies to gain their independence, Britain's economy would suffer a crippling blow from the loss of this major market. The loss of Canada for France would be as nothing compared to Britain's privation. Moreover, the British would be saddled for generations to come with the expensive and onerous task of defending Canada and Nova Scotia against the constant threat of American invasion.[5] This was to be a cornerstone of French foreign policy for the ensuing twenty years. The main thrust of that policy was simple and straightforward: *revanche*, the abasement of Great Britain, which alone could restore French prestige after the humiliating defeat that France had suffered in the Seven Years' War. In Europe Choiseul's aim was to restore the balance of power. To this end Britain had to be kept isolated, the Family Compact with Spain had to be strengthened, and all other continental entanglements—wars above all—had to be avoided. To achieve this the country's economic strength first had to be restored, the navy rebuilt, and sweeping reforms made in the army. Next, at the first opportunity, Britain had to be struck hard. Choiseul declared that he had "only one foreign policy, a fraternal union with Spain; only one policy for war, and that is England." His objective, he estimated, might be achieved in five years.[6] It was to take fifteen.

Britain faced more problems after 1763 than Choiseul dared to imagine.

Following the Seven Years' War France retained her allies, with the exception of Russia, while Britain lost all of hers. There was no need for Choiseul to strive to keep Britain isolated. By their conduct in the past war the British had isolated themselves. In addition, victory created greater problems for Britain than defeat did for France. The national debt had almost doubled to £137,000,000; the interest on it ran to £5,000,000 a year and the government's revenues did not exceed £8,000,000. The costs involved in the administration of the newly acquired territories were immense. The maintenance of twenty battalions, 10,000 men, to defend the American western frontier cost £350,000 a year, and the American colonial assemblies refused to share that burden. The constantly changing ministries found themselves striving to cope with massive problems in a worldwide empire: possessions in India, Africa, America from the Arctic to the Caribbean and Central America, not to mention that permanent festering sore, Ireland, and then in the 1770s, Australia. As never before, Britain desperately needed skilled leadership, but the shiftless men who formed the shifting governments were pathetically inadequate for the tasks they had to face.

Meanwhile the economic resurgence of France was nothing short of miraculous. Overseas trade soared to new heights, old markets were recaptured, new ones gained. Even before the Peace of Paris was ratified, Choiseul had set about rebuilding the navy. By 1763 there were forty-seven ships of the line in service, by 1770, sixty-four ships of the line and fifty frigates. Major reforms were effected in the army, particularly in the artillery. The ink was barely dry on the peace treaty when Louis XV ordered the duc de Broglie to have a careful survey made of the English coasts in order to revise the existing plans for an invasion. Some months later secret agents, including Major-General the Baron de Kalb, were dispatched to America to urge the radicals on.[7]

In 1774, when Louis XVI acceded to the throne, the conduct of French foreign policy was given into the hands of a competent, experienced diplomat, Charles Gravier, comte de Vergennes, who adopted the views of Choiseul. His policy was simple: Britain was the enemy, had been since 1689; France, therefore, had to strive to maintain peace in Europe, keep Britain isolated, and then pounce at the first favorable opportunity. He intended that when war came it should be fought overseas, preferably on British territory, certainly not in Europe. His war aim was equally clear cut: the break up of the British empire. Not only would American independence be a crippling blow to London, Vergennes also hoped that the American market could be acquired for French industry. There was one significant caveat. This future independent republic in America would have to be restricted to the area between the Appalachians and the Atlantic, just as Louis XIV had decreed in 1701. It could not be allowed to seize the western territories, Florida, Canada, or Nova Scotia. A too powerful republic in North America could conceivably become as great a menace to the interests of the European maritime powers as Britain then was. Were Spain to enter the anticipated conflict alongside France, it could expect to receive either Gibraltar or Minorca, perhaps both, and to regain Florida. For its part France hoped to gain control of the Grand Banks fishery and secure commercial bases in India.[8] Like Choiseul, Vergennes had no desire to regain Canada, and for exactly the same reasons.

As relations between Britain and its American colonies deteriorated, the French watched and waited. In 1774 the House of Commons passed the Quebec Act that, among other things, granted the Canadians freedom to practice their Roman Catholic religion and placed the lands lying between the Great Lakes and the Ohio River under the jurisdiction of the governor of Quebec. Despite the fact that the Canadians had been practicing their religion all along, the New Englanders were enraged. To them the Roman faith was blood-stained anathema. Although the colonies that coveted the Ohio valley lands had refused to bear any of the burdens of their administration, the land speculators of Virginia and Pennsylvania, men such as George Washington, the Lees, and Benjamin Franklin, were livid. The Royal Proclamation of 1763 that had denied them the lands of the Indian nations had been bad enough, but it was regarded as merely a temporary expedient "to quiet the minds of the Indians," at least so Washington and Franklin had viewed it.[9] The Quebec Act went much further; it consolidated the Proclamation, thereby snatching away irrevocably the Americans' prospect of one day acquiring the lands in question. Britain, it appeared, had stepped into the shoes of the French. The independence of the colonies therefore seemed all the more necessary to these influential speculators.

Later that year some Americans in London intimated to a member of the French embassy staff that in the event of hostilities erupting between the British and the colonists, French aid would be welcome. Vergennes did not bite, but sometime between mid-March and early May a plan to provide aid secretly to the Americans was drawn up. Then in April 1775 came the first clash of arms between the Americans and British troops at Lexington and Concord, followed in June by the far more serious encounter at Bunker Hill. It appeared that the Americans were in earnest, that their cause was not a mere jacquerie. The following September Vergennes sent an agent, Julien-Alexandre Achard Bonvouloir, to Philadelphia to establish relations and encourage the Continental Congress to press on. Bonvouloir was also instructed to let the Americans know that their ships were free to use French ports. In August 1775 George III had declared the American colonies to be in a state of rebellion, thus the French action at that juncture could have been deemed a hostile act by Great Britain. Since the British government had earlier openly provided the forces in Corsica rebelling against French rule with funds, arms, and munitions, they were not in a strong position to complain but, of course, they did.[10]

Vergennes must have been encouraged when he learned that the Americans had invaded Quebec in September, and he must have been even happier when the American army was compelled to flee from Quebec the following year. That failure made plain their military ineptitude, that they were no more able to conquer Canada now than they had been in their previous attempts. Moreover, it ensured that they would have to depend on French aid, or be crushed. "Let us not disturb them in their desperate eagerness to wage war with their fellow citizens," Vergennes remarked. "Let them wear themselves down in this civil war while we reserve our strength to be used as best suits us."[11]

In September 1775, before the outcome of the Canadian adventure was known, and well before the signing of the Declaration of Independence, Vergennes entered into an arrangement with Pierre-Augustin Caron de Beaumarchais, author of the *Barber of Seville*, among other things, to provide covert aid to the Americans through the agency of the trading company, Roderigue Hortalez and Company. Later, Spain, too, provided clandestine aid through Beaumarchais's company. The Spanish acted in the hope that their aid would enable America to continue the war until both Britain and her colonies were ruined.[12]

By the autumn of 1776 the revolutionary cause appeared to be on the point of collapse. The ill-conceived invasion of Quebec had been an unmitigated disaster, succeeding only in alienating the Canadians. When forced to choose between their self-proclaimed American liberators and their British conquerors, they now opted for the latter, seemingly the lesser of two evils. In August the British government made plain its intention to crush the rebellion. General William Howe trounced Washington's much larger force at Long Island, drove the demoralized rebels helter-skelter to the south and secured the port of New York.

The fear in France now was that the prospect of American independence and the break up of the British empire was proving to be a chimera. The Americans had demonstrated that they were incapable of achieving it on their own by force of arms. Vergennes's response was to fan the flickering embers of rebellion by dispatching massive supplies of arms and ammunitions. In March, 1777, ships began arriving at New Hampshire ports bearing some 22,000 muskets, tons of gunpowder, military equipment, clothing, boots, blankets, tents, cannon, everything needed to keep an army in the field. It was those supplies that enabled the American forces to stop General John Burgoyne's army at Saratoga.[13]

Burgoyne there found himself and his army ensnared, surrounded, hopelessly outnumbered, unable to advance, victims of his incompetence. All that remained for him was to salvage the honor of British arms, even at the expense of mass slaughter. He therefore gave General Horatio Gates a choice. His army would lay down its arms, march to a British-held port and sail for England with the understanding that they would not serve again in America. This was a customary eighteenth-century military practice. Or,

Burgoyne threatened, his army would attempt to fight its way through the American lines, indubitably taking heavy casualties but inflicting far heavier ones on its adversary. Fearing both the effect such heavy casualties would have on the rebel cause, and concerned lest General Henry Clinton should soon appear from the south with an army to relieve Burgoyne, Gates agreed to the Convention of Saratoga. Once the British army had laid down its arms the American Congress repudiated the Convention and had the troops marched into a prison camp. One historian has made the odd comment: "Congress was neither honorable nor foolish enough to keep" the agreement.[14] This was not the first time the Americans had dishonored a cartel under somewhat similar circumstances.[15]

It has become conventional wisdom that the American victory at Saratoga convinced the French and Spanish that an independent American republic was indeed a possibility, hence it was worth risking war with Britain to achieve it. It has, however, been argued, quite convincingly, that it was not the American victory at Saratoga but General Washington's defeats—the latest, at Brandywine, had occurred at almost the moment of Burgoyne's surrender—that convinced Vergennes that the Americans could not achieve their, and his, aims without direct military intervention by France and Spain.[16]

By January, 1778, France was prepared to recognize the United States and to ally itself with the new nation. That France had achieved a near naval parity with Britain by this time made Louis XVI's decision easier, even though the French government recgnized that France could achieve the naval superiority required only if Spain entered the war. In February, France and the American commissioners signed two treaties, the Treaty of Amity and Commerce, and the Treaty of Alliance. The latter treaty stipulated that were war to break out between France and Great Britain, France and the United States would make common cause. It also stated that the purpose of the treaty was to maintain the independence of the United States, that if the allies succeeded in reducing the northern parts of America held by Britain, or the Bermuda Islands, the United States should retain those territories. It went on to state in Article six that France renounced forever the Bermudas and those parts of America claimed by France prior to 1763. This was inserted to quell American fears that France intended to regain Canada, for that surely would have driven them back into the arms of their mother country.

Vergennes explained to the Spanish ambassador that France had no need of more colonial possessions. They were, in his view, more of a liability than an asset. Moreover, were France to attempt to regain Canada she would merely revive the old fears that had kept the English colonies submissive to Britain for so long.[17] Not only did the Treaty of Alliance stipulate that if France seized any of Britain's islands in the West Indies she would retain them, the Treaty of Amity and Commerce also bluntly stated that the United States were not to infringe on the French fishing grounds off Newfoundland. Finally, Article eight of the Treaty of Alliance stated categorically that "Neither of the two Parties shall conclude either Truce or Peace with Great Britain, without the formal consent of the other obtain'd, and they mutually engage not to lay down their arms until the independence of the united states shall have been formally or tacitly assured by the Treaty or Treaties that shall terminate the War."[18] The Americans promptly offended French diplomatic sensibilities by publishing the text of the treaties before France had ratified them. The Continental Congress was new at the game and had much to learn.

In Britain those treaties offended more than diplomatic niceties. The French clearly were aiding and abetting the king's enemies, thus the treaties were regarded as virtually constituting a declaration of war. Without His Britannic Majesty bothering to go through the formality of declaring war, as was its wont, the Royal Navy began seeking out and attacking French ships wherever they were to be found. To the chagrin of the Admiralty the French fleet gave a very good account of itself and saw the Royal Navy off. From this point on the British were haunted by fear of the French navy, where its squadrons were, where they might next appear. The Royal Navy was spread thin over the oceans. Conceivably the French could muster naval superiority in one theater or another, as indeed they were to do three years later. Twenty ships of the line and some 10,000 troops had to be held back in England to fend off a possible invasion. Meanwhile French and neutral ships poured supplies and money into America to keep Washington's forces in the field.

In 1779 Spain entered the conflict. Russia, Denmark and Sweden, outraged by Britain's apparent determination to lay down the law to the entire European community, formed the League of Armed Neutrality. Hubris-laden Britain did not have a friend in the world, not even the Dutch, their nominal ally, who had long been providing the Americans with supplies from their islands in the Caribbean. They posed a greater threat to Britain as neutrals than as declared foes, therefore in December 1780 the Royal Navy began attacking their ships.

The American Revolution had thus escalated into a global conflict and the American theater became little more than a sideshow. What loomed larger were Gibraltar, Minorca, the Caribbean, India, Senegal, and an end to Britain's arrogant dominance of Europe's shipping lanes. Indeed to 1780 it began to look as though the revolution in America soon would be crushed as Washington's forces suffered defeat after defeat. Horatio Gates's army was destroyed at Camden. In May the British took Charleston, taking prisoner ten regiments, capturing 400 cannon and three of the Americans' seven frigates. The South appeared to be lost to the rebel cause, although a vicious, murderous, civil war raged on with neither side giving quarter. As one historian has put it: "The war in America trembled constantly on the knife-edge between civilized conventions and atrocious barbarity."[19]

Washington's forces were now reduced to a northern army of some 10,500 men, with an annual desertion rate of 20 to 25 percent, while Generals Sir Henry Clinton and the Earl of Cornwallis had 30,000 British and German regulars. The only thing that kept the American army in the field was French money, loans and subsidies, amounting to forty-eight million livres by 1782, plus more for French naval support.[20] In May 1780 the first segment of a proposed 8,000-man expeditionary force, 5,500 in all, under the command of Donatien-Marie-Joseph de Vimeur, vicomte de Rochambeau, set sail for America. Admiral the chevalier de Ternay, commander of the convoy, baffled the Royal Navy and landed the French army unscathed at Newport, Rhode Island. They were there because it had become abundantly clear to Vergennes and to Jose Monino y Redondo, comte de Floridablanca, the astute Spanish foreign minister, that the Americans could not hope to win their independence without direct military intervention by France and Spain.[21]

By September, 1780, the French Council of State was divided as to whether or not its commitment to the war in America could be continued, or indeed was worth continuing. Some members of the Council advised negotiating for peace with Britain. Vergennes refused to give way. He wanted peace, but an honorable peace, one that included the independence of the United States as an essential clause. In December Catherine II of Russia and the Hapsburg Emperor, Joseph III, proposed that mediation should be undertaken to end the conflict, but the ensuing negotiations, marked by insincerity by all the parties, were inconclusive. Diplomacy having resolved nothing, the issues in the conflict had to be settled, as usual, by the military, which meant putting everything to hazard.

Fortunately for Rochambeau's newly arrived army, the Royal Navy failed to attack before they were securely entrenched at Newport. Had the British done so, General Sir Henry Clinton later lamented, the "almost expiring embers" of the Revolution could have been extinguished.[22] The French troops received a frosty welcome from the Americans and relations between the officers of the two armies rapidly deteriorated. For the Americans, memories of the attacks on New England by the French in Canada and their Indian allies in previous wars, religious bigotry, and xenophobia that equated the Roman Catholic monarch of France with the Anti-Christ, made for an uneasy relationship. For their part, the French were appalled by the sloveliness and manifest lack of training and discipline in the American army. As for the militia, the French quickly concluded that they were worthless, more of an encumbrance than a military asset.[23] The French were also upset by the merchants of Newport who charged them outrageous prices for everything they had to sell. Nor were the French officers pleased by the disparaging remarks addressed to them by senior American officers. The marquis de Lafayette was so outraged by the slurs cast on his countrymen by an American general that he had to be restrained from calling him out.[24] The comte de Clermont-Crevecoeur, a lieutenant in the artillery, looking down his aristocratic nose, noted in his journal, "one may reasonably state that the character of this nation is little adapted to society."[25]

Rochambeau, upon taking stock of the situation, began to fear that the Americans were about to throw in the towel. Five days after his arrival he sent his son off to France with an urgent dispatch: "Send us troops, ships and money, but do not count on these people or on their resources, they have neither money nor credit, their forces exist only momentarily."[26] To Rochambeau it was clear that if the war in America was to be won, the French army and navy would have to do it. Then, in January, 1781, came the mutinies of the Continental armies of New Jersey and Pennsylvania. Mutiny was endemic in the American forces; ill-fed, ill-clad, undisciplined, their pay always in arrears, relations between officers and men hostile, to say the least, it was a wonder that Washington managed to keep the semblance of an army in the field.[27] These particular mutinies, given the juncture of events, were far more serious then previous such outbursts and they certainly gave the French pause.

Bleak as was the situation early in 1781, events were occurring that would soon radically alter matters. In March a French convoy with twenty ships of the line uder the command of Admiral Francois-Joseph-Paul, comte de Grasse, sailed for the West Indies. His orders were to support the Spanish forces against British attempts on either the French or Spanish possessions, and to launch assaults on Florida and Jamaica. He also had been given a free hand to commit his forces to a campaign in mainland America if the circumstances appeared propitious and the Spanish commander in the Caribbean theater concurred. Moreover, the mutinies in the American army during the past winter had so shaken the confidence of the French in their ally's ability to hold out that de Grasse had to be prepared to go to the rescue of Rochambeau's army and transport it to safety in the West Indies.[28]

In the meantime Anne-Cesar, chevalier de La Luzerne, French minister plenipotentiary to the Continental Congress, urged Louis, comte de Barras, commander of the French naval squadron at Newport after the death of Admiral Ternay, to send his ships and the French troops to support the Americans in the south before the British army under the command of the Earl of Cornwallis reduced Virginia as he had the Carolinas. Luzerne feared that the demoralized Americans were preparing to enter into peace negotiations, hoping to save their necks and retain possession of as much territory as they could on the basis of *uti possedetis*.[29]

That same spring Rochambeau was instructed by the Council of State to merge his army with that of the Americans under Washington's command. On May 6 Rochambeau's son arrived back from France with the disappointing news that no more troops would be sent to Newport, but he did bring six million livres for the American army's overdue pay, and word that the French West Indies fleet would cooperate with the allied armies in the forthcoming offensive. The French government was convinced that a hard blow had to be struck at the British forces before it was too late. Washington was eager to launch a attack on New York, claiming that to march the armies south would result in heavy losses from disease.[30]

Rochambeau was of the opinion that a combined operation with de Grasse's fleet offered the best opportunity for military success. His maxim was eminently sound: the destruction of Britain's armies would end the war, but the conquest of towns and territory would not force the enemy to give up, as the British were discovering to their cost. In late spring Rochambeau received word from de Grasse that he hoped to be off the American coast by mid-July. From this point on the French were completely in command of the campaign.[31]

Washington and Rochambeau and their staffs surveyed the British fortifications at New York and concluded that they were too formidable to warrant attempting an assault. The French naval officers considered the forcing of New York harbor to be out of the question, and Washington had to acknowledge that his own forces were too meager, the various states having failed to provide the men he had demanded in sufficient numbers.[32] On August 15 Rochambeau received confirmation that de Grasse expected to be at the Chesapeake shortly with some twenty-five to twenty-nine ships of the line, 3,200 troops, and 1,200,000 livres, provided by the Spanish. De Grasse warned that he would have to return to the Caribbean by mid-October to rejoin the Spanish forces, whose commander, Bernardo de Galvez, had graciously agreed to release the French fleet and troops for the campaign in mainland America.

De Grasse had taken a dangerous gamble. He had ordered the annual convoy of island produce to remain in the West Indian ports, putting it at risk to an attack by Admiral George Rodney's fleet. This was something that no British admiral would have dared to do, hence Rodney never dreamed that de Grasse would be so reckless.[33] Thus the French fleet suddenly appeared where, in the view of the Royal Navy, it had no right to be. The ensuing tactical surprise would prove to be one of the more important events in the history of the last two centuries.

Washington gave way to Rochambeau and agreed that the allied armies would march south to Virginia to face Cornwallis. On August 19 the French army set off from Phillipsburg. They had tarried long enough near New York to convince Clinton that an assault on Staten Island was impending; consequently, obtuse as always, the British commander convinced himself that he could not spare any of his troops to relieve Cornwallis. The French artillery, the great siege train, was transported by Barras's ships along with some of the troops. By September 26 the French army was encamped at Williamsburg where Lafayette, with a small motley force awaited.

A few miles away, at Yorktown, Cornwallis's men were digging entrenchments in the soft earth and constructing redoubts while waiting for the New York fleet to bring reinforcements and block the bay to any French ships that might venture south from Newport. With those British ships in place to fend off whatever Barras might bring, Cornwallis and his army would have had nothing to fear, for he could then easily evade the allied armies ensconced on his doorstep. Moreover, by controlling the Chesapeake and the narrow belt of land between its headwaters and the mountains Britain would, at last, have split the colonies and penned Washington in to the north. Such a strategical defeat could well have put an end to the rebel cause. All that they could then have hoped for would have been a negotiated peace, leaving the British in control of New York and all land south of Pennsylvania. An independent republic restricted to what remained under its control, and denied expansion to the west, would have had a bleak, and likely brief, future.

As events turned out, Admiral Thomas Graves discovered upon his arrival at the mouth of the Chesapeake that he was facing, not just Barras, but also the entire French West Indies fleet. Against twenty-four ships of the line, 1,800 guns, he had only nineteen ships of the line and one fifty-gun warship, mounting 1,400 guns in all. The ensuing battle on September 5 for control of the bay was, in one sense, a draw. Both fleets were badly mauled, but Graves was unable to renew the engagement the next day and was forced to retire to New York to refit. The French were left in control of the Chesapeake. The British fleet could now do nothing for Cornwallis, the French fleet everything for Rochambeau and Washington. The trap had been sprung on Cornwallis, with just over 6,000 rank and file, including four loyalist regiments. Opposing him were 7,800 French, 5,800 American Continentals, and 3,000 Virginia militia.

On September 7 Barras sailed up the bay with seven ships of the line and landed the guns, ammunition, and provisions for the allied armies. By September 28 they had marched out from Williamsburg, driven the British from their advanced posts, and established themselves before the British lines. From this point on the siege was directed by the French corps of engineers, an elite unit, employing eighteenth-century military textbook tactics. Neither Washington nor any other American officer had had any training for, or experience in, this type of set piece warfare. In fact, the only engineers in the Continental army were French officers, on loan to the Americans at the request of the Continental Congress.[34] And so the work proceeded in methodical fashion; first the artillery park was established, then the first parallel of entrenchments and gun emplacements were dug and the gun batteries—the cannon, mortars, howitzers—sited. The village of Gloucester, across the river from Yorktown at then arrows, held by 1,100 British to guard a field hospital and supply depot, was taken by assault. That prevented Cornwallis from getting his army across, outflanking the Franco-American armies, and slipping north to New York. Two advanced British redoubts were stormed, then incorporated in the second parallel. This brought the heavy guns and mortars some 1,000 paces closer to the British entrenchments, which were bombarded without let up, night and day.

His situation manifestly hopeless, his army reduced to 3,273 men fit for duty, on October 17 Cornwallis offered to capitulate. It made no sense to go on. Two days later the Articles of Capitulation were signed. The British army, regulars, Hessians, loyalists, marched out and laid down their arms as a band played the mournful tune, "The World Turned Upside Down." This crucial and decisive victory, deserving to rank with the British victory at Quebec in 1759, had been achieved by incredible tactical timing and strategic surprise, the French fleets from Newport and the West Indies arriving together at the Chesapeake ahead of the British fleet, just as the French and American armies reached nearby Williamsburg.

Two of Rochambeau's officers, the comte de Clermont-Crevecoeur and Jean-Baptiste-Antoine de Verger, relate in their journals that immediately after the surrender the French officers entertained the English and Hessians and got on well with them, which infuriated the Americans. Clermont-Crevecoeur wrote:

> The English and French got on famously with one another. When the Americans expressed their displeasure on this subject we replied that good upbringing and courtesy bind men together and that since we had reason to believe that the Americans did not like us, they should not be surprised at our preference.[35]

The French had come to regard the American officers as uncouth and arrogant, with nothing to be arrogant about, not fit to keep company with gentlemen, let alone members of the nobility. Arrogant as they themselves were, the French undoubtedly made little effort to dissemble on this score. The American officers could not grasp that these European professional soldiers regarded themselves as members of an international confraternity sharing the same values, the same code of conduct. The British, French, and Hessian officers were, in short, brothers in arms. Since the American commander-in-chief, George Washington, had failed conspicuously throughout his military career to grasp this concept, there was small chance that his subordinate officers would, or ever could, subscribe to the notion.[36]

One example of the European officers' mores was revealed when Cornwallis found himself without sufficient funds to pay his troops. He appealed to the French, whose generals and colonels immediately pooled their resources and loaned him 100,000 *ecus* (300,000 *livres* or £125,000 sterling).

Upon his arrival at New York he repaid the debt and added 100 bottles of porter to express his appreciation for the favor rendered.[37] In contrast, some months later, when Rochambeau's troops were encamped near Peekskill on the Hudson and built huts for themselves, the local inhabitants demanded exorbitant sums for damages they claimed had been done to their fields and fences. They finally agreed to settle for a more reasonable sum. Subsequently the local sheriff asked to speak to Rochambeau and, clapping his hand on the general's shoulder, attempted to arrest him, declaring that since the bill for damages had not been settled Rochambeau would have to be lodged in gaol until it was. Washington swiftly intervened to prevent such an unseemly occurrence. Rochambeau must have wondered, what next?[38]

After the Yorktown victory the Americans pressed Rochambeau to join his army with theirs for an assault on Canada, but he demurred stating that he first would have to obtain the authorization of the Council of State. He knew that Vergennes wanted the British to remain there as a counterpoise to keep a incipient American republic in check. Earlier Congress had proposed such an assault with the French volunteer, the marquis de Lafayette, in command of the invasion army, but Washington had rejected the proposal, fearing that a successful incursion might result in the reacquisition of Canada by France. Congress then abandoned the project, for not only did Britain have a formidable army in Quebec, but the legislators realized that during the 1775–76 invasion of the province the Americans had so mistreated and alienated the Canadians that they could be counted on to support the British in defense of their homeland.[39] Thus Canada retained its independence from the United States because the French would not allow the Americans to have it, and the Americans most definitely did not want the French to regain it. More to the point, the French most definitely did not want the territory.

Militarily, Britain was by no means yet defeated. By the spring after Yorktown she still had 30,000 troops in America, held Quebec, Nova Scotia, New York, Charleston, Savannah and Saint Augustine. Moreover, not only had de Grasse's fleet been shattered in the Battle of the Saintes off Guadeloupe in April, but the American forces were in poor shape and France teetered on the edge of bankruptcy. The British people, however, were no longer determined to see it through. The taxpayers had had enough. The national debt had soared to insupportable heights, the war had lasted seven years and nothing appeared to have been accomplished. Minorca had been invaded, its garrison, decimated by scurvy, would shortly be forced to surrender; West Florida and Tobago had been lost, Fort Prince of Wales and York Factory in Hudson Bay had been captured and destroyed by the French, and what was far more menacing, a combined French and Spanish fleet cruised in the Channel with 15,000 troops assembled, ready to be embarked for the crossing. The opposition, anything but loyal to Lord North's government, saw its chance. A resolution was introduced in the House of

Commons on March 4, 1782, declaring that all who sought to continue to prosecute the war against the American colonies should be regarded as enemies of their country. It passed, and Lord North's ministry was forced to resign. The hands of the new government, headed by Charles Watson Wentworth, Marquis of Rockingham, were tied. There was only one thing to do: end the war in America and concentrate the country's resources against the European foes who, for the first time since 1588, posed a serious threat of invasion.

This new government, with the devious Earl of Shelburne serving as secretary of state for home, colonial, and Irish affairs, made contact with the American commissioners in Paris, using a British merchant, Richard Oswald, as his emissary. The commissioners agreed to negotiate a preliminary peace treaty without informing Vergennes, despite the fact that their official instructions and the Treaty of Alliance expressly forbade them to do any such thing. They also had the effrontery to demand that in addition to Britain's recognition of the independence of the United States, Canada—that is, the provinces of Quebec and Nova Scotia as then constituted—be ceded to them, and that they be given the territory west of the Alleghenies to the Mississippi, freedom of navigation on that river, and the access to the Newfoundland fisheries that they had previously enjoyed as British subjects. What is more, they expected to be granted access to the British West Indies markets.

These demands came from delegates of a people who had conspicuously failed to obtain anything of significance by force of their own arms, a people whose hope for gaining their independence came as the result of a French military victory. The Americans could never have reached this point without French aid, yet here they were negotiating behind the backs of their ally. That they were extraordinary men goes without saying, but that they could seriously expect Britain to grant such outrageous demands boggles the mind. The Americans had no viable claim to any territory beyond that which they had held in 1750, yet they now demanded half the continent, lands occupied by peoples who wanted nothing to do with them.

Shelburne was perfectly willing to recognize the independence of the United States. He had three objectives. He sought to drive a wedge between France and the United States and he hoped to break up their alliance. In addition he wanted a reconciliation with the Americans for purely economic reasons. The American market, present and potential, for cheap British manufactured goods was, in his view, well worth a humiliating swallowing of pride. All that was required for the garnering of that commerce was the cession to the Americans of other peoples' lands in the trans-Appalachian west. That this would be a betrayal of Britain's Indian allies, who were now doomed to extinction, meant nothing to Shelburne.[40] In similar fashion he betrayed the loyalists, making only a feeble demand for compensation on their behalf, knowing full well that the Americans would never honor it.[41]

He did draw back when asked to cede Quebec and Nova Scotia. Neither he, his cabinet colleagues, nor Parliament could have been expected to swallow that. Access to the Newfoundland fisheries he was willing to concede to make sure that New England did not oppose the prospective treaty; besides, it would have required the stationing of a naval squadron at Newfoundland permanently to keep the Americans out. The self-righteous New Englanders were convinced that the cod of the Grank Banks had been put there by God for their express use "and woe unto the wretch who dared to interfere with God's will."[42] Shelburne would not grant the Americans entree to the West Indies market; that had to be reserved for the merchants of Britain, Nova Scotia, and Quebec. The American commissioners agreed to these terms and signed the "Preliminaries of Peace," but made them conditional on a peace treaty being concluded between Britain and France. They thereby forced Vergennes's hand, for should he not agree to end the war on British and American terms he could be under no illusions that the Americans, consulting only their own interests, would surely sign a separate treaty with Great Britain, thereby releasing the British naval and army forces then in America for assaults on vulnerable French and Spanish territorial possessions in other parts of the world.

On November 29, Franklin, a past master of duplicity, unabashedly informed Vergennes of what had transpired, brazenly terming it "a mere breach of etiquette." Vergennes was outraged, but he could not have been surprised. He had never trusted the Americans. In his view it was, at the very least, an inexcusable act of bad faith. He wrote bitterly to Luzerne at Philadelphia, predicting that if "we can judge the future by what passes presently before our eyes we shall be paid badly for what we have done for the United States of America, and for having assured them of that title."[43] Vergennes was a diplomatist of the old regime. Shortly after his death in 1787 the world that he had known was swept away. For some five years he had dealt with men of an emerging new regime, men with new values, or no values.

All that Vergennes could now do was try to salvage as much as possible for France. He was astounded by the terms that Shelburne had offered the Americans, in particular his cession of the trans-Appalachian West and access to the Newfoundland fisheries. To his first secretary he declared that the "English bought the peace rather than negotiate[d] it. Their concessions exceeded all that I would have thought possible. What could be the motive that would result in clauses such that they could be interpreted as a form of capitulation?"[44] He also considered that Shelburne's failure to protect and gain compensation for the loyalists was dishonorable.

In the negotiations that ensued Vergennes sought to have Shelburne withdraw the cession of the western lands south of the Great Lakes. He wanted the region between the mountains and the Mississippi left to the Indians, the rightful owners, for it would then serve as a buffer zone between the new republic and Louisiana.[45] As for the Newfoundland fisheries, one of his war aims had been the acquisition of the island and sole control of the fishing grounds. He resented the fact that French fishermen would now have to share this fishery with the Americans as well as the British.[46]

In this war the Americans possessed of white skins were the only winners. They gained their independence and far more territory than they had any right to expect. Great Britain sacrificed its sovereignty over the original thirteen colonies but retained possession of the territories that comprise present-day Canada. The Spanish ambassador to France, the Count de Aranda, in a dispatch to the king prophesied: "This federal republic is born a pygmy but a day will come when it will be a giant, a colossus, formidable for this country."[47]

Immediately after the peace treaties were signed British ships began pouring goods into American ports while Beaumarchais was experiencing great difficulty recovering what he claimed was owed him by the Americans. Just as Shelburne had anticipated, trade with the burgeoning republic grew by leaps and bounds, vastly exceeding what it had been before the war. France, on the other hand, had only wines, spirits, and expensive luxury goods to offer, for which there was little demand.

Although the debt Britain had incurred—on top of that from the previous war—was staggering, it was about the same as that of the French government. Britain's credit and tax structure was such, however, that it was able to retire its debt with relative ease, whereas within six years the French government had to admit virtual bankruptcy, which led directly to the collapse of the ancien régime. All that the French could claim was that the independence of the United States represented a humiliating defeat for Great Britain. The French, nothing if not a proud people, thus had some solace, some compensation for the bitter defeat they had suffered at the hands of the British in the Seven Years' War. Yet, despite all, Britain emerged from the conflict more powerful than ever, soon to rule over the greatest empire the world has ever seen and to remain the dominant world power for a century, the century of the Pax Britannica.

There can be no question but that the United States of America owes its independence, its very existence as a nation, mainly to French support: logistical, financial, and military. It was the French navy, French cannon, and French troops that had made the crucial victory at Yorktown possible. The French could have defeated Cornwallis's army on their own; the Americans most certainly could not. American independence was bound to have come sooner or later, but not necessarily when, or in the way that it did. After all, George III merely attempted to do that which Abraham Lincoln also decided to do some eight decades later. In short, George III sought to prevent, by force of arms, the secession of his thirteen American colonies from the British Empire. He failed. Likewise, Lincoln sought to prevent, by force of arms, the secession of the southern states from the American empire. He succeeded. Had George III used the methods employed by Lincoln and those of his generals, Grant and Sherman, then the American Revolution would surely have been crushed before the French could have intervened.

The War over, independence gained, the Americans displayed a singular lack of gratitude to the French. The Treaty of Alliance had served their purpose. It could now be disregarded, tossed into discard.[48] Thus when the Treaty was put to the test in 1793, President Washington, without a qualm, abrogated it. By then too, the mythmakers were hard at work, fashioning their teleological, Whig interpretation of the colonial period of American history, making it appear that the American people, perhaps with a little help from their allies, but mainly by their own valiant efforts, had achieved their independence. For surely it had been preordained by God from the moment that the first settlers arrived on the shores of Virginia and New England. The French, after all, had merely been one of His instruments. Therefore it was God, not the French, who deserved thanks.

10

British Armed Forces
and the American Victory

Sylvia R. Frey

The immediate, and one might argue, the general cause of the American Revolution was military. In 1763 the British ministry decided to assign fifteen infantry battalions to North America so as to guarantee the security of Nova Scotia, Canada, and Florida; manage Indian affairs; and police the older American colonies. Still riding the tide of euphoria created by British and American military victories in the French and Indian War, Americans lodged only muted objections. But the passage of the Stamp Act and the Quartering Act in 1765, followed by the decision to centralize control of the army under a military officer and to separate its administration from colonial politics, produced a storm of protest that reached critical proportions after the arrival of regular troops in 1768. Within an astonishingly short time many Americans, most of them in New England, had come to hate their recent comrades in arms and to view the army as a political and moral menace. Fear and resentment of the urbane and dissolute officer corps and of potential violence by the soldiery were widespread in garrison towns like Boston. Adding to the sense of insecurity was a commonly held belief in the inherently corrupt nature of any standing army. The Boston Massacre on March 5, 1770, seemed to confirm popular fears that the British troops were, in the words of Dr. Joseph Warren at the fifth commemorative celebration, "the ready engines of tyranny and oppression," a view that came to be widely shared as the colonial protest turned into open warfare.[1]

In fact the British army sent to America was the result of a century and a half of struggle by an essentially unmilitaristic society to create a army that would not subvert the British constitution. An institution of the states, the British army in America reflected the political will of the British people and, in its broad outlines, the overall character of a society in transition.

Although professional armies were emerging in Europe in the course of
the sixteenth century, the England of Queen Elizabeth had no permanent,
professional military institutions. For purposes of home defense the nation
relied primarily on its militia system. For external defense, the insular,
maritime nation depended upon a navy, most of whose officers and crews
were commissioned in wartime and discharged in peacetime. In peace and
in war, military policies and management of external defense were in the
hands of the queen and the Privy Council.[2] The emergence of a professional
standing army in Britain was the result of processes set in motion following
Elizabeth's reign, and came about largely as a reaction to the centralizing
tendencies of the Stuart monarchs.

At the time of Elizabeth's death in 1603, England possessed no military
power. Because of the geographical isolation provided by the English Channel, her foreign policy was essentially one of isolation. The army did not
therefore become a matter of political concern until the 1620s, when the
Thirty Years' War forced Charles I to resort to the billeting of troops in
private homes, to forced loans, and to martial law to discipline civilians.[3]
The antimilitarism such actions engendered found their voice in the Petition
of Right of 1628, which condemned, among other things, the use of martial
law and the quartering of soldiers on private householders. Charles continued to exercise the military prerogatives historically reserved to the crown,
however, until controversy over the army raised to fight the Irish Rebellion—
and the accompanying fear that it would be turned against Parliament—
motivated members of the legislature to bring in the Militia Bill, legislation
that would have transferred ultimate command of the militia from crown
to Parliament. Noting that "Kingly Power is but a shadow" without command of the militia, Charles unequivocally rejected the Militia Bill.[4]

The Militia Bill, of course, comprehended the even larger questions of
sovereignty and the relationship between power and sovereignty, and it
implied a radical change in the English constitution. One of the precipitating
issues of the English civil wars, it became identified with opposition to the
monarchy. During the tumultuous years of the civil wars the pervasive
suspicion of the dangers of a standing army were exacerbated by Oliver
Cromwell's use of the army as an instrument of personal power. The New
Model Army created by Cromwell in 1645 to make the revolution, and
later maintained to secure the government of the Commonwealth and Protectorate, was England's first standing army. Democratic in structure but
inspired by religious fanaticism, the army was radical in its politics. Its
support for universal manhood suffrage and abolition of the king and House
of Lords, among other things, put it distinctly at odds with its titular head,
Parliament. The New Model Army's refusal to disband at Parliament's
order, its resort to the use of martial law, its efforts to set up and bring
down governments, intensified the general prejudice against a standing army
and made of it a major political and intellectual issue.[5]

Essentially the controversy centered on two issues. Should the army be an instrument of executive power or subject to parliamentary government? Was military service a responsibility of citizenship? Although anti–standing army arguments included concern about the cost of maintaining a military establishment and the methods employed for billeting troops, the principal objections were to the potentially corrupt and tyrannical power that a standing army implied by its very existence. Classical republicans in general composed the opposition, but it was the ideas of the political philosopher James Harrington, articulated in *Commonwealth of Oceana*, that provided the intellectual framework for the debate. Drawing upon the ideas of Niccolo Machiavelli, Harrington argued that, by enhancing the power of the throne, the existence of a standing army would become a vehicle for absolutism and corruption, and spell the death of the free, balanced constitution. Harrington's alternative was a militia composed of propertied citizen-soldiers. Properly trained and educated in military science, the citizen militia would stand as the principal component in the free state, the safeguard of liberty and constitutional stability.[6]

Both the disbanding of the Cromwellian army in 1660, which temporarily allayed public fears, and the absence of effective leadership in Parliament, led to a decline in interest in the standing army question. At the Restoration the old constitution was reestablished. Even the Militia Act, passed by Parliament in 1661 as part of the Restoration settlement, reaffirmed the king's military prerogatives. It declared that "the sole supream government, command and disposition of the militia, and of all forces by sea and land, and of all forts and places of strength, is, and by the laws of England ever was the undoubted right of his Majesty, and his royal predecessors, Kings and Queens of England...; and that both, or either of the houses of parliament cannot, nor ought to pretend to the same."

Soon, however, the standing army issue was rekindled. One cause was the preference of Charles II, and later James II, for standing armies—widely believed to be permeated with Catholics—and their neglect of the militia, ideally composed of Protestant freeholders. Other factors that reinvigorated the standing army debate included Charles' efforts early in the Restoration to disarm dissenters as a means of snuffing out political and religious dissent; his veto of a bill to embody the militia and rely less on the standing army; James's plans after Monmouth's Rebellion to disband the militia as inadequate for national defense and his decision to rely upon a standing army instead; and his orders to confiscate militia weapons in Ireland. Scotland, and to some extent in England. Ultimately, the widespread impression arose that the Stuart kings were intent on disarming Protestants and creating a standing army dominated by Catholics, a perception that played a major role in the Glorious Revolution of 1689.[7]

The military settlement of the Glorious Revolution produced a fundamental change in the British constitution. After declaring the throne vacant, the Convention Parliament convened to settle the government, and to read to William of Orange and Mary, the Declaration of Rights. Later given statutory form as the Bill of Rights, the Declaration clearly defined the constitutional place of military forces and established constitutional checks on royal military authority. It reaffirmed the rights of Englishmen, including the right of Protestants to bear arms, and confirmed the prohibition against billeting troops upon private citizens without their consent. In the most important section of the Bill of Rights, Article VI described as "ancient law" the revolutionary assertion that "the raising or keeping a standing army within the kingdom in time of peace, unless it be with consent of parliament, is against law," the effect of which was to shift sovereignty from the Crown, where it had resided historically, to Parliament, where republican theorists had argued it should rest in a free state.[8]

The Mutiny Act, passed by the House of Commons in 1689, completed the transfer of power from Crown to Parliament. It also made the standing army permanent but subject to the annual vote of Parliament. By its terms, martial law was established and procedures for its administration were instituted. While the act preserved some of the royal military prerogatives, such as the authority to grant commissions and to convene courts-martial and oversee general discipline, it reserved for Parliament budgetary control over the army. Significantly, the Mutiny Act declared that no officer or soldier was to be exempt from the ordinary process of law, thus in effect stating Parliament's intention that soldiers should remain citizens, although concurrent changes in the social and economic structure of England clearly implied a separation of military service from the responsibilities of citizenship.[9]

The Mutiny Act gave to the British army a certain legal status, but it also created problems of administration that became more acute as the size of the army increased and as the scope of military operations expanded as a result of the renewed warfare with France that commenced in 1689. Questions arose such as which government ministers should exercise responsibility toward the army, and what should be the political parameters within which military officers should operate. In short how should military administration be organized so as to reconcile philosophical and constitutional concepts with the practical powers necessary for defense.[10] Eighteenth-century British efforts to devise a rational and reasoned military administrative system were shaped by the suspicion of unchecked military force now ingrained in parliamentary thought; the system additionally grew from that century's continuing preoccupation with subordination of the military to the civil power. In developing the administrative machinery of the army, politicians resorted to the system of checks and overlapping responsibilities practiced in British public administration generally. In the process military administration, historically the Crown's constitutional prerogative, came increasingly under the control of Parliament.

Although some European states had begun to concentrate administrative powers and to develop special functional ministries, the British army administration that developed during the reign of Queen Anne was almost totally lacking in cohesion. Command of the army was in the hands of military officers, while general administrative functions were carried out by civilian ministers, some of whom had only tenuous links with the military, and who for constitutional reasons not only shared areas of overlapping responsibility but were responsible either to the Crown or to Parliament. At the head of the army stood the king as captain general of all land and naval forces. It was customary, however, for him to delegate his executive military powers to some prominent military officer as commander-in-chief. Although the commander-in-chief was the chief military administrator, the office was not occupied continuously in war and peace until 1793, on the occasion of the outbreak of war with France. As a result his powers were not accurately defined, although they were generally assumed to include command of the regular infantry and cavalry and the reserve forces when embodied, coordination of national defenses, and supervision of army discipline, including training establishments, except for Woolich Military Academy, which fell within the province of Ordnance.[11]

Transport and supply, the most vital part of military administration, were concentrated in two entirely separate departments: the Commissariat and Ordnance. The Commissariat, which was responsible for food and forage, was entirely civilian and was controlled by the Treasury, and was not therefore subject to military discipline. Ordnance, which had its roots in the medieval practice of hiring wagons and contracting for food, had by the eighteenth century developed as a distinct corps with its own uniform, discipline, and promotion structure. The master general of the Ordnance, a military officer, provided certain supplies for the army, including arms, ammunition, ordnance, and wagons, supervised the construction and maintenance of fortifications, magazines, hospitals, and barracks throughout the Empire, and exercised complete control over artillery, engineers, sappers, pontoonists, and artificers. Assisted by a board of officers, the master general was directly responsible to the king, the Privy Council, or the two secretaries of state. The dispersal of authority in two separate departments and between military and civilian personnel, though highly inefficient, was regarded as a constitutional safeguard, the underlying philosophy of which was that military reliance on a civilian commissariat for sustenance would curb the political adventurism of the army.[12]

Ministerial responsibilities were shaped by the same constitutional pressures, with the result that military administration was shared by the secretaries of state, the Treasury, Admiralty and Ordnance boards, the paymaster general and regimental agents, as well as the secretary at war. The government minister most intimately concerned with military administration was the secretary at war, a post created by Charles II in 1661 as a kind of military secretary. Although he was usually a member of Parliament, until 1794 no secretary ever sat in the cabinet; however, because all secretaries held their commissions from the Crown under the sign manual and were responsible to the Crown, they generally enjoyed access to the closet. On the other hand, by law the secretary of war presented the military estimates to the House of Commons, thus creating a link between royal administration of the army and parliamentary control. In theory the two secretaries of state were responsible for policy questions, the secretary at war for carrying them out. In practice the secretary at war exercised independent control only over his special spheres of financial and legal matters. All of his other functions were affected by the overlapping jurisdictions of the Treasury, the Ordnance, and the Paymaster's office.[13] By modern standards, and even by contemporary European standards, the whole system was chaotic and contained numerous opportunities for the very fraud and corruption they were meant to eliminate.[14] In certain fundamental respects, however, it was an accurate reflection of eighteenth-century British political assumptions, the most fundamental of which was that administration means power and, to avoid abuse, power must be subject to checks and functional separation. The constitutional controls established by the military settlement of the Glorious Revolution and the administrative reforms completed during the reign of Anne, resolved most of the issues that had occupied republican thinkers since the 1620s. To be sure, a legacy of fear persisted in Britain through the eighteenth century among a minority of the British population, albeit a vocal one, and the inherited dislike of soldiers continued unabated. The anti–standing army tradition survived in the efforts of opposition politicians to keep the size of the standing army small, in their regular efforts to revitalize the militia, and in their reluctance to increase military professionalism in national training institutions.[15] By and large, however, the majority of citizens were satisfied with the safeguards that Britain had instituted during the previous century. This general confidence led to the growing acceptance of a professional army. Even so, the army remained small, and despite the annual renewal of the Mutiny Act, its existence as a permanent land army was not officially recognized until 1755, when the first of the continuous series of army lists was published. Although the army would never attain the status of a major national institution, such as the Royal Navy or the French and Prussian armies enjoyed, changes in the domestic economic and social structures guaranteed it a growing role in eighteenth-century British politics.[16]

Isolated from the continental wars that had ravaged Europe during the seventeenth century, England took an early lead in the expansion of heavy industries. Unrivalled deposits of coal seams located near navigable streams led to the rapid expansion of mining enterprises. Rich supplies of iron ore formed the basis for a remarkable increase in metals production. Two technical inventions, the "puddling" process used in the manufacture of bar iron, and the adaptation of steam power, produced a phenomenal growth in industrial output. The single most important cause of economic growth in the eighteenth century, however, was the series of wars against France that began in 1740 and culminated in 1783. The wars, which necessitated large field armies and expensive military expeditions to Europe, Africa, India and America, created a demand for munitions and textiles, and stimulated the large-scale production of military clothing and the manufacture of standardized weapons, which in turn encouraged the development of banking and finance.[17]

Britain's unprecedented economic expansion had repercussions on every aspect of its financial, social, political, and military history. It led to the rise of the factory system, which permanently altered English home industry. It contributed to the widespread replacement of manual labor with machines, and rendered numerous skills and crafts obsolete. It stimulated the growth of new urban centers in the developing north and west, where water, coal, iron, roads, and canals were readily available. It produced dramatic demographic shifts, as an increasingly mobile population migrated from areas of relative decline to the booming North. The new enthusiasm for scientific inquiry and practical application led to agricultural experimentation and the development of large-scale consolidated farms, and displaced countless small farmers in the process. It promoted improvements in armaments and munitions to accommodate the growth in the size of military forces and the increase in their need for equipment, and it gave rise to the mercantile classes—adventurers, traders, financiers, wealthy gentlemen clothiers—who owed their wealth and success to the new war orders.[18]

The massive dislocations caused by rapid social and economic change, and the glaring inequalities in wealth and power that it produced, led to a period of prolonged mob disorder in England. Beset by growing social violence and sharpening class distinctions, the harassed government turned to the army as the only effective police force available in most instances. Since the early decades of the eighteenth century, the army had been employed to apprehend large smuggling gangs. From that small beginning, the use of troops to cope with civil disorder gradually expanded. By the 1760s the government was employing the army, conformable with the advice and consent of local magistrates, to curb prison riots; break up disorders at fairs, cockfights, and other sporting events; and to disperse rural and urban mobs. The use of the army for internal security was viewed as unconstitutional by some and was considered inappropriate by the army itself. But the army's compliant obedience to its political masters encouraged the view that it was a politically reliable, even a docile instrument of the state, a tool that could be safely used for broad constitutional purposes such as the protection of private property and the maintenance of civil order. By 1763, when the decision was made to deploy British troops in American towns, the new constitutional premise of coercive police power was well established in Britain. Ironically, the British crowds against whom soldiers were most frequently used were composed of members of the working class, the same common laborers, weavers, colliers, and coal heavers from which the army increasingly satisfied its manpower needs.[19]

What a society gets in its armed forces tends to be a reflection of what society is. Britain's standing army was small by continental European standards, befitting perhaps an insular, maritime society. At the outbreak of the American Revolution the total land force, excluding militia, amounted to only 48,647 infantrymen, cavalry, and artillerymen, although by 1781 the numbers had increased to 110,000 men, about one-half of whom were stationed in America and the West Indies.[20] Like all eighteenth-century armies, the social structure of the British army reflected the intensely hierarchical nature of society. Commissioned positions were dominated by the upper ranks of society, while noncommissioned officers and common soldiers were drawn from the main body of the nation. European armies traditionally were composed of landless peasants, unemployed laborers, drifters, and common criminals. The British army had its share of highway robbers, rogues, and vagabonds, and men conscripted against their will, but after 1750 the massive changes in the British economy began to produce a different reservoir of manpower. Increasingly, mature, ordinary men from economically marginal groups, in most cases the victims of economic dislocations, were brought into the army.

A variety of methods were employed to recruit men into eighteenth-century European armies. Levies of rogues and vagrants, common since the time in Elizabeth's rule when prisoners in Newgate were freed to reinforce beseiged troops in Le Havre, now were used less frequently. For instance, during the period of the American Revolution, Britain resorted on only two occasions to the press system to raise troops, in 1778 and again in 1779, justifying its strong-arm methods of recruiting on the premise that the state had the right to conscript unproductive citizens, who were a burden to society, or to dragoon malefactors who disturbed the social order. But compared to Elizabethan times, or to the contemporary Prussian army, which was heavily reliant on the press system, the British army had relatively few involuntary recruits. As a result principally of constitutional developments, methods of inducting men into the army by violence or subterfuge fell into discredit in England. During the 1750s the anti-Pitt element in Parliament tried unsuccessfully to extend the right of habeas corpus to pressed men on the constitutional grounds that it was as wrong to condemn a man to military service without recourse to legal procedures as it was to detain him in prison without a trial. Those men who were pressed into the land forces seldom saw conventional service, more often facing assignment to foreign posts, such as the West Indies or Gibraltar, from which desertion was difficult.[21]

The great majority of British recruits were found through a process known as "beating up for volunteers." Recruiting parties beat drums through the towns, villages, and shires trying to induce volunteers to sign enlistment papers. Each potential enlistee was enticed by a bounty of one and a half guineas. In Scotland, a system known as "raising men for rank" also was used. Peers or wealthy men of local reputation were authorized to raise an established quota of men, in return for which they were granted a commission and the right to nominate some or all of the officers. During the American Revolution the War Office allowed a number of towns to raise regiments by private subscription. But the practice was viewed as an unconstitutional breach of parliamentary privilege and led to the adoption of a resolution requiring all private subscriptions to state explicitly that any corps raised by such methods would be employed "for such uses as the Parliament should think fit."[22]

Thus, by midcentury Britain was able to raise its army by voluntary enlistment, a development due chiefly to a surplus of manpower, and perhaps to the fact that the military calling was slowly rising in esteem among ordinary men. Eighteenth-century British military records are scarce and often incomplete, but such records as do survive suggest that regions experiencing economic decline contributed heavily in manpower to the service. Recruits tended to be around twenty years of age and averaged 5' 7" in infantry regiments, a bit taller in elite regiments such as the dragoons.[23] Most were urbanites either by birth or migration, of lower or lower-middle class background, and possessed of occupational skills no longer in great demand. The textile industry, for example, early on felt the impact of industrialization, and a high percentage of eighteenth-century soldiers were former textile workers, especially weavers, perhaps because the weaving sector of the industry was in chronic depression. Shoemakers, pliers of a craft that also had begun to feel the effects of mechanization and overcrowding, likewise enlisted in extraordinary numbers. As in continental armies the British army, particularly the infantry, also contained a large number of unskilled workers, or casual laborers. Cottagers, squatters, and numerous marginal farmers, driven from the land by the enclosure movement or rack-renting, joined the army in large numbers as did many seasonal workers, such as carpenters, bricklayers, and masons, many of whom were hard-hit by static wages and rising prices.

In addition to involuntary recruits and economically marginal groups, Britain's army, like most contemporary armies, included a large number of foreigners. By contrast to continental armies, however, foreign troops in British service usually served in their own units and were commanded by their own officers. During the Revolutionary War approximately 30,000 German mercenaries saw service with the British army in America, comprising about 2 percent of elite corps and slightly over 10 percent of infantry regiments. Although they were not regular troops, approximately 5,000 women camp followers and tens of thousands of blacks served as part of the operational apparatus of the British army in that war. It had been a custom since ancient times for women to accompany their husbands on military campaigns, but their numbers had declined by the eighteenth century, and many of the functions once performed by the females now were increasingly taken over by the commissariat and the medical corps. No effort was made to recruit blacks, but thousands of slaves fled to British service after the seat of the war was transferred to the South. Small numbers were armed and fought as regular soldiers on land or in actions at sea, but the vast majority did the work usually assigned to poor local peasants by armies in European wars. They served as pioneers, or guides, as military laborers on fortifications and public works, and as agricultural laborers on the farms and plantations in Georgia and South Carolina that produced food and supplies for the army.[24]

The eighteenth-century notion that the qualities essential to command—natural genius, honor, courage, and loyalty—were to be found only in gentlemen, guaranteed that the officer corps would remain the preserve of the upper classes. As was the practice in most European armies the highest military positions, major general, lieutenant general, and general, were reserved to the highest nobility. Sir William Howe, Thomas Gage, John Burgoyne, and Sir Henry Clinton all were members of noble families. Howe, Clinton, and Burgoyne also were members of Parliament, as were numerous other officers. Most of the regimental officers in the British army, the lieutenants, captains, and majors, sprang from the country gentry and from the mercantile classes, and a disproportionately high percentage were of Scottish origin, perhaps because of the region's tradition of military service. Perhaps as many as one-third of the officers in the British army in America were Scots, the great majority of whom were men of social rank and landed property, and who, like their English counterparts, were involved in politics or had political connections.[25] A high proportion of all officers were either sons of army officers or the younger sons—and therefore subject to disinheritance by the laws of primogeniture—of aristocratic or gentry families. As the century progressed, larger numbers of middle-class families, which increasingly looked upon the army as a means to achieve status and financial security, also sent their sons into the army's officer corps. In addition, many noncareerist officers joined as a temporary expedient, and a host of "gentlemen volunteers" enlisted in the hope of earning a commission.[26]

Although a handful of officers in the army came up from the ranks, the normal method of obtaining a commission and of subsequent promotion, was through the purchase system, a purely private transaction between individuals. Prices of commissions, which were subject to no government regulation, varied according to rank from the elite corps to the infantry. Another method was "recruiting for rank," a device by which men who undertook to raise recruits to form a new company or complete an existing one were granted a commission. The method favored by ambitious officers who could not raise the money for promotion to the senior ranks was to fill a place vacated by death during war, which provided the cheapest and speediest access to the commissioned ranks. From the rank of colonel up, however, officers generally had to rely on patronage and political connections to advance their military careers.[27]

Generals Howe and Clinton, the British commanders-in-chief for most of the war, are examples of officers whose ancestry and political connections helped them to advance up the ladder of rank. Both were drawn from the peerage. Howe was the younger son of Emanual Scrope Howe, second viscount Howe, by his wife Mary Sophia, who was reputed to be the illegitimate daughter of George I. Clinton was the only son of Admiral the Honorable George Clinton, second son of the sixth earl of Lincoln. Both Howe and Clinton were protégés of powerful men. Howe's older brother was Admiral Richard Lord Howe, one of England's most distinguished naval officers and, as fourth viscount Howe, a formidable influence in arranging for seats in the House of Commons and in procuring sinecures for his brothers and other relations. Clinton's principal patrons were his cousins, the first and second dukes of Newcastle, through whose influence he was elected M.P. for Boroughbridge in Yorkshire in 1772, and who in 1774 also returned him for Neward in Nottinghamshire.

Both Howe and Clinton rose to high command without benefit of a military education or even intensive training. After four years at Eton, Howe purchased a lieutenancy at age eighteen, a captaincy at twenty-one, and a lieutenancy-colonelcy at twenty-eight. Clinton began his military career at age fifteen. One year later he was commissioned a captain by his father, who was then Royal Governor of New York. Clinton spent the next twenty-six years in London, much of it in the waiting room of the Duke of Newcastle, at whose intercession he was awarded a commission in the elite Coldstream Guards.

Both Howe and Clinton received their military training in the Seven Years' War. Howe commanded a light infantry battalion in the expedition to Quebec and emerged from the war with a distinguished military reputation. Clinton saw active service for the first time in 1760, when his regiment was ordered to Germany. Appointed aide-de-camp to one of Europe's most famous soldiers, the twenty-five year old Charles, Hereditary Prince of Brunswick, Clinton made a name for himself when he was wounded in the campaign of 1762. After the war he was promoted to full colonel, four months after William Howe was promoted for gallantry in the conquest of Canada. Although veterans of the German campaigns considered themselves members of an elite group of officers, Clinton, as a consequence of the order of seniority, was compelled to serve beneath Gage and Howe.[28]

The same burdens of class restriction for career advancement existed in the Royal Navy, but the nation's reliance on the navy for national security guaranteed that it would not exercise the same degree of influence. Long after the purchase system had fallen into disuse on the continent, it continued

to flourish below the general ranks in the infantry and cavalry branches of
the British army.[29] Although it allowed men with no military experience
and meager talents to rise to high command by buying their promotions,
all efforts to abolish or reform the system were ineffectual before the late
nineteenth century. In part, the system was defended on the grounds that
men who were willing to spend large amounts of money for a commission
would have a stake in maintaining the status quo and would not therefore
become a threat to the established order. It also was argued that military
efficiency rested in large measure on the respect of the rank and file for their
socially superior officers. That the system survived for so long attests to the
economic and political influence of the British aristocracy, as well as to the
fact that the army in the eighteenth and nineteenth centuries was an important source of government patronage. Indeed, the desire to secure and
maintain the social status of "deserving" officers who wanted to keep their
pay, pensions, and rank, was a factor in the decision of 1763 to maintain
a large army in America.[30]

By the beginning of the eighteenth century soldiers lived increasingly in
large, self-contained communities, scattered through villages and towns of
England. The separation from family and community was compensated in
part by the fellowship soldiers found in the regiment, which was usually
named after the regimental colonel or the geographic area from which the
recruits were drawn, or was simply given a number, as was common in
infantry regiments. The basic unit of the army, the regiment, was the foundation of the morale and tenacious loyalties that distinguished British service. The sense of group solidarity that developed was derived from several
sources, the most obvious being the experiences and traditions of each
regiment that were embodied in uniforms and rituals.[31]

Before the rise of the standing army each soldier fitted himself in clothing
according to his own taste and means. In the 1640s Cromwell introduced
uniforms in the New Model Army, and thereafter troops of all nations wore
uniforms manufactured according to government specifications. Most British regiments wore scarlet jackets, but each regiment was distinguished by
different color facings on collars and cuffs. Each regiment had its own
distinctive color waistcoat and breeches, its own peculiar pattern of lace,
its own design for the lapels, loops, and arrangements of the buttons. The
uniform had a functional purpose, of course, but it had a symbolic one as
well. It marked the transformation from private citizen to professional soldier, and implied the severing of most family ties and the surrender of
individuality to the group, which henceforth became the principal source
of emotional security against the stress of combat and daily life. Regimental
colors—large silk flags carried on half pikes—played a similar role in the
bonding process. At the formation of the regiment formal religious services
were held to consecrate the flags, thus imbuing them with an almost mystic
quality. On the field of battle each regiment carried two flags, one displaying

the king's colors, the other the regimental facing color. Embroidered with battle honors, or decorated with medals, they embodied the traditions of the regiment and recalled its glories.[32]

Military society was above all founded on a network of friendship and kinship, actual and implied. Each regiment contained a substantial number of men who had been born in the regiment, grew up in it, and as adults remained in it to become professional soldiers. Because military life was inconsistent with the performance of family obligations, and because of the cost of maintaining additional dependents, the British army deliberately recruited unmarried men. Although soldiers were recruited all over Britain, regiments often limited their efforts to particular counties or areas in order to take advantage of friendships and family connections. Recruiting teams frequently included local men who had advanced from the ranks to become noncommissioned officers. Their success inspired young men and boys to volunteer for the service. Contrary to the modern practice of separating members of the same family, the British army deliberately united relatives and friends in the same units as "nothing binds them more strongly to the service." Finding a home and friends in the regiment, young, unmarried men without family obligations tended to remain in the service. In the eighteenth century the average infantryman had more than ten years of service, the average dragoon or grenadier almost nine years. The permanence of personnel helped to weld together the bonds of loyalty forged among friends and relations in the barracks and on the battlefield.[33]

Despite, or perhaps because of the exaggerated distinctions in rank in the eighteenth-century British army, the aristocratic officer corps played a crucial role in shaping the regimental ideology that not only linked men, but which instilled in them the habit of obedience. It is clear that cultural norms derived from patterns of behavior characteristic of British society habituated soldiers to a status system. By contrast to the Continental soldiers' frequent rejection of authority, which finds precedence in the institutionalized ideals of the Declaration of Independence, British soldiers had no precedent for revolt and no institutionalized approval for defiance of authority. Habituated by working-class habits of deference, they generally accepted discipline and authority, and perhaps even found security in the definite hierarchical structure of the army. The moral authority of the officer corps sprang from sources other than cultural norms, however. In part it derived from the economic power entrusted to them by the state to pay and equip the troops.[34]

One of the results of the contest between Parliament and the Crown over the control of finance and of the army, was the creation of a primitive and chaotic system of finance that made the regimental colonel responsible for clothing, feeding, and housing his regiment through deductions from the soldier's pay. According to procedures established by Parliament, the soldier's daily pay of eight pence was divided into two parts. "Subsistence" pay, which amounted to six pence, was supposed to cover his food, and certain items of clothing such as shoes, stockings, and gaiters; the remaining two pence, or "off reckonings," suffered various other deductions to cover the cost of clothing and to support the Royal Hospital at Chelsea, the paymaster general of the forces, and the regimental agent. In contrast to the occasional soldier, the professional soldier was thus entirely dependent upon the regimental officer for his sustenance and support.[35]

The leadership of the officer corps was above all else founded on attributes peculiar to their class. The eighteenth-century officer corps was in a sense an exclusive club or a cohesive brotherhood, whose members were bound together by family ties and distinctive values. The status and relative security provided by the military often induced all male members of the same family to follow in the footsteps of a father, a brother, or some other relative in choosing an army career. Moreover, vacancies created by deaths, promotions, or augmentations were eagerly sought by ranking officers for family members and friends. As is the case with most exclusive organizations, the officer corps had its own rigid code of honor which regulated behavior. Gentlemanly conduct, personal fealty to Crown and country, intense group loyalty, and the pursuit of glory were the chief components of the code. Above all other military values officers prized courage and fortitude, qualities that were functionally indispensable in warfare until bureaucratic command replaced personal leadership. Officers took and shared risks with the men they led, and often acted with extraordinary heroism, which produced a high rate of officer battle casualties in the eighteenth century. By their actions officers came to symbolize regimental esprit, which significantly enhanced their authority.[36]

Inspired by an heroic ethos, eighteenth-century officers were often brave amateurs. Professionalism in the modern sense of the word did not exist, except perhaps in the Prussian officer corps. Although changes in military technology necessitated the training of officers, it did not occur without great resistance. By contrast to the Royal Navy, which placed a high premium upon competence and training, and which therefore developed an adequate system of professional education much earlier, Britain's only academic institution for military tutelage was the Royal Military Academy at Woolich, established in 1741. Founded for cadets who aspired to careers in the artillery or engineers, the academy offered a minimal amount of technical instruction, although cadets underwent a rigorous course of study, principally in mathematics and science. But the fear of creating a class of professional officers who might become a threat to the established order militated against formal and systematic training. There was, however, considerable interest in military art and a number of treatises appeared in Britain over the century. As a result of the interest generated by military writers, the professionalism of officers improved. Although a system of uniform drill in the movement of bodies of troops was not adopted until the 1790s, practical training in tactical drill for new recruits was in wide use by the

American Revolution, which both improved military proficiency and sub-ordination, and inculcated esprit.[37]

The advances made in group cohesion and solidarity, as well as the growth in technical or tactical expertise, were apparent in the performance of British field armies, among the most consistently successful forces of the eighteenth century. The French commander at the battle of Dettingen in 1743 compared the British infantry to a wall of brass "from which issued so brisk and well sustained a fire that the oldest officers owned that they had never seen anything like it, incomparably superior to our own." Although the battle of Fontenoy in Flanders ended in defeat, British and Hanoverian battalions marched in unwavering lines into a sustained fire until they reached the enemy camp, where they were stopped by a total lack of support. In an astonishing, if futile, demonstration of discipline, they then retired with stoical courage through the same nightmare of grape and musket balls.[38] In the American Revolution, the most notable defeat in modern British history, British troops led by able, if not brilliant, officers, fought with fire and spirit, and exhibited all of the military virtues—obedience, subordi-nation, and patient endurance. The humiliating defeat of Burgoyne's army at Saratoga and four years later the surrender of the Earl of Cornwallis at Yorktown produced bitter debate in print and in Parliament. Members of Parliament blamed ministers for the army's failure; ministers blamed gen-erals, generals blamed each other, ministers, and admirals. Significantly, all agreed that the British failure in America was not for lack of will or readiness in her forces.[39]

British military failures in America, in fact were due to a variety of factors, including inept conduct of the war by the home government and poor generalship. Perhaps the central reason for the loss of the war was the fact that the constitution and mentality of the British army made it peculiarly unsuited for the suppression of a mass democratic revolt. The civil-military foundations upon which Britain's professional army had been built were fundamentally sound. Although there remained crucial areas of controversy, by and large the army not only reflected the political will, but it was in harmony with the national character and attitudes of eighteenth-century Britain. In European wars it remained a formidable instrument. But envi-ronmental differences and divergent social developments and constitutional perceptions destined its failure in America.

The British army sent to America faced the task of restoring imperial authority in a society of four million politically minded people, provincials who were, by their own definition, "deep into Principles." That distinctive feature made the American Revolution a political war, It was "not a war of posts," as Nathanael Greene, the American general, carefully distin-guished, "but a contest for States dependent on public opinion." The dif-ference was at least dimly perceived by the secretary of state for the colonies, Lord George Germain, who was in charge of grand strategy, and the British army high command, which was responsible for the direction of operations. Accordingly they tried to shape a political policy of conciliation designed "to gain the hearts and subdue the mind of America."[40] Paradoxically, the constitutional safeguards evolved over a century and a half and the class aspects of British constitutionalism made it perhaps inevitable that they would lose the battle, and ultimately the war.

In the wars of Europe the purpose of the army was the destruction of the enemy, a fact that determined the way wars were fought. In America, too, the British army sought to defeat its provinicial adversaries, but the pursuit of that objective was modified by the conviction of ministers and generals that the overwhelming majority of Americans were loyal to the Crown. The orderly application of force and the containment of violence would, they believed, reap handsome political rewards. The problem was that under the British system of military administration, the exercise of authority was more or less discretionary, and to a large degree depended upon the talents and personality of the officeholder. The campaign of 1777 is an example in point.

In the aftermath of the Hessians' humiliating defeat at Trenton late in 1776, the ministry was concerned over the possibility that France and Spain might enter the conflict. In order to forestall the intervention of its European rivals, Whitehall expected its armies to capture American territory during the campaign of 1777. Only after it had achieved substantive military victories, the goverment had concluded, would it be feasible to discuss reconciliation with the colonists. General William Howe, in command of Britain's army in North America, thought otherwise. He preferred pacification to a devastating offensive, a view that colored his conception of strategy for 1777.

From the outset, therefore, the government and its principal commander in America worked at cross purposes in 1777. The strategy devised in London by February, 1777, called for General John Burgoyne to lead an invasion of the Hudson Valley from Canada, so as to isolate New England from the rest of the provinces. At that point the ministry presumed that Howe would cooperate with the Canadian army. However, in the course of authoring four separate plans for 1777, Howe settled on a different course. His first scheme, conceived in November, 1776, envisaged an assault against New England and upper New York. His final plan, which he did not forward to London until April, 1777, anticipated a campaign to take Philadelphia. It seems inconceivable that the general—or Whitehall—could seriously have believed that Philadelphia might be taken in sufficient time for Howe to assist Burgoyne that same year, but Lord Germain and George III approved his last plan with that very understanding. Not that their concurrence counted for much, for Howe had already launched his plan by the time Germain's endorsement arrived. The result, of course was disaster. In a campaign plagued by lack of cooperation and coordination, Howe won

a meaningless victory at Philadelphia, while Burgoyne suffered the pernicious defeat at Saratoga that induced France to ally with the United States.[41]

Throughout this war Britain often would suffer for the constitutional
peculiarities of its military administration. The most sensational instance
after Saratoga, of course, occurred in 1781, when the Earl of Cornwallis
was able to invade Virginia contrary to the orders of his commander, Sir
Henry Clinton. Because of limitations on the powers of the high command,
even regimental officers enjoyed enough local autonomy to frustrate the
will of ministers and generals.[42]

Although many of the estimated 3,500 to 4,000 officers who served in
America favored the policy of political pacification, the majority either
supported or were converted to a program of violent pacification. The
socially elitist assumption that birth alone entitled one to military command
predisposed many officers to look on American military institutions and
values with contempt.[43] Their attitudes shaped by class values of obedience
and subordination, the majority of officers took a dim view of rebellion,
the ultimate subversion of hierarchical values. Trained for complex drill
evolutions, not for riot duty or guerrilla warfare, they found the war in
America, particularly in the southern theater, frustrating and unprofitable.[44]
Acting on their own initiative, field commanders, who still enjoyed wide
discretionary powers over the possessions of the conquered, regularly ordered systematic plundering operations, either to seize or destroy war material, or to procure provisions. The collective booty then was deposited in
a common pool to be shared among the officers and the poorly paid men
who made up the expedition, a practice commonly condoned by European
powers reluctant to incur added financial liability for the support and maintenance of military forces. Excesses committed by the British army sometimes turned an apparently loyal populace into patriots, as in Queens
County, New York.[45] The strategy of violent pacification pursued by the
Prevost brothers in Georgia after 1779, as well as Cornwallis's reluctant
resort to terror tactics in South Carolina beginning in the summer of 1780,
produced the same fatal results. Not only did it alienate white loyalist
support, but in Georgia and South Carolina it prompted a successful in-
surgency.[46]

British difficulties were compounded by the unfitness of military administration to deal with the overwhelming problem of supply in America.
Constitutional mechanisms developed in Britain as a defense against the
concentration of power in military hands, such as divided responsibility for
supply, produced what the historian of the British army, Sir John Fortescue,
called "a hopeless organization for war." The army in America consumed
an estimated 300 tons of food a week, most of it sent from Europe, from
one to two months' sail away. The inefficiency of the state bureaucracy, the
inadequacy of the commissary system, and a critical shortage of land and
sea transport caused long delays in the shipment of supplies. Away from

the coastal areas, where the Royal Navy could provide assistance, logistics became a nightmare. Although the army generally tried to avoid indiscriminate private plundering because of its harmful effects on military discipline, the system of supply in the field was heavily reliant on impressment, which caused acute distress and ultimately widespread disaffection among American farmers.[47]

In an effort to solve the urgent problem of food and provender the army in Georgia and South Carolina resorted to the sequestration of approximately 100 rebel estates and over 7,000 rebel-owned slaves. One of the primary objectives was to produce supplies for the army, thus relieving it of dependence on the hazardous and unreliable trans-Atlantic system. Slaves were employed both as agricultural laborers and as military workhands, but the systematic exploitation of slave labor, at least from a political standpoint, can only be judged an utter failure. To a generation of white southerners passionately committed to the guiding values of liberty, equality, and property enshrined in the Declaration of Independence, the appropriation of their chattel constituted a general attack on the rights of property.[48] As much as any other single factor, the British army's confiscation of property, which in the South above all meant slaves, caused the failure of Britain's southern strategy and the loss of the thirteen colonies.

From the outset British ministers and the army high command recognized that the American Revolution represented both a military and a political problem. Consequently, they tried to develop a war policy based upon the restrained use of military force. The execution of the policy differed significantly from the design, leading to an astonishing paradox: in most major battles the British army outfought the Americans, but it lost the war. The failure to a significant degree was a necessary result of ancestral British fears of militarism and the class nature of the officer corps. Although the army, or military power, had faded away as a social or political issue, Britain still tolerated a chaotic and primitive system of military administration rendered quaint by the passage of time. Developed during the reign of Queen Anne, when antimilitarism was high, the system of divided administration and separation of functions no longer was an effective form of military organization even in European wars. For extended overseas operations it was positively obsolete. The diffused authority and decentralized responsibility, the watchwords of British constitutionalism, were inadequate to the huge logistical effort necessary to successfully conduct extended overseas operations. Obliged to live off the land, the army often showed a calloused disregard for American rights, and in the process it alienated the popular support essential to British war plans.

The sharp fears of the governing classes that army officers might become a dangerous political and social force led to the development of exclusive caste requirements for entry into the officer corps and persistent resistance to systematic professional education in peacetime. Dominated by a hierarchy of birth, wealth, kinship, and political connections, the officer corps was dedicated to an extraordinary degree to hierarchical order, tradition, and obedience, moral virtues desirable perhaps in an eighteenth-century soldiery, but completely unsuited to the resolution of problems posed by a democratic revolution. Their conduct of the war—undisciplined, vengeful, and destructive—was a dangerous, double-edged, self-destructive weapon, which polarized and hardened attitudes and exposed the differences between two opposed kinds of societies. Superior in leadership, tactical skills, and discipline, but lacking in political judgment, the army command was capable of a military victory, but not of winning a political war.

The American Revolution demonstrated the need for new organizational forms and administrative procedures. It revealed the necessity for a professionally educated officer corps and for a structure of promotion in which competence was a condition for advancement. In short, the War of Independence indicated that a general remodeling of the British army was in order. Such reforms, however, were essentially alien to the nature of eighteenth-century British society. Deep-seated faults of the army, the purchase system, aristocratic dominance of the officer corps, and a cumbersome bureaucratic system designed for constitutional security, were imbedded in eighteenth-century British society and could only be cured by time and changes within that society. To be sure, patterns of society in Britain were evolving, and the pattern of the army would evolve in conformity with it. In the meantime, Britain had cut the path in establishing civilian control over the military. Although Americans of the revolutionary generation rejected the product, they eagerly embraced the principle.

11

Naval Warfare
and the American Victory

Mary B. Wickwire

That the American, or Continental, navy accomplished very little of value during the Revolution should occasion no surprise. Begun from a base of zero, chronically short of funds for building, maintaining, manning, and supplying ships, and lacking both the traditions of a service and the administrative organization to manage it, the American navy probably accomplished as much as reasonably could have been expected of it.

Yet there remains something pathetic about its record, for by war's end virtually all its ships had been lost and it had failed both as an offensive force and for the most part as a defensive arm. So meager were its accomplishments, John Adams once remarked, that he nearly was moved to tears at the mere thought of its performance.[1]

Its defensive tasks were basically the protection of rebel coasts and commerce, occasional convoy duty, and the conveyance of goods and messages. For these duties the Continental navy was inadequate. If the Royal navy mustered in force against either shore or shipping, the American navy could not successfully interpose itself. The use of American naval vessels for convoy duty usually meant dispatching the vessels to the West Indies, but in the performance of this duty the Americans at best could successfully defend only against attack by privateers or a small enemy force. In an age when men served for glory or profit, the navy's attempt to provide a transport arm probably was doomed from the outset.[2]

It was in its offensive role—the harassment of British ports and commercial shipping—that the American navy most nearly achieved success, and, perhaps, some modicum of glory. Even in this role, however, the Americans more early resembled a horde of gnats than a swarm of wasps. True, some of their more successful raiders "terrorized" the coasts of the

British isles and elicited from British merchants a clamorous plea for naval protection. True also, the Americans took between 200 and 250 prizes, although most of these successes occurred in the early period of the war, before the British began to use armed convoy protection.

The exploits of some individual American captains, such as Lambert Wickes, Gustavus Conygham, and John Paul Jones, evoked consternation in Britain and admiration among Britain's enemies-to-be, yet their activities, however much vaunted in American histories, were only a distraction for the Royal navy and had no effect on the outcome of the war. Perhaps the ineffectual nature of the Continental navy can best be exemplified by looking at the defeats it suffered at Penobscot Bay and on Lake Champlain.

Lake Champlain became the scene of utmost importance in 1776, after the American army's retreat from Canada. Fort Ticonderoga, taken by troops under Ethan Allen and Benedict Arnold the preceding spring, could not by itself defend the lake. Control of Champlain required a fleet, and during 1776 both the Americans and the British worked to construct one.

Unfortunately for the Americans, Major General Philip Schuyler, in command at Lake Champlain in 1776, committed his efforts to the building of small vessels, principally bateaux for the transport of troops and supplies, and armed craft called gundalows and galleys. Together with three small schooners captured from the British in 1775, these diminutive craft would have to contest passage of the lake with the British.

Under the charge of Captain Charles Douglas, the British meanwhile had contrived to acquire a far more formidable fighting force. They brought vessels from Canada to the lake by carting them overland at the portage from the Richelieu River. Douglas also had built at Saint Johns another craft known as a radeau, which carried more armament than the largest of the American schooners.

Benedict Arnold, because of his experience at sea, took command of the small American fleet. He faced a British squadron under Lieutenant Thomas Pringle, whose guns could throw almost twice as much metal as those of the Americans. Arnold skillfully chose a defensive position at Valcour Island, yet in the action on October 10 he used up three-quarters of his ammunition and was compelled to withdraw. The British caught up with him on October 13, whereupon he lost all but four vessels and suffered heavy casualties, but reached Ticonderoga.

Some historians have asserted that Arnold's action won the Americans a valuable prize, one year in which to gather the strength to win at Saratoga in October 1777. However, a recent study of British logistics has revealed that even had the engagement occured earlier in the year, Sir Guy Carleton did not have the provisions to besiege and then hold Ticonderoga, or even to maintain troops at Crown Point over the winter.[3]

While it may thus be doubted that Arnold's defeat on Lake Champlain was actually a sacrifice of value to the Americas, there is no doubt about

Penobscot Bay, the worst American naval defeat of the Revolution. Yet the way to it was prepared by the successes of its "irregular" navy, the privateers. From the beginning, enterprising Yankees had fitted out their ships as privateers to take advantage of British laxness. Their successes helped supply the American armies with captured goods, and kept enthusiasm for the cause alive with tales of easy booty "for the taking." Nova Scotia shipping especially suffered. Yankee privateers not only grabbed nearly every vessel they came upon bound to or from that province, but they also swooped down upon Nova Scotia coasting vessels and raided into small harbors and up rivers and inlets. They even poached around Halifax, Britain's big, supposedly "safe" port, prompting Vice Admiral Marriott Arbuthnot to write from Halifax in 1778 that "the Trade and intercourse by Water have suffer'd greatly from the Number of Armed Vessels fitted out from new England; even at the Mouth of this Harbour many vessels are taken."[4] Royal naval vessels found it difficult—and often impossible—to stop many of the privateers, which were so small and of such shallow draft that the larger British ships could not follow them inshore without fear of grounding.

To eliminate Maine as a base for privateering, as well as to stop periodic Yankee incursions by land into Nova Scotia and to establish a refuge for loyalists, the British sent an expedition to Maine in June of 1779. A British force of 750 regulars under Brigadier General Francis Maclean landed at Penobscot Bay, halfway up the Maine coast, where they proceeded to dig in at the Bagaduce Peninsula (now Castine), and to erect works they dubbed Fort George. Massachusetts immediately responded with an expedition of militia under the command of General Solomon Lovell. The militiamen were loaded aboard twenty transports and escorted by a fleet that consisted of some twenty-two armed vessels, including more than a dozen privateers carrying sixteen to twenty guns each, the frigate *Warren*, two brigantines, a brig, and a sloop. Command of the fleet went to Commodore Dudley Saltonstall, a Continental naval officer from Connecticut. The British had precious little with which to stop the Americans when they arrived off Penobscot. Their naval commander, Captain Henry Mowat, could only place his three sloops of war across the mouth of Bagaduce Harbor, and anchor behind these vessels his four small transports, each of which he was fully prepared to turn into a fireship. The Americans landed their soldiers and besieged the fort, but Saltonstall, despite his advantage of numbers, was excessively cautious and did little but maneuver about the mouth of the Penobscot River for two weeks. Lovell, meanwhile, refused to storm the fort until Saltonstall eliminated the British ships, for their gunfire could destroy American ground forces if they ventured into the open. In the end, Saltonstall's and Lovell's irresolution proved fatal when a British squadron of seven vessels under Sir George Collier arrived. What ensued was not battle but flight, and it resulted in a huge loss for the Americans: fourteen ships destroyed, another twenty-eight captured, 500 casualties, and $7 million wasted.[5] The feckless Saltonstall, when asked by the Committee of Inquiry why he had not attacked a British warship at Penobscot, replied: "If I had fired, then the enemy would have fired back." He was dismissed from the service, having been found "ever after" incompetent to hold a government office.[6]

Despite the magnitude of the American losses, the disaster resulted in only a brief lull in New England's privateering activity against Nova Scotia. On the other hand, Britain's brilliant victory at Bagaduce ended rebel hopes of making a conquest of Nova Scotia.[7]

If American victory in the Revolution owed nothing to its navy, did Britain's failure owe to the Royal Navy? For the most part the British navy performed indifferently, often incompetently, during the revolutionary war. It did have some bright moments, although generally it failed to live up to its traditions or to perform up to its capabilities, and it must share the blame for the failure of British arms during the American Revolution.

In its previous test, the Seven Years' War which ended in 1763, the British navy had performed superbly. British armies had floated to victory around the globe. The navy had taken Wolfe's troops to Quebec and Draper's to the Philippines, and it had cleared the West Indies of its foes. Moreover, the navy would rise to even greater heights during the French Revolutionary and Napoleonic Wars. Why, then, did Britain's navy perform so poorly during the American Revolutionary War?

Blame for failure must rest in the first instance on the shoulders of England's principal ministers, including those responsible for the navy. The triumvirate of Lord North as prime minister, Lord George Germain as American Secretary, and Lord Sandwich as first Lord of the Admiralty invited failure. Indeed, one historian even went so far as to call Sandwich and Germain "a gift without price to the American cause."[8]

Even so, Britain faced such innumerable difficulties in suppressing the American rebellion that it is doubtful that a cabinet containing men of the highest caliber could have succeeded. Perhaps there was not a statesman then alive in Britain who could have won this contest, for the problems it presented were without precedent in British history. Today it seems clear that no mere military solution was possible. Instead, only a strategy that included the enlightened utilization of the colonial loyalist population, the most sagacious employment of propaganda weaponry, and a thorough understanding of colonial issues, could have won the war.

Within North's cabinet, immediate responsibility for Britain's naval activities fell to John Montagu, fourth earl of Sandwich. He combined real strengths as an administrator with a love of the navy and a desire to forward its interests. Although hampered by inadequate funds from Lord North, he worked hard and well to repair the woeful inadequacies of the fleet and dockyard stores he had inherited from his predecessor. The legacy left by Sir Edward Hawke in January of 1771 was inauspicious for the new Sandwich administration. Vessels lay rotting in harbor, their timbers not even visible until the toadstool-like fungi of dry rot was cleared away. This state of affairs was the result of building with green timber during the Seven Years' War and of "repairing" with unseasoned timber in the postwar years. Hawke bequeathed yet other naval weaknesses: storehouses stood half empty, corruption and inefficiency remained unchecked, and the implications of earlier experiments with copper sheathing awaited development and exploitation in times of greater administrative vitality.[9]

Although Sandwich fought unsuccessfully with Lord North before 1778 for funds to commission more ships, he was able to increase sixfold the supply of timber in the dockyards and to lay down rules to insure the proper seasoning of timbers and masts used in building and repairing ships.[10] His energies also deserve credit for the coppering of the fleet. When he took office in 1771 only six ships had received copper sheathing as an experiment, but by 1779 coppering of the navy's fleet had become "almost general."[11] Coppering preserved the hull from attack by worms and barnacles, making the ship cleaner, more weatherly, and able to remain at sea for longer periods of time without returning to port for refitting. In 1779 Sandwich helped introduce a new piece of naval ordnance, the carronade, a short large-caliber cannon, which could give overwhelming superiority of fire power to a ship so armed. Indeed, even forty-gun ships could carry thirty-two-pounder carronades. His administration also saw the beginnings of a new system of signaling, which, by allowing greater flexibility in the commands that could be given in signals, allowed greater flexibility in tactics.

Sandwich's failures largely were due to matters beyond his control. It is true that his reputation as a rake and a gambler laid him open to criticism and even to undeserved charges of corruption and malfeasance. In addition, his past political activities, including his role in the Wilkes affair in the previous decade, made him enemies and caused others to view him with suspicion. Nor was Sandwich a superb judge of talent. Yet his greatest problem was the misfortune to have been placed during wartime at the head of a branch of the military that had become riddled with faction and ideological dispute. The domestic reform movement, as well as the issues raised by the American Revolution, were so divisive that some of the ablest naval officers refused to serve at all, and others declined to serve in American waters. Sandwich's effectiveness also suffered because of the infamous Keppel-Palliser dispute, a quarrel that arose out of personal heat and party fervor, yet which proved so divisive that it "almost ruined the Navy," according to Admiral George Rodney.[12]

As if these problems were not sufficient to complicate Sandwich's task, the Royal Navy still was not a thoroughly professional service. Too often prickly personal pride and purely personal considerations caused some officers to give less than their utmost. At times, political considerations and personal animosities resulted in conduct characterized by a slowness to move, and something less than a spirit of cooperation. Even the most able officers sometimes showed poor judgment or acted with seeming indifference.

For example, when Admiral Rodney went home sick in 1781, he not only did not bother to report the intelligence he possessed concerning the French fleet under Admiral de Grasse, but he also took with him three ships of the line that could have reinforced his successor. Similarly, Richard Lord Howe, who served as commander-in-chief of the navy from 1776 to 1778, was an able officer before and after this war, but he seemed unable to put his heart into fighting the Americans. His family had affectionate ties to Massachusetts, which had erected a monument to his brother, killed in the Seven Years' War; moreover, Howe considered the war a tragedy, which he hoped to end not by a crushing military victory but by negotiation, for he and another brother, Sir William, were peace commissioners as well as army and navy commanders. Howe's principal failure in the revolutionary war was his inability to institute a strong blockade when the Americans were desperately short of military stores. Indeed, his most brilliant service only came after he had resigned, when badly outgunned by Comte d'Estaing's preponderance of larger ships with their greater weight of metal, he defended Sandy Hook, relieved Rhode Island, and by maneuvers that showed great tactical skill began to gain the weather gauge for an attack when a strong storm intervened to prevent it. Howe had at last shown initiative in American waters. But, overall, his performance scarcely resembled that of the captain in the Seven Years' War who had hunted French ships among the rocks of Quiberon Bay, or the "Black Dick" Howe of the French Revolutionary and Napoleonic Wars who led the Channel fleet to a great victory over the French in 1792, or the retired admiral on the fleet who served his country again by winning over the mutineers at Portsmouth in 1797.[13]

Nor was the service of most of the other leading British admirals particularly distinguished. Indeed, one scholar has termed Admirals Marriot Arbuthnot, James Gambier, and Thomas Graves the "old women" of the navy, a pejorative term that might also have been directed at Admiral Samuel Hood, who contributed to the debacle at Chesapeake Bay by giving less than his utmost.[14]

One exception to this lackluster performance by Britain's naval leaders was the role played by Sir George Collier. He served brilliantly, although naturally enough in this perverse war his achievements went unrewarded. Collier had successfully organized the naval defense of Nova Scotia in 1776, and that same year he landed a force that helped save Fort Cumberland from an American siege operation. In 1779, during a brief stint as commander of the North American squadron, he convoyed to Virginia an expedition that captured or burned some 127 enemy vessels. He returned to New York to help capture Fort Lafayette (now Verplanck), and later he led a squadron that destroyed an American naval force vastly superior in numbers in Penobscot Bay. His heroics prompted George III to remark that it was "remarkable that Sir G. Collier, with so scanty a force, should have been during the five months able to effect more objects against the rebels than the admirals that commanded such large fleets."[15] Nevertheless, Collier did not make flag rank until long after the revolutionary war ended.

Sandwich, therefore, had a large measure of bad luck, but he was far from blameless. As a cabinet minister with an important voice in the planning and conduct of the war, his greatest shortcomings were his inability to comprehend the politics behind the colonial revolt and, partly as a consequence, his lack of an imperial strategy. These failures would have been of less significance had either North, who was responsible for Britain's overall policy, or Germain, whose office oversaw American affairs, proved capable statesmen. Alas, neither did, and those two, together with Sandwich, became the infirm basis upon which British policy stood.

But it is Lord North, the prime minister, who must bear final responsibility for the decisons that resulted both in the strategic weaknesses and the operational deficiencies that inhibited the Royal Navy. Had North heeded Sandwich's timely pleas for greater naval preparations the damage might have been avoided. Over a period of years beginning in 1771 Sandwich had frequently urged North to allow naval preparations for war. On one of those many occasions he warned that if Britain delayed while the French continued to build, she would at last find herself "reduced to the necessity of either leaving our distant possessions undefended or seeing France and Spain in the Channel with a superior fleet."[16] Sandwich's prophecy came true.

Britain in 1778 first faced the consequence of her previous inactivity in building naval strength, for France entered the war against Britain that year with "*effective* naval parity."[17] That spring the French prepared a fleet at Brest, an army at Normandy, and another fleet under d'Estaing at Toulon. As d'Estaing prepared to sail, the British ministers debated how to meet the threat. Possessed of enough ships they need not have debated the matter. They would undoubtedly have kept a powerful Channel fleet to watch the French at Brest while sending another to bottle up d'Estaing. But lacking the necessary strength, the question of priorities arose. Where should the cabinet send the ships it had? Sandwich and Germain disagreed.

Sandwich perhaps naturally viewed the defense of England and Ireland as the admiralty's "principal object," and the loss of America as "by far the inferior consideration" compared to the security of Lord Howe's fleet.[18] Germain, on the other hand, fearing for his armies in America, was desperate to prevent d'Estaing's getting to sea, and he proposed detaching a sufficient number of craft from the Channel fleet to stop the departure of France's Toulon navy. Sandwich strongly opposed any detachment from the fleet in home waters. He pointed to the French at Brest and the Spanish at Cadiz, and argued that a weakened Channel fleet could not withstand a force so superior in numbers.[19] Germain's plan, he said, would open Britain to invasion.

When Sandwich prevailed in the cabinet council, Germain pressed for a detachment from Keppel's Channel fleet to reinforce the British ships in American waters, whither it seemed d'Estaing was bound. Sandwich again objected to a decrease in Keppel's force until he could be certain of d'Estaing's intentions. He gained support for his position—indeed was influenced in taking that position—by the concurrence of prominent naval officers, including the commander-in-chief of the home fleet. The arguments of naval officers for preserving intact the strength of the Channel fleet similarly influenced the king, who judged that "Keppel, Palliser, Parker, and Hood, are men whose knowledge in that science may be trusted."[20] Sandwich thus prevailed.

D'Estaing sailed unopposed to North America in the spring of 1778, but his mission hardly proved fatal to Great Britain. Not only did he fail to seize either Rhode Island or Savannah, his principal objects, but he did not succeed in destroying a single important British warship in 1778. Moreover, the invasion of Britain did not occur, for by 1779 France and Spain had aborted as hopeless their plans for such an undertaking.

If Britain had escaped its peril in 1778–79, it was not so fortunate in 1781. By that year it had reestablished naval parity, but mere parity, as Sandwich had warned before the war, was not enough. That spring the ministry had to choose between relieving Gibraltar, under siege by French and Spanish forces, or of seeking to prevent still another French fleet from sailing out of Brest. Lacking the resources to accomplish both goals, the North government decided that, regardless of the danger to its American interests, it must attempt the relief.[21] Thus reinforcements went to Gibraltar, and Admiral François de Grasse slipped out of Brest with twenty ships of the line. He was bound for America. The road to Yorktown had begun.

It has become almost an article of faith with historians that the cabinet's— or Sandwich's—great mistake was in not preventing de Grasse's voyage by blockading French ports, a strategy Britain had successfully pursued in the Seven Years' War, and which she again would accomplish during the French Revolutionary and Napoleonic Wars. Those who make this argument overlook a host of considerations. First, Britain's other blockades were less effective than they are generally reputed to have been. In the Seven Years' War, for instance, a French fleet reached New France every year until after the fall of Quebec, while in the Napoleonic conflict the French fleet managed to slip out of Nelson's attempted blockade before the Battle of Trafalgar. Second, at the time of the American Revolution, Britain had no experience of blockading the French coast while it simultaneously waged war with America. Third, Britain faced overwhelming odds in 1781. To have blockaded Brest and Toulon effectively would have required more ships than Britain possessed, and it could have been accomplished only at the cost of leaving her trade unprotected from the North Sea to Africa, while at the same time it allowed Gibraltar to fall for want of provisions. Contemporaries seemed to understand what historians have been unable to grasp. For example, even Lord Barrington, no friend of Sandwich, appreciated the true cause of the admiralty's embarrassments, for he admitted that Britain's "marine difficulties at home and on stations abroad do not arise from want of ability or care in him [Lord Sandwich] but solely from our being at war with France, Spain and North America at the same time without any ally, or diversion in our favor."[22]

Regardless of whether Britain could have attempted a blockade, what she needed in the summer of 1781 was intelligent cooperation between her army and navy. By the time Admiral Thomas Graves took command of the British Navy in New York, both he and Sir Henry Clinton, the commander of the British army in America, had learned that a French fleet under the Comte de Grasse intended to sail from the West Indies. Britain's Caribbean fleet under the command of Rear Admiral Sir Samuel Hood was following him. Hood did not know that de Grasse had taken his entire fleet of twenty-eight ships north, leaving the French West Indies unprotected, in order to gamble on a victory in North America. But he did know, and so did Clinton and Graves, that if de Grasse reached Newport, lifted the British blockade of that port, and joined his fleet to the one already there under the command of Louis, Comte de Barras, the French would have a formidable navy in North American waters. Clinton and Graves also knew that General Jean Baptiste Rochambeau, commander of the French army in America, had marched from Newport to join his army to General Washington's. They knew the Earl Cornwallis was in Virginia with an army of around 5,000 men. The situation called for some sort of decisive action on their part. None was forthcoming.

Clinton did nothing to stop the junction of Washington and Rochambeau, and after the allied armies had started marching south on August 19 he continued to believe they intended to attack him in New York, even though he possessed "intelligence" to the contrary. Graves, meanwhile, also tarried in New York, neither sailing to join Hood in order to establish the alliance that would have cut up de Grasse, nor blockading Barras, who slipped from Newport carrying to the Chesapeake the siege guns that Rochambeau would need to batter Cornwallis at Yorktown. Only after Hood, Graves's junior, arrived in New York, did the combined British fleets put to sea. By then the odds were stacked against the British. Should Barras and de Grasse combine, the French would outgun them nearly two to one. If Barras delivered the siege guns to the combined French and American armies, and the British navy could not reach Yorktown to embark Cornwallis's army, the British general's fate was sealed, and with it the fate of Britain in its original thirteen colonies.

When Graves and Hood reached the mouth of the Chesapeake they discovered their real difficulties. Twenty-four French sail of the line drifted out to challenge them, while four others guarded the anchorage. The battle that followed between the British and French off the Virginia Capes did not by any means bring glory to the British navy. At best a draw in tactical terms, strategically it was a failure for the British. While the fleets maneuvered for a week, Barras slipped into the bay. Graves eventually broke off the action and returned to New York. There he did very little, learning by message from Cornwallis that de Grasse and Barras had indeed combined, and now had thirty-six sail of the line in Chesapeake Bay. Those were daunting odds, since Graves could at best count upon twenty-five of his own. While trying to decide what to do, the British navy did nothing until October 19, the day that Cornwallis surrendered.

The admiralty had made official ship dispositions that taken together might have brought victory, but a peculiar concatenation of circumstances that included freakish weather, lost messages, ill health, and obstinate personalities nullified those preparations. As a result, only about one-half of Britain's American fleet fought off Yorktown.[23] Fifteen ships of the line in the West Indies had returned to England between March and August of 1781, and for one reason or another nine others in American waters were not with Graves at Chesapeake Bay. None of those ships had been dispersed owing to admiralty orders, however. Thus, it is difficult to blame London for the fact that when Graves confronted de Grasse he had nineteen ships of the line against twenty-four French.[24] The British naval force would at least have equalled de Grasse's fleet had the various admirals obeyed orders and had "strange fatalities" not dogged the British. Rodney took with him to England three ships of the line thus depriving Hood of them; Sir Peter Parker erred in not sending any aid to Graves and also in detaining the *Torbay* and *Price William* at Jamaica; some of Hood's dispatches to Graves arrived only a day before Hood himself, while others were never delivered; Graves should have kept his ships collected and ready, as he had promised, and should have moved sooner to the Chesapeake. Retrospect makes clear these and other errors.[25]

The failure to save Cornwallis's army in the autumn of 1781 was the most spectacular display of Britain's naval bungling, but far from the first. In 1775 and 1776 the British navy threw away four opportunities to halt the rebels' progress. Their first chance came in June 1775 at the Battle of Bunker Hill. When the American siege army entrenched itself in the heights upon Charleston neck overlooking Boston, it chanced its own destruction. With their complete naval superiority, the British merely had to land sufficient forces behind the rebels to seal off the neck of land and to prevent the colonists from relieving their comrades dug in on the hill. Instead, the British used their naval superiority to land troops at the foot of the peninsula, men who then had to take the elevated ground. The redcoats eventually carried the American position, but only after suffering the loss of nearly half the 2,400 soldiers they committed to the engagement.[26]

Incredibly, the Americans gave the British navy yet more chances to capture their principal army during the campaign for New York in 1776. Sir William Howe's army, rebuilt and reorganized in Nova Scotia after evacuating Boston, and augmented with reinforcements until it numbered over 30,000 men, the largest expeditionary force Britain had ever sent overseas, began landing on Long Island in late August. The fleet that landed it was a huge armada, comprising over thirty warships and 400 transports. To oppose this force Washington had no navy and only about 19,000 men, split between Manhattan and Long Island. By thus dividing his forces in the face of vastly superior numbers, Washington had invited disaster, and following the initial engagement on Long Island the American army appeared to be doomed. It had straggled into the prepared defenses at Brooklyn, but the British navy under Admiral Howe needed only to send a sufficient force up the East River to cut off any possible American retreat to Manhattan. Howe could thus bag half of Washington's army. A northeast storm blew up to prevent any sort of easy sailing up the East River, and it rained incessantly for two days. But that need not have stopped Lord Howe from bringing up enough frigates to have prevented an American escape. Howe's ships would have had to pull themselves up the river by their anchors, a dreary, backbreaking labor, but a tactic that the British had used often before and would use again. Instead, the admiral was less determined to defeat the Americans than to placate them, and the British navy was nowhere to be seen when, under cover of storm and fog on the night of August 29, Washington managed to evacuate his besieged American defenders. Strangely, the American general could get boats into position, but, apparently, the commander of the British fleet in North America, heir to a proud naval tradition, could not.

The British navy had, together with the army, produced the failures at Bunker Hill and Long Island. However, it managed all by itself to lose an opportunity to reverse the war in the South. The instance occurred in Georgia. At the onset of the Revolution, Georgia had a large number of loyalists, as well as a popular and able royal governor, Sir James Wright. But to secure Georgia for the Crown the British needed to take Savannah. Early in 1776 circumstances gave the British navy an opportunity to do just that.

General William Howe, cooped up in Boston after Britain's pyrrhic victory at Bunker Hill, was kept alive during the winter of 1776 by the British navy, which he kept busy with forage operations, along the coast of North America. One of these expeditions included armed schooners, transports with 200 marines, and a frigate, the *Scarborough*, sent to Savannah to secure rice. What they sought was indeed there. Some twenty ships loaded with rice rested at anchor near Hutchinson's Island in the south branch of the Savannah River above the capital.

Scarborough and its convoy rendezvoused with another force of four smaller armed craft and several auxiliary vessels, and the whole force reached the mouth of the river and dropped anchor near Cockspur Island early in February, 1776. Their arrival threw the Whigs, who had managed to seize control of the town and put Governor Wright under house arrest, into a panic. The council of safety issued several hurried proclamations, and Lachlan McIntosh, commander of Georgia's tiny continental regiment, assumed command of Savannah's defenses. He had at his disposal a slovenly militia of 300 to 400 men on the verge of mutiny. He was desperate, for as he later told Washington, Savannah was then an "open, straggling, defenseless, and deserted town." Wright made it more deserted when he escaped with his family on the night of February 11 and boarded the *Scarborough*.

Had the British acted decisively, Savannah could have been taken. Wright, fully aware of the situation, urged the navy to send its marines ashore to storm the town, but Naval Captain Andrew Barclay, the expedition's commander, settled for using his marines as foragers. His orders had told him to get rice, so he would get rice. Fooling the militia defenders ashore by some apparently aimless maneuvers, he managed by skillful navigation to bring a schooner, a sloop, and some boats up the north branch of the river to the "back," or northeast end of Hutchinson's Island. Then some 170 marines landed on the island, walked across it to the anchored riceboats, and seized them. Loyalist sailors rendered the task absurdly easy, another measure of sentiment in Savannah at the time. The patriots sought to stop the operation by shoving fireboats toward the captured vessels, but managed to burn only two. The British then brought off eighteen riceboats by some more skillful navigation, bringing them back through a passage that, according to one of the marine commanders, had been "never before attempted for ships of their draft of water."[27]

Britain had garnered the rice, but nothing else. Indeed, soon after the rice boats were dispatched, McIntosh's militia opened fire on the British marines still on Hutchinson Island. A rout ensued, and the militia found itself looking at marines, to quote McIntosh, "running in the marsh in a laughable manner for fear of our rifles." Soon after Barclay sailed away, leaving the Whigs to believe they had won a clear victory. The British had not dared land, the militia had seen the backs of redcoats, and the naval representatives of His Majesty's government seemed to appear as cowardly thieves. By March 8, after it was all over, McIntosh thought the whole thing a patriot victory. The British had lost rather than gained "any reputation" and had done the province of Georgia an "honor" by harassing it.[28] "And thusly," Wright observed, "you see what a difference a few days have made in the state of affairs here."[29]

Still another lost opportunity occurred in 1776. During the previous year, Governor Josiah Martin of North Carolina had taken refuge aboard a British sloop of war. From that secure position he had urged the British to send a contingent of regular troops to North Carolina. To assist the regulars, Martin went on, he would arm 30,000 loyalists. The governor overestimated, but he did believe that he could muster about 3,000 people, mostly recent Highland immigrants or persons of Highland Scots descent, to serve the king. They needed arms, but the expedition could deliver weapons.

The idea had merit. The British army and navy would have the chance to cooperate with loyal civilians. Moreover, the result of any military triumph would mean the restoration of proper civilian government. Once loyal rule was established in one colony in the middle of the South, the British could think of reestablishing it all over the South. "The vast advantages," Martin assured London, "that I apprehend are to be made of the strength which this Province yields within itself, for the support of His Majesty's Government, not only here but in the neighboring Provinces are in my opinion of the greatest importance and such as I think cannot sufficiently recommend to your lordship's attention."[30]

The British commander-in-chief in Boston, General Thomas Gage, liked the idea and dispatched two Scots, both regular army officers, to recruit. The ministry also responded favorably, and by the middle of October prepared to implement the scheme. The king earmarked four regiments of infantry and two companies of artillery to leave from Cork for North Carolina, and ordered William Howe (who had replaced Gage in August) to send down from Boston what forces he could spare. All that was an auspicious start. If the loyalists could now organize, and the British expedition could land and support them, loyalty might prevail before rebellion acquired much chance.

Soon, however, everything went wrong. Not only were the reinforcements slow to leave Cork, but the force that sailed from Boston was terribly weak, consisting of from only 1,200 to 1,500 "boys," and it also proceeded south at a snail's pace. By the time it at last reached the Cape Fear River in mid-March, disaster had struck, rendering the whole point of the expedition fruitless.[31]

Expecting the British regulars to be on North Carolina soil by mid-February, Governor Martin issued a proclamation against rebellion and urged the loyalists to join with the British army. Soon, approximately 1,400 Highlanders were mustered. Unfortunately, they received no support, for the British navy did not arrive with the promised redcoats. Patriots, informed of the plan through a spy, mustered to battle the Highlanders, whom they defeated at Moore's Creek Bridge on February 27. Loyalist hopes in North Carolina were shattered.[32]

Almost two more months elapsed before the reinforcements at last arrived from England. By late May they were in place under General Henry Clinton, but there were no armed loyalists remaining in North Carolina. Clutching at straws, Clinton and the fleet commander, Sir Peter Parker, opted to move against South Carolina, where they thought they might establish some kind of post near Charleston on Sullivan's Island. If they left a garrison of redcoats there, it could perhaps serve as a rallying point for loyalists. The scheme was nonsensical. The garrison would have been terribly isolated, and it would only have served to anger patriots rather than intimidate them. But so incompetent was the joint command at this time that they did not even land on the island. Protected at its southern end by a fort of palmetto logs, an installation whose big guns could bring under deadly fire any British ships attempting to menace the city, the island's northern end was nearly defenseless. Instead of landing his forces on it, however, Clinton landed them on Long Island, to its north, after reconnoitering Sullivan's Island in a small boat and concluding the surf was too rough for an amphibious landing. He simply took the word of some local people that his troops could wade from Long Island to Sullivan's. In fact they could not; even at low tide pools were well over the heads of his men, and cross currents made them difficult to negotiate even in small boats. Thus, Clinton's men got ashore at Long Island, then they sat idly and waited for something to happen. There followed a series of comic-opera interchanges between Clinton and Parker, in which each promised a diversion if the other would do something. In the end Parker decided to "do" something. He sought to reduce the fort on Sullivan's Island by bombardment, but he could not move his ships in close enough to be effective. So he lost three ships and sixty-one men killed and wounded, and with nothing to show for it, for his cannon fire did virtually no damage to the fort. With all its mobility and naval power, the British navy had managed to suffer a defeat.[33] These two southern failures were significant for British fortunes. In their aftermath the Whigs preserved their power and the loyalists remained cowed. The British navy's ineffectivness, therefore, had proven a crucial detriment to Britain's cause from the very beginning.

Of course, the British navy's record was not one of unmitigated failure during the revolutionary war. It performed more than adequately in the difficult areas of transporting men and materials across the Atlantic. It played a remarkable role in establishing complete mastery of Lake Champlain in 1777, affording General John Burgoyne with an excellent start for his invasion of New York. That his campaign ended in failure at Saratoga that autumn was due to the general's shortcomings, not to those of the Royal Navy.[34] Finally, the navy scored spectacular victories in the Caribbean in the seldom remembered year that followed the British disaster at Yorktown.

Thus the Royal Navy's record during the American Revolution, like the army's, was inconsistent. There was much to blame, as well as some success. But in the end, the government, the king and cabinet, must take responsibility for the failure in America. Its attempt to coerce the colonies involved it in a war that it did not understand. It wanted to rule America, but it did not know how. It could not formulate a winning strategy, and it could not inspire in most of its naval officers a desire to strive with the resolution that might have brought victory.

Notes

The following abbreviations are used throughout in each citation of the publications and scholarly societies listed below.

AHR	*American Historical Review*
APS	American Philosophical Society
AQ	*American Quarterly*
C 11A	Archives Nationales, Colonies, Series C 11A
CHR	*Canadian Historical Review*
CHS	Connecticut Historical Society, Hartford
CO	British Public Record Office Papers, Colonial Office (All references are to Series 5)
CVSP	William P. Palmer et al., eds., *Calendar of Virginia State Papers and Other Manuscripts, 1652–1781*, 11 vols. (Richmond, 1875–1883)
CWRL	Colonial Williamsburg Research Library, Williamsburg, Virginia
EHR	*English Historical Review*
GHQ	*Georgia Historical Quarterly*
HHL	Henry Huntington Library
HLQ	*Huntington Library Quarterly*
HSP	Historical Society of Pennsylvania
IHS	Indiana Historical Society, Indianapolis

JCC	Worthington C. Ford et al., eds., *Journals of the Continental Congress*, 34 vols. (Washington, D.C., United States Government Printing Office, 1904–1937)
JMH	*Journal of Modern History*
JSH	*Journal of Southern History*
LC	Library of Congress, Washington, D.C.
LD	Paul H. Smith, ed., *Letters of Delegates to Congress* (Washington, D.C., Library of Congress, 1976–)
LGV	H.R. McIlwaine, ed. *Official Letters of the Governors of the State of Virginia*, 3 vols. (Richmond, Virginia State Library, 1931–1932)
LMCC	Edmund C. Burnett, *Letters of Members of the Continental Congress*, 8 vols. (Washington, D.C., Carnegie Institution of Washington 1921–1936)
LP	Lee Papers, New York Historical Society *Collections*, 4 vols., (New York, 1871–1874)
MHM	*Maryland Historical Magazine*
MHS	Massachusetts Historical Society, Boston
MHSQ	*Maine Historical Society Quarterly*
MVHR	*Mississippi Valley Historical Review*
NA	National Archives, Washington, D.C.
NCHR	*North Carolina Historical Review*
NEQ	*New England Quarterly*
NJH	*New Jersey History*
NJHS	New Jersey Historical Society, Newark
NYHS	New York Historical Society,
PCC	Papers of the Continental Congress, National Archives, Washington, D.C.
PG	Richard K. Showman et al., eds., *The Papers of General Nathanel Greene* (Chapel Hill, N.C., University of North Carolina, 1979–)
PGW	W. W. Abbot et al., eds., *The Papers of George Washington* (Charlottesville, Virginia, University Press of Virginia, 1983–)
PH	*Pennsylvania History*
PMHB	*Pennsylvania Magazine of History and Biography*
PSQ	*Political Science Quarterly*
RAPQ	*Report de l'Archiviste de la Province de Québec*
RIsH	*Rhode Island History*

SCHS   South Carolina Historical Society, Columbia
VMHB   *Virginia Magazine of History and Biography*
VSL   Virginia State Library, Richmond
WMQ   *William and Mary Quarterly*
WW   John C. Fitzpatrick, ed., *The Writings of George Washington from the Original Manuscript Sources, 1745–1799*, 39 vols. (Washington, D.C., United States Government Printing Office, 1931–1944)

Chapter 1:
The Colonial Background to the American Victory

1. Ralph Waldo Emerson, "Concord Hymn," lines 1–4, in Sculley Bradley et al., eds., *The American Tradition in Literature*, 2 vols. (New York, W.W. Norton, 1967), 1:1211.

2. Henry Wadsworth Longfellow, "Paul Revere's Ride," lines 111–18, in Henry Wadsworth Longfellow, *Tales of a Wayside Inn* (1872; reprint Little, Brown, Boston; 1915), 29.

3. On the Elizabethan military system see Lindsay Boynton, *The Elizabethan Militia, 1558–1638* (London, Routledge and K. Paul, 1967); William L. Shea, *The Virginia Militia in the Seventeenth Century* (Baton Rouge, Louisiana State University, 1983), Introduction; and T. H. Breen, "The Covenanted Militia of Massachusetts Bay: English Background and New World Development," in T. H. Breen, *Puritans and Adventurers: Change and Persistence in Early America* (New York, Oxford University Press, 1980), 27–33. Elizabeth's reforms dated from 1573; the militia itself had been formally established in the Assize of Arms, 1181.

4. On the origins of the British army see J. W. Fortescue, *A History of the British Army*, 13 vols. (London, Macmillan, 1899–1930), 1:3, 204–28, 279–331; Michael Carver, *The Seven Ages of the British Army* (New York, Beaufort, 1984), 1–38; John Childs, *The Army of Charles II* (London, Routledge & K. Paul, 1976), 1–20.

5. J. R. Western, *The English Militia in the Eighteenth Century: The Story of a Political Issue, 1660–1802* (London, Routledge and K. Paul, 1965), 3–74 et seq.

6. An early, but still useful, attempt to describe the evolution of American military institutions in terms of regression to medieval practice can be found in Daniel Boorstin, *The Americans: The Colonial Experience* (New York, Random House, 1958), 341–74. On the Virginia system, see Shea, *Virginia Militia*; on Massachusetts, see Jack S. Radabaugh, "The Militia of Colonial Massachusetts," *Military Affairs* 18 (1954): 1–18, and Douglas E. Leach, "The Military System of Plymouth Colony," *NEQ* 24 (1951): 342–64. An important brief treatment of the whole range of colonial military practice is John Shy, "A New Look at the Colonial Militia," *WMQ*, 3d ser., 20 (1963): 175–85; reprinted and revised in John Shy, *A People Numerous and Armed: Reflections on the Military Struggle for American Independence* (New York, Oxford University Press, 1976), 23–33. The best general account of the development of colonial military institutions in the colonial wars is Douglas Edward Leach, *Arms for Empire: A Military History of the British Colonies*

in North America, 1607–1763 (New York, Macmillan, 1973). Slaves were armed and trained as soldiers in South Carolina during the Yamassee War; see Peter Wood, *Black Majority: Negroes in Colonial South Carolina from 1670 through the Stono Rebellion* (New York, Knopf, 1975), 124–30.

7. For class animosity as an element in the cause of Bacon's Rebellion, see Edmund Morgan, *American Slavery, American Freedom* (New York, W.W. Norton, 1975), 215–92; for alternative views, see Darrett Rutman and Anita Rutman, *A Place in Time* (New York, W.W. Norton, 1984), 86; and Shea, *Virginia Militia*, chap. 6. Governor Berkeley is quoted in Boorstin, *Colonial Experience*, 353. On the growth in exclusiveness of the Virginia militia, see Shea, *Virginia Militia*, 139.

8. The literature on the origins of slavery is vast; a good place to start is with Morgan, *American Slavery, American Freedom*, and Gloria L. Main, *Tobacco Colony* (Princeton, Princeton University, 1982), 97–106. On the militia as a police force for the slave system, see Rutman and Rutman, *A Place in Time*, 175; Rhys Isaac, *The Transformation of Virginia* (Chapel Hill, University of North Carolina, 1982), 106.

9. Shy, *A People...Armed*, 27, 264, n. 18. The adaptation of lines from Dryden's "Cymon and Iphiginia" was by Edward Kimber; quoted in Isaac, *Transformation of Virginia*, 107.

10. Breen, *Puritans and Adventurers*, 25–45; Harold E. Selesky, "Military Leadership in an American Colonial Society: Connecticut, 1635–1785" (Ph.D. diss., Yale University, 1984).

11. Archibald Hanna, Jr., "New England Military Institutions, 1693–1750" (Ph.D. diss., Yale University, 1951), 121, 283–90. See also Leach, *Arms for Empire*, chap. 1.

12. Alan Guy, *Oeconomy and Discipline: Officership and Administration in the British Army, 1714–63* (Manchester, Manchester University, 1985), 91. The comparative annual rent and profit on a farm of 100 acres are from Joan Thirsk, ed., *The Agrarian History of England and Wales*, 5 vols. to date (Cambridge, Eng., Cambridge University, 1967–), vol. 5, pt. 2, 88–89. (The ensign who invested £170 in his commission could expect to collect £66 18s 4d *per annum* as a salary, almost twice the profit on the farm, but less than the rentier's income from the lease.)

13. This description is derived from John Ferling's careful analysis of the social composition of the Virginia Regiment in 1756 and 1757, "Soldiers for Virginia: Who Served in the French and Indian War?" *VMHB* 94 (1986): 307–28. For another important study that reaches different conclusions from the same sources, see James R. W. Titus, " 'Soldiers When They Choose to Be So': Virginians at War, 1754–1763" (Ph.D. diss., Rutgers University, 1983). On Washington's role in constituting and shaping the Virginia Regiment, see Don Higginbotham, *George Washington and the American Military Tradition* (Athens, Ga., University of Georgia, 1985), chap. 1.

14. The estimate of Massachusetts participation is from Fred Anderson, *A People's Army: Massachusetts Soldiers and Society in the Seven Years' War* (Chapel Hill, University of North Carolina, 1984), 58–60. On Connecticut, see Selesky, "Military Leadership," 295–96. The men most eligible for service were those aged between sixteen and twenty-nine; such men made up nearly three-fourths of the Massachusetts provincial soldiers in 1756.

15. This summary is based on a more complete account of how the provincial armies of Massachusetts functioned in Anderson, *A People's Army*, 26–62.

16. Ibid., 39–48, 111–41, 162–64, 167–96.

17. Diary of Major Seth Pomeroy, entry for June 21, 1745, in Louis Effingham de Forest, ed., *The Journals and Papers of Seth Pomeroy* (New Haven, Yale University, 1926), 37. I have modernized the spelling and punctuation of this and all subsequent quotations from eighteenth-century journals.

18. Diary of Captain Samuel Jenks, entry for August 30, 1760, in Henry F. Jenks, ed., "Samuel Jenks, his Journal of the Campaign in 1760," MHS *Proceedings* 25 (1889–90): 374.

19. In this connection see John Ferling, "The New England Soldier: A Study in Changing Perceptions," *AQ* 33 (1981): 26–45. He argues for a greater secularization in this view by the French and Indian War than I believe was the case for most New England provincials. See Anderson, *A People's Army*, chap. 7.

20. David Perry, "Recollections of an Old Soldier," *Magazine of History* 137 (1928): 23. Perry was describing an incident from 1762.

21. Diary of James Henderson, entry for July 20, 1759, New England Historic and Genealogical Society Library, Boston. Figures on punishments in Amherst's 1759 expedition are from Anderson, *A People's Army*, 137, n. 80.

22. Diary of Gibson Clough, entries of July 4 and September 30, 1759, Essex Institute, Salem, Massachusetts.

23. Massachusetts's casualty rate can be inferred from the death rate of 51.1 per thousand sustained by its troops from 1756, the only year of the war for which a reasonably accurate statistical series has been developed. Deaths in this year were almost wholly from disease and accident, and evidence indicates that they were substantially underreported; thus to apply the death rate per thousand from 1756 to enlistment figures for the other war years yields a highly conservative estimate. The number of dead for the war arrived at by this method amounts to between 0.6 and 0.7 percent of the province's maximum estimated population in 1764, of 259,000. Deaths among men aged 16 to 29 during the war would have amounted to 5 or 6 percent of the total age cohort. (See Anderson, *A People's Army*, 58–60, 106–7, 239–41). For comparative figures from the Civil War and the two World Wars, see Richard B. Morris et al., eds., *The Encyclopedia of American History* (New York, Harper & Row, 1976), 292, 372, 443, 649.

24. This theme has been developed by John Murrin in an important essay, "The French and Indian War, the American Revolution, and the Counterfactual Hypothesis: Reflections on Lawrence Henry Gipson and John Shy," *Reviews in American History* 1 (1973): 307–18. See also Jack P. Greene, "The Seven Years' War and the American Revolution: The Causal Relationship Reconsidered," in Peter Marshall and Glyn Williams, eds., *The British Atlantic Empire before the American Revolution* (Totowa, N.J., F. Cass, 1980), 85–105.

Chapter 2:
The Continental Army and the American Victory

1. George F. Scheer, ed., *Private Yankee Doodle: Being a Narrative of Some of the Adventures, Dangers, and Sufferings of a Revolutionary Soldier* (Boston, Little, Brown, 1962), p. 291.

2. Don Higginbotham, "The American Militia: A Traditional Institution with Revolutionary Responsibilities," in Don Higginbotham, ed., *Reconsiderations on the Revolutionary War: Selected Essays* (Westport, Conn., Greenwood Press, 1978), 83–103.

3. Scheer, *Private Yankee Doodle*, 290.

4. See Eric Robson, *The American Revolution in Its Political and Military Aspects, 1763–1783* (New York, W. W. Norton, 1966), 93–174. The problem of space became more obvious to British forces as the war lengthened. Wrote Hessian General Friedrich Wilhelm von Lossberg in early 1778: "It seems that we are far from an anticipated peace because the . . . land is too large, and there are too many people. The more land we win, the weaker our army gets in the field." Quoted in Ernst Kipping, ed., *The Hessian View of America* (Monmouth Beach, N.J., 1971), 34.

5. John Adams to Hezekiah Niles, February 13, 1818, in Charles Francis Adams, ed., *The Works of John Adams*, 10 vols. (Boston, 1850–56), 10:282–83. On the problem of localism, see Lawrence Delbert Cress, *Citizens in Arms: The Army and Militia in American Society to the War of 1812* (Chapel Hill, N.C., University of North Carolina, 1982), 3–14; E. Wayne Carp, *To Starve the Army at Pleasure: Continental Army Administration and American Political Culture, 1775–1783* (Chapel Hill, N.C., University of North Carolina, 1984), 3–15; and James Kirby Martin and Mark Edward Lender, *A Respectable Army: The Military Origins of the Republic, 1763–1789* (Arlington Heights, Ill., Harlan Davidson, 1982), 173–79.

6. Dartmouth to Gage, January 27, 1775, in Clarence E. Carter, ed., *The Correspondence of General Thomas Gage . . . 1763–1775*, 2 vols. (New Haven, Conn., Yale University, 1933), 2:179–83.

7. James Thacher, *Military Journal of the American Revolution* (Hartford, Conn., 1862), 16–17.

8. Ibid., 21.

9. Robert K. Wright, Jr., *The Continental Army* (Washington, D.C., Center of Military History, United States Army, 1983), 15–20.

10. Ibid., 21–29; See also proceedings of the Continental Congress, June 14–17, 1775, in Worthington C. Ford., ed., *JCC*, 2:89–97.

11. Quoted in Charles Royster, *A Revolutionary People at War: The Continental Army and American Character, 1775–1783* (Chapel Hill, N.C., University of North Carolina, 1979), 25, 25–53 for a detailed discussion of the *rage militaire*.

12. Ford, *JCC*, June 30, 1775, 2:111–23.

13. "Address From the General Officers to the Soldiery of the Grand Continental Army," November 24, 1775, in Peter Force, ed., *American Archives*, 4th ser., 6 vols. (Washington, D.C., 1837–46), 3:1666–67. See also "To the American Soldiery," November 14, 1775, and "To the Worthy Officers and Soldiers in the American Army," November 24, 1775, in Force, *American Archives*, 4th ser., 3:1557–59, 1667–68. Throughout this essay, manpower estimates are based on the Continental army's monthly strength reports compiled in Charles H. Lesser, ed., *The Sinews of Independence* (Chicago, University of Chicago, 1976).

14. Washington to Joseph Reed, February 1, 1776, in John C. Fitzpatrick, ed., *WW*, 4:299–301.

15. Washington to John Augustine Washington, December 18, 1776, Fitzpatrick, *WW*, 6:396–99.

16. On Howe's confusion, see Howe to Germain, December 31, 1776, April 2, May 31, June 3, and July 16, 1777, in Great Britain, Royal Historical Manuscripts Commission, *Report on the Manuscripts of Mrs. Stopford-Sackville, of Drayton House, Northhamptonshire*, 2 vols. (Hereford, England, Mackie, 1904–10), 2:53–55, 63–65, 68, 72–73.

17. Washington to John Augustine Washington, December 18, 1776, Fitzpatrick, *WW*, 6:399.

18. On Washington's plans, see his letters to the President of Congress, September 24 and December 16, 1776, Fitzpatrick, *WW*, 6:106–16, 379–81. Congress basically approved Washington's plans when it provided for long-term enlistments. See Ford, *JCC*, November 12, 1776, 6:944–45.

19. Adams to James Warren, January 7, 1776, in Worthington C. Ford, ed., *The Warren-Adams Letters*, 2 vols. (Boston, MHS, 1917–25), 1:197–98. See also the essay by "Caractacus" entitled "On Standing Armies," August 21, 1775, in Force, *American Archives*, 4th ser., 3:219–21, and Cress, *Citizens in Arms*, 53–66.

20. Martin and Lender, *A Respectable Army*, 65–97.

21. For the text of the Articles of War, see Ford, *JCC*, September 20, 1776, 5:787–807. See also General Orders, October 3, 1776, Fitzpatrick, *WW*, 6:151, announcing the implementation of the new Articles.

22. Washington to Philip Schuyler, June 25, 1775, Fitzpatrick, *WW*, 3:302–4; Ford, *JCC*, July 20, 1775, 2:194.

23. See Ford, *JCC*, 5:448–49, 526, and Jonathan G. Rossie, *The Politics of Command in the American Revolution* (Syracuse, Syracuse University, 1975), 96–117. Also see Rossie's essay later in this collection.

24. Howe to Carleton, April 5, 1777, *Stopford-Sackville Mss.*, 2:65–66.

25. Focused as he was on Washington's army, Howe could not fathom Burgoyne's entrapment. He had failed to reckon with the Continental army's regionalized command structure. On Howe's confusion in 1777, see Howe to Germain, October 22 and November 30, 1777, and Germain to Howe, February 4, 1778, *Stopford-Sackville Mss.*, 2:79–81, 92–93, and Frey's essay later in this collection.

26. Germain to Clinton, March 8, 1778, *Stopford-Sackville Mss.*, 2:94–101.

27. Ira D. Gruber, "Britain's Southern Strategy," in W. Robert Higgins, ed., *The Revolutionary War in the South: Power, Conflict, and Leadership* (Durham, N.C., Duke University, 1979), 205–38; Piers Mackesy, "The Redcoat Revived," in William M. Fowler, Jr., and Wallace Coyle, eds., *The American Revolution: Changing Perspectives* (Boston, Northeastern University, 1979), 172–88.

28. On February 27, 1776, Congress established the Southern Department to consist of Virginia, North Carolina, South Carolina, and Georgia. See Ford, *JCC*, 4:174. On partisan war in the region, see Clyde R. Ferguson, "Functions of the Partisan-Militia in the South during the American Revolution: An Interpretation," in Higgins., ed., *Revolutionary War in the South*, 239–58, and various essays in Ronald Hoffman et al., eds. *An Uncivil War: The Southern Backcountry during the American Revolution* (Charlottesville, Va., University Press of Virginia, 1985).

29. Greene to Washington, December 28, 1780, in George Washington Greene, *The Life of Nathanael Greene, Major-General in the Army of the Revolution*, 3 vols. (New York, 1867–71), 3:131–32.

30. Cornwallis advocated that all British forces be concentrated in Virginia. The British then would "have a Stake to fight for and a successful battle may give us

America." See Cornwallis to General William Phillips, April 10, 1781, Cornwallis Papers, P.R.O.30/11.85.

31. Scheer, ed., *Private Yankee Doodle*, 284–85.

32. "Deserters from the Rebels and Others," June, 1778, *Stopford-Sackville Mss.*, 2:116. On the propblem more generally, see Thad W. Tate, "Desertion from the American Revolutionary Army" (M.A. thesis, University of North Carolina, 1948), and James Howard Edmonson, "Desertion in the American Army during the Revolutionary War" (Ph.D. diss., Louisiana State University, 1971).

33. Germain to Clinton, March 8, 1778, and Clinton to Germain, January 11, 1779, *Stopford-Sackville Mss.*, 2:98, 123; Benedict Arnold to Samuel Holden Parsons, September 8, 1780, Peter Force Transcripts, Library of Congress. See also James Kirby Martin, "Benedict Arnold's Treason as Political Protest," *Parameters* 11 (1981): 63–74.

34. "A Jersey Soldier," *New Jersey Journal*, May 16, 1779, in *Documents Relating to the Revolutionary History of the State of New Jersey*, 2d ser., 5 vols. (Trenton, John Murphy, 1901–1917), 3:307–9. See also James Kirby Martin, "A 'Most Undisciplined, Profligate Crew': Protest and Defiance in the Continental Ranks, 1776–1783," in Ronald Hoffman and Peter J. Albert, eds., *Arms and Independence: The Military Character of the American Revolution* (Charlottesville, Va., University Press of Virginia, 1984), 119–40.

35. Washington to the President of Congress, January 23, 1781, Fitzpatrick, *WW*, 21:135–36.

36. Alexander McDougall to Greene, March 24, 1779, Nathanael Greene Papers, APS.

37. Richard H. Kohn, "The Inside History of the Newburgh Conspiracy: America and the Coup d'État,"*WMQ*, 3d ser., 27 (1970):187–220.

38. Quoted in Douglas Southall Freeman et al., *George Washington: A Biography*, 7 vols. (New York, Scribners, 1949–1957), 5:435.

39. Martin and Lender, *A Respectable Army*, 194–208. See also Richard H. Kohn, "American Generals of the Revolution: Subordination and Restraint," in Higginbotham, ed., *Reconsiderations*, 104–23.

40. John Shy, "The Military Conflict Considered as a Revolutionary War," in Shy, *A People Numerous and Armed: Reflections on the Military Struggle for American Independence* (New York, Oxford University Press, 1976), 195–224. See also Martin and Lender, *A Respectable Army*, 171–79, and John Ellis, *Armies in Revolution* (New York, 1974).

41. Elias Boudinot, *An Oration, Delivered at Elizabethtown, New Jersey...on the Fourth of July, 1793, Being the Seventeenth Anniversary of the Independence of America* (Elizabethtown, N.J., 1793), 16.

Chapter 3:
The American Soldier and the American Victory

1. Mark Edward Lender, "The Enlisted Line: The Continental Soldiers of New Jersey" (Ph.D. diss., Rutgers University, 1975), chap. 1; Charles Royster, *A Revolutionary People at War: The Continental Army and American Character, 1775–1783* (Chapel Hill, N.C., University of North Carolina, 1976), 28, 32–33.

2. James Thacher, *Military Journal of the American Revolution* (Hartford, Conn., 1862), 59–60; John C. Dann, ed., *The Revolution Remembered: Eyewitness Accounts of the War for Independence* (Chicago, University of Chicago, 1980), 8; Frank Moore, *The Diary of the Revolution*, 2 vols. (Hartford, Conn., 1876), 1:270; Hezekiah Niles, *Principles and Acts of the Revolution in America* (Baltimore, 1822), 305–6.

3. George F. Scheer and Hugh F. Rankin, eds., *Rebels and Redcoats* (Cleveland, World Publishing, 1957), 92; Aaron Wright, "Revolutionary Journal . . . , 1775," *Historical Magazine* 6 (1862), 209; Thacher, *Journal*, 59–60; Charles K. Bolton, *The Private Soldier Under Washington* (New York, Scribners, 1902), 13; Jesse Lukens to John Shaw, Jr., September 13, 1775, *American Historical Record* 1 (1872): 547–48; Sidney Kaplan, "Rank and Status among Massachusetts Continental Officers," *AHR* 56 (1951): 320–22.

4. Royster, *Revolutionary People*, 25–53; Thacher, *Journal*, 60; James Kirby Martin, "A 'Most Undisciplined, Profligate Crew': Protest and Defiance in the Continental Ranks, 1776–1783," in Ronald Hoffman and Peter Albert, eds., *Arms and Independence: The Military Character of the American Revolution* (Charlottesville, Va., University Press of Virginia, 1984), 122; Simeon Lyman, "Journal . . . ," *CHS Collections* 7 (1899): 128–31; Alexander Garden, *Anecdotes of the Revolutionary War in America* (Charleston, S.C., 1822): 199–200.

5. Thacher, *Journal*, 60; Don Higginbotham, "The American Militia: A Traditional Institution with Revolutionary Responsibilities," in Don Higginbotham, ed., *Reconsiderations on the Revolutionary War* (Westport, Conn., Greenwood Press, 1978), 84; Nathanael Greene to Jacob Greene, September 18, 1776, Richard K. Showman, *PG* 1: 303; Worthington C. Ford, ed., *JCC*, 5:762–63, 788; John Shy, *A People Numerous and Armed: Reflections on the Military Struggle for American Independence* (New York, Oxford University Press, 1976), 173.

6. Martin, "Undisciplined Crew," in Hoffman and Albert, *Arms and Independence*, 124–25; Lender, "Enlisted Line," iii, 110–39; Mark Edward Lender, "The Social Structure of the New Jersey Brigade: The Continental Line as an American Standing Army," in Peter Karsten, ed., *The Military in America: From the Colonial Era to the Present* (New York, Free Press, 1980), 36–38; Lender, "The Mind of the Rank and File: Patriotism and Motivation in the Continental Line," in William C. Wright, ed., *New Jersey in the American Revolution* (Trenton, N.J. Historical Commission, 1976), 21–34; John R. Sellers, "The Virginia Continental Line, 1775–1780" (Ph.D. diss., Tulane University, 1968), 50–54; John R. Sellers, "The Common Soldier in the American Revolution," in Stanley Underdal, ed., *Military History of the American Revolution* (Washington, Office of Air Force History, 1976), 153–55; John R. Sellers, "The Origins and Careers of the New England Soldier: Noncommissioned Officers and Privates in the Massachusetts Continental Line" (Unpublished paper, American Historical Association Convention, 1972); Edward Papefuse and Gregory A. Stiverson, "General Smallwood's Recruits: The Peacetime Career of the Revolutionary War Private," *WMQ*, 3d ser., 30 (1973): 131–32; James Kirby Martin and Mark Edward Lender, *A Respectable Army: The Military Origins of the Republic, 1763–1789* (Arlington Heights, Ill., Harlan Davidson, 1982), 90–93; Robert A. Gross, *The Minutemen and their World* (New York, Hill and Wang, 1976), 146–53; Shy, *People Numerous and Armed*, 173.

7. Royster, *Revolutionary People*, 132–33; Robert C. Bray and Paul E. Bushnell,

eds., *Diary of a Common Soldier in the American Revolution, 1775–1783: The Military Journal of Jeremiah Greenman* (DeKalb, Ill., Northern Illinois University, 1978), 72–73; George F. Scheer, ed., *Private Yankee Doodle: Being a Narrative of Some of the Adventures, Dangers, and Sufferings of a Revolutionary Soldier* (Boston, Little, Brown, 1962), 197–98.

8. Bolton, *Private Soldier*, 21; William Gilmore Sims, ed., *The Army Correspondence of Colonel John Laurens in the Years 1777–1778* (New York, 1867), 108, 115–18; Benjamin Quarles, *The Negro in the American Revolution* (Chapel Hill, University of North Carolina, 1961), ix, 68–80; Scheer, *Private Yankee Doodle*, 245–46.

9. Bolton, *Private Soldier*; Royster, *Revolutionary People*; Higginbotham, "American Militia," in Higginbotham, *Reconsiderations*; Robert Middlekauff, *The Glorious Cause: The American Revolution, 1763–1789* (New York, Oxford University Press, 1982), 334–36, 364–65, 510–12; Middlekauff, "Why Men Fought in the American Revolution," *HLQ* 43 (1980): 135–48; Allan R. Millet and Peter Maslowski, *For the Common Defense: A Military History of the United States of America* (New York, Free Press, 1984).

10. Mark E. Lender and James Kirby Martin, eds., *Citizen Soldier: The Revolutionary War Journal of Joseph Bloomfield*, NJHS *Collections* 18 (1982): 37–38; Thomas Ewing, ed., *The Military Journal of George Ewing (1754–1824)* (Yonkers, N.Y., T. Ewing, 1928), 13; Enoch Anderson, "Personal Recollections" Historical Society of Delaware *Papers* 16 (1896): 38.

11. Herbert T. Wade and Robert A. Lively, eds., *This Glorious Cause: The Adventures of Two Company Officers in Washington's Army* (Princeton, Princeton University, 1958), 224; Scheer, *Private Yankee Doodle*, 57–61, 196; Joseph Collins, *Autobiography*, in S. G. Miller, *Sixty Years in the Nueces Valley* (San Antonio, Tex., Naylor, 1930), 236–37; Thacher, *Journal* 188; MHS *Proceedings* 13 (1874): 244.

12. See authors and titles in n. 6 above.

13. Fitzpatrick, *WW*, 2:286; Frederic R. Kirkland, ed., *Journal of Lewis Beebe* (New York, New York Times, 1971), 27; William Young, "Journal," *PMHB* 8 (1884): 277.

14. Bolton, *Private Soldier*, 39, 53; Lender, "Mind of Rank and File," in Wright, *New Jersey in the Revolution*, 21–23; Lender, "Enlisted Line," 140–45; Royster, *Revolutionary People*, 268, 373–78; Higginbotham, "American Militia," in Higginbotham, *Reconsiderations*, 86–87; Millett and Maslowski, *Common Defense*, 56–57. For a negative assessment of the "traditional" viewpoint, see Richard H. Kohn, "The Social History of the American Soldier: A Review and Prospectus for Research," *AHR* 86 (1981): 553–67.

15. Middlekauff, *Glorious Cause*, 335–36.

16. Howard H. Peckham, ed., *Memoirs of the Life of John Adlum in the Revolutionary War* (Chicago, Caxton Club, 1968), 55–56; John McAuley Palmer, *General Von Steuben* (New Haven, Yale University, 1937), 157; Royster, *Revolutionary People*, 224–28; Middlekauff, *Glorious Cause*, 419; Greene to Governor Reed, March 18, 1781, Nathanael Greene Papers, HHL.

17. Scheer, *Private Yankee Doodle*, 289–90; Middlekauff, "Why Men Fought," 142–43.

18. Middlekauff, "Why Men Fought," 135–37; Sergeant R———, "The Battle of Princeton," *PMHB* 20 (1896): 518; *Archives of the State of New Jersey*, 2d ser.

(Newark, John Murphy, 1901), 17; "Elijah Fisher's Journal While in the War for Independence," *Magazine of History* 2 (1909): 31; Wade and Lively, *Glorious Cause*, 168, 195.

19. Scheer, *Private Yankee Doodle*, 280; Middlekauff, "Why Men Fought," 140; Richard Holmes, *Acts of War: The Behavior of Men in Battle* (New York, 1985), 25.

20. Middlekauff, "Why Men Fought," 147–48; Worthington C. Ford, ed., *Correspondence and Journals of Samuel Blachley Webb*, 3 vols. (New York, 1893), 2:231–32; Robert Cooper, *Courage in a Good Cause* (Lancaster, Pa., 1775), 24–25; John M. Roberts, ed., *Autobiography of a Revolutionary Soldier [James P. Collins]* (Clinton, La., 1859), 259–61; Scheer, *Private Yankee Doodle*, 24–25.

21. Howard H. Peckham, ed., *The Toll of Independence: Engagements and Battle Casualties of the American Revolution* (Chicago, University of Chicago, 1974), 133; Scheer and Rankin, *Rebels and Redcoats*, 92; Wade and Lively, *Glorious Cause*, 170–71; Bray and Bushnell, *Greenman*, 23; John Joseph Henry, *Account of Arnold's Campaign Against Quebec* (Albany, 1877), 107–15.

22. Dann, *Revolution Remembered*, 50; Anderson, "Personal Recollections," 21; Moore, *Diary*, 298; William H. W. Sabine, ed., *The New-York Diary of Lieutenant Jabez Fitch* (New York, Colbourn and Teague, 1954), 31–34.

23. Anderson, "Personal Recollections," 25; William S. Powell, ed., "A Connecticut Soldier Under Washington: Elisha Bostwick's Memoirs of the First Years of the Revolution," *WMQ*, 3d ser., 6 (1949): 101; Jared C. Lobdelb, ed., "The Revolutionary War Journal of Sergeant Thomas McCarty," NJHS *Proceedings* 80 (1964): 45; Elisha Stevens, *Fragments of Memoranda Written by Him in the War of the Revolution* (Meriden, Conn., Stevens, 1922), 2; Joseph Clark, "Diary," NJHS *Proceedings* 7 (1885): 98–99.

24. James Collins, *Autobiography*, 264–65; Steven E. Kagle, ed., *The Diary of Josiah Atkins* (New York, New York Times, 1975), 19, 25, 38, 40; Dann, *Revolution Remembered*, 81.

25. Scheer, *Private Yankee Doodle*, 68–69, 215–17; Henry Steele Commager and Richard B. Morris, eds., *The Spirit of 'Seventy-Six*, 2 vols. (Indianapolis, Bobbs, Merrill, 1958), 1:192–201; Wade and Lively, *Glorious Cause*, 198; Walter Clark, ed., "Diary Fragment," *State Records of North Carolina, 1777–1790*, 16 vols. (Winston and Goldsboro, 1895–1905), 16–606; Bray and Bushnell, *Greenman*, 24.

26. Wade and Lively, *Glorious Cause*, 174; Daniel Barber, *The History of my own Times* (Washington, 1827), 14; "Journal of Bayze Wells of Farmington, May, 1775–February, 1777," CHS *Collections* 7 (1899):296; "Revolutionary Dairy Kept by George Newton of Ipswich, 1777–1778," Essex Inst., *Historical Collections* 74 (1938): 339–40; Henry B. Dawson, ed., *Diary of David How* (Morrisania, N.Y., 1865), 36; Scheer, *Private Yankee Doodle*, 66–67, 70, 110; Dann, *Revolution Remembered*, 9–12, 19–22; Bray and Bushnell, *Greenman*, 76; Thomas Williams Baldwin, ed., *The Revolutionary Journal of Col. Jeduthan Baldwin, 1775–1778* (Bangor, Me., C.H. Glass, 1906), 43–54; Bolton, *Private Soldier*, 177–84; Thacher, *Journal*, 68–69; Ebenezer Elmer, "Journal Kept During an Expedition to Canada in 1776," NJHS *Proceedings*, 1st ser., 3 (1844): 51.

27. "Diary of Lt. James McMichael of the Pennsylvania Line," *Pennsylvania Archives*, 2d ser., 15 (1890): 202; Kenneth Roberts, ed., *March to Quebec: Journals of the Members of Arnold's Expedition* (New York, Doubleday, 1938), 547; Alex-

ander Graydon, *Memoir of a Life* (Harrisburg, 1811), 108; W. Croghan to Barnard Gratz, March 4, 1779, *Historical Magazine*, 1 (1857): 180; John Sanger Dexter to Samuel Blachley Webb, November 2, 1782, Ford, *Webb*, 2:429; Bray and Bushnell, *Greenman*, 186–87, 210–11; Ewing, *Ewing*, 44–45; Jabez Fitch, Jr., "A Journal," MHS *Proceedings*, 2d ser., 9 (1895): 61; Dann, *Revolution Remembered*, 34–35; Scheer, *Private Yankee Doodle*, 161; Fitzpatrick, *WW*, 14:28.

28. Sergeant R_____, 515; Albigence Waldo, "Valley Forge," *PMHB* 21 (1897):306–7; Fisher quoted in Bolton, *Private Soldier*, 77; Scheer, *Private Yankee Doodle*, 102–3, 186.

29. Bray and Bushnell, *Greenman*, 171, 175–76; Scheer, *Private Yankee Doodle*, 124, 151, 222–23, 284, 287; Samuel Cogswell to Father, July 15, 1780, *Historical Magazine*, 2d ser., 8 (1870):102.

30. John Shy, *Toward Lexington: The role of the British Army in the Coming of the American Revolution* (Princeton, Princeton University, 1965), 396–97; Louise Rau, ed., "Sergeant John Smith's Diary of 1776," *MVHR* 20 (1933–34):256–57, 266; Barber, *History*, 16; Scheer, *Private Yankee Doodle*, 285; Thacher, *Journal*, 186; Fitzpatrick, *WW*, 7:47, 8:465–66.

31. Thacher, *Journal*, 188; Rau, "Smith's Diary," 264; Royster, *Revolutionary People*, 296; Wade and Lively, *Glorious Cause*, 208, 238.

32. Scheer, *Private Yankee Doodle*, 100–01, 158–59, 284.

33. Fitzpatrick, *WW*, 14:28; *New Jersey Journal*, May 6, 1779, in *New Jersey Archives*, 2d ser. 3 (1906): 307–9.

34. Elisha Stevens, *Fragments*, 12; Rau, "Smith's Journal," 259; Scheer, *Private Yankee Doodle*, 148, 193, 225; Barber, *History*, 12.

35. Lemuel Roberts, *Memoirs of Captain Lemuel Roberts* (1809, reprint, New York, New York Times, 1969), 39–40; Fitzpatrick, *WW*, 8:152–53, 12:118–19, 16:13; "Orderly Book of the Second Pennsylvania Continental Line," *PMHB* 35 (1911): 342, 474–75, 36 (1912): 249; Muhlenberg's "Orderly Book," *PMHB* 34 (1910):455.

36. "The Revolutionary Journal of James Stevens of Andover, Mass.," Essex Inst., *Historical Collections* 46 (1912): 44; Martin, "Undisciplined Crew," in Hoffman and Albert, *Arms and Independence*, 130; Scheer, *Private Yankee Doodle*, 165, 186.

37. Marshall Smelser, *The Winning of Independence* (New York, Franklin Watts, 1973), 105; Scheer, *Private Yankee Doodle*, 182–86; Martin, "Undisciplined Crew," in Hoffman and Albert, *Arms and Independence*, 133–37; Royster, *Revolutionary People*, 299–301.

38. Scheer, *Private Yankee Doodle*, 279, 283, 292. Don Higginbotham, *The War of American Independence: Military Attitudes, Policies, and Practice, 1763–1789* (New York, Macmillan, 1971), 412.

Chapter 4:
George Washington and the American Victory

1. John Adams to Abigail Adams, May 29, 1775, in L.H. Butterfield et al., eds., *Adams Family Correspondence*, 4 vols. (Cambridge, Mass., Harvard University, 1963–), 1:347.

2. Eliphalet Dyer to Joseph Trumbull, June 16 and 17, 1775, in Paul H. Smith, ed., *LD*, 1:495–96, 499; Silas Deane to Elizabeth Deane, June 16, 1775, Smith, *LD*, 1:494; Deane to Trumbull, June 18, 1775, Smith, *LD*, 1:506; John Hancock to Elbridge Gerry, June 18, 1775, Smith, *LD*, 1:507; Robert Treat Paine to Artemas Ward, June 18, 1775, Smith, *LD*, 1:509.

3. Dyer to Trumbull, June 19, 1775, Smith, *LD*, 1:499; L. H. Butterfield et al., eds., *The Diary and Autobiography of John Adams*, 4 vols. (Cambridge, Mass., Harvard University, 1964), 3:321; Marshall Smelser, *The Winning of Independence* (New York, Franklin Watts, 1973), 59.

4. Washington C. Ford et al., eds. *JCC*, 2:91.

5. Paul David Nelson, *General Horatio Gates: A Biography* (Baton Rouge, La., Louisiana State University, 1976), 6–9; Willard Sterne Randall, *A Little Revenge: Benjamin Franklin and His Son* (Boston, Little, Brown, 1984), 54–56; John E. Ferling, " 'Oh That I was a Soldier': John Adams and the Anguish of War," *AQ* 36 (Summer 1984): 258–75; Adams to Abigail Adams, February 13, 1776, Butterfield, *Adams Family Correspondence*, 1:347; Alexander Hamilton to Edward Stevens, November 11, 1769, in Harold C. Syrett and Jacob E. Cooke, eds., *The Papers of Alexander Hamilton*, 26 vols. (New York, Columbia University, 1961–1979), 1:512.

6. For the most extensive treatments of Washington's early years see the appropriate volumes in Douglas Southall Freeman, *George Washington: A Biography*, 7 vols. (New York, Scribners, 1948–1957), and James T. Flexner, *George Washington*, 4 vols. (Boston, Little, Brown, 1965–1972).

7. Washington to Dr. James Craik, August 4, 1788, John C. Fitzpatrick, ed. *WW*, 30:36; Washington, "Sentiments on a Peace Establishment," Fitzpatrick, *WW*, 26:389; John R. Alden, *George Washington: A Biography* (Baton Rouge, La., Louisiana State University, 1984), p. 5.

8. Washington to Governor Dinwiddie, April 7 and 24, September 23 and 28, April 29, 1756, April 29 and May 30, 1757, W. W. Abbot et al., eds. *PGW*, 2:332–35; 3:44–46, 414–18, 420–21; 4:149–50, 171–72.

9. Bernhard Knollenberg, *George Washington: The Virginia Period* (Durham, N.C., Duke University, 1964), 44–45.

10. *Virginia Gazette*, September 3, 1756; Dinwiddie to Washington, October 19, 1757, in Robert Dinwiddie, *The Official Records of Robert Dinwiddie, Lieutenant-Governor of Virginia, 1751–1758*, 2 vols. (Richmond, Va., 1883–1884), 2:707–8.

11. "The humble Address of the Officers of the Virginia Regiment to George Washington," December 31, 1758, in Stanislaus Hamilton, ed., *Letters to George Washington and Accompanying Papers*, 5 vols. (Boston, 1898–1902), 3:143–46; Paul Kopperman, *Braddock at the Monongahela* (Pittsburgh, University of Pittsburgh, 1977), 130–31.

12. Washington to Robert Stewart and the Gentlemen Officers of the Virginia Regiment, January 10, 1759, in Flexner, *Washington*, 1:349–50; Washington to John A. Washington, May 31, 1754, Fitzpatrick, *WW*, 1:70.

13. Paul Ford, *The True George Washington* (Philadelphia, 1896), 138–45.

14. Washington to Jonathan Boucher, May 21, 1772, Fitzpatrick *WW*, 3:83–84.

15. General Orders, July 4, 5, 6, 7, 10, 11, 14, 15, 16, 18, and 23, August 11 and 18, and September 6, 1775, Fitzpatrick, *WW*,3:309, 312–17, 332–34, 338, 340–41, 346, 357, 414, 429, 475; Washington to Lund Washington, August 20,

1775, Fitzpatrick, *WW*, 3:432; Washington to Richard Henry Lee, July 10, and August 29, 1775, Fitzpatrick, *WW*, 3:331, 450.

16. Washington to Congress, November 8 and 11, 1775, Fitzpatrick, *WW*, 4:73–74, 82–83; James K. Martin and Mark E. Lender, *A Respectable Army: The Military Origins of the Republic, 1763–1789* (Arlington Heights, Ill., Harlan Davidson, 1982), 69–78.

17. On Washington's life-style, see: Freeman, *Washington*, 3:290; 4:413; 5:44, 408, 443, 483; Flexner, *Washington*, 2:283; Marquis de Chastellux, *Travels in North America in the Years 1780, 1781, and 1782*, 2 vols. (New York, 1968), 1:117–28.

18. Gordon Wood, *The Creation of the American Republic, 1776–1789* (Chapel Hill, N.C., University of North Carolina, 1969), 30–73, 91–124; Garry Wills, *Cincinnatus: George Washington and the Enlightenment* (Garden City, NY., Doubleday, 1984).

19. Henry Laurens to John Laurens, October 16, 1777, Smith, *LD*, 8:125; Robert Morris to Richard Peters, January 21, 1778, Smith, *LD*, 8:650; Peters to Morris, January 21, 1778, Smith, *LD*, 8:651n; Adams to Benjamin Rush, February 8, 1778, *Microfilm Edition of the Adams Papers*, 608 Reels (Boston, MHS, 1954–1959), Reel 89; Freeman, *Washington*, 5:436; Lafayette to Washington, December 30, 1777, in Stanley J. Idzerda et al., eds. *Lafayette in the American Revolution: Selected Letters and Papers, 1776–1790*, 5 vols. (Ithaca, N.Y., Cornell University, 1977–1983), 1:204.

20. Washington to Joseph Reed, February 10 and 26, 1775, Fitzpatrick, *WW*, 4:319, 321, 348; Flexner, *Washington*, 2:13.

21. Washington to John A. Washington, October 13, 1775 and March 31, 1776, Fitzpatrick, *WW*, 4:26, 446, 450.

22. Washington to Congress, July 3, 1776, Fitzpatrick, *WW*, 5: 214–15.

23. Joseph Reed to Esther Reed, September 2 and 6, 1776, Reed Mss., NYHS, 4:56, 57.

24. Washington to Lund Washington, December 17, 1776, Fitzpatrick, *WW*, 6:347; Washington to John A. Washington, December 18, 1776, Fitzpatrick, *WW*, 6:398; Washington to Congress, December 5 and 11, 1776, Fitzpatrick, *WW*, 6:330–31, 351.

25. Reed to Washington, December 22, 1776, in William B. Reed, *The Life and Correspondence of Joseph Reed*, 2 vols. (Philadelphia, 1847), 1:271–73.

26. Washington to Congress, September 8, 1776, Fitzpatrick, *WW*, 6:28.

27. Chastellux, *Travels*, 1:119–26, 137; Evelyn M. Acomb, ed., *The Revolutionary Journal of Baron Ludwig von Closen, 1780–1783* (Chapel Hill, N.C., University of North Carolina, 1958), 241; Mercy Warren to Adams, October 25, 1775, in Robert J. Taylor et al., eds. *Papers of John Adams* (Cambridge, Mass., Harvard University, 1977–), 3:269; Abigail Adams to Adams, July 16, 1775, Butterfield, *Adams Fam. Corres.*, 1:246; "Mrs. Theodorick Bland's Reminiscences on George Washington's Headquarters at Morristown," *NJHS Proceedings* 51 (1933): 250–53.

28. Lafayette to Adrienne de Noailles de Lafayette, January 6, 1778, Idzerda, *Lafayette in America*, 1:223.

29. Flexner, *Washington*, 2:30; Rupert Hughes, *George Washington*, 3 vols. (New York, William Morrow, 1926–1930), 2:365–66; Charles Martyn, *The Life*

of Artemas Ward: First Commander-in-Chief of the American Revolution (New York, A. Ward, 1921).

30. Washington to Charles Lee, June 30, 1778, Fitzpatrick, *WW*, 12:132–33; Theodore Thayer, *The Making of a Scapegoat: Washington and Lee at Monmouth* (Port Washington, N.Y., Kennikat, 1976); John Alden, *General Charles Lee: Traitor or Patriot?* (Baton Rouge, La., Louisiana State University, 1951), 194–227.

31. Washington to John Jay, April 14, 1779, Fitzpatrick, *WW*, 14:383–86; Alexander Hamilton to Elias Boudinot, July 5, 1778, Syrett and Cooke, *Papers of Hamilton*, 1:512.

32. Adams to Abigail Adams, February 21, 1777, Butterfield, *Adams Fam. Corres.*, 2:165; Page Smith, *A New Age Now Begins*, 2 vols. (New York, McGraw-Hill, 1976), 2:1134.

33. Washington to Congress, June 17, 1776, Fitzpatrick, *WW*, 5:152.

34. Butterfield, *Adams Diary and Autobiography*, 3:387; John H. G. Pell, "Philip Schuyler: The General As Aristocrat," in George Athan Billias, ed., *George Washington's Generals* (New York, William Morrow, 1964), 54.

35. Theodore Thayer, *Nathanael Greene: Strategist of the American Revolution* (New York, Twayne, 1960), 20–51, 56, 91.

36. Nelson, *Gates*, 170–71.

37. Washington to Thomas Nelson, February 8, 1778, Fitzpatrick, *WW*, 10:433; Washington to John Fitzgerald, February 28, 1778, Fitzpatrick, *WW*, 10:529.

38. Nelson, *Gates*, 189, 197–205; Ford, *JCC*, 12:1042–48.

39. Washington to Congress, November 11, 1778, Fitzpatrick, *WW*, 13:223–24; Washington to Henry Laurens, November 14, 1778, Fitzpatrick, *WW*, 13:254–57; Ford, *JCC*, 13:11–13.

40. Washington to Conrad Gerard, May 1, 1779, Fitzpatrick, *WW*, 14:470–73; Washington to Gouveneur Morris, May 8, 1779, Fitzpatrick, *WW*, 15:24–25.

41. "Conference at Hartford," September 22, 1780, Fitzpatrick, *WW*, 20:76–81; Washington to James Duane, October 4, 1780, Fitzpatrick, *WW*, 20:118; Washington to John Cadwallader, October 5, 1780, Fitzpatrick, *WW*, 20:122.

42. Washington to James Warren, March 31, 1779, Fitzpatrick, *WW*, 14:313; Washington to Moses Hazen, January 21, 1780, Fitzpatrick, *WW*, 17:418–19; Washington to Congress, November 11, 1778, Fitzpatrick, *WW*, 19:235; Washington to G. Morris May 8, 1778, Fitzpatrick, *WW*, 15:24.

43. John Shy, "George Washington Reconsidered," in Henry S. Bausum, ed., *The John Biggs Cincinnati Lectures in Military Leadership and Command, 1986* (Lexington, Va., Virginia Military Institute Foundation, 1986), 39–52; William S. Stinchcombe, *The American Revolution and the French Alliance* (Syracuse, N.Y., Syracuse University, 1969), 142. Shy's criticism is not founded on Washington's personality but on the commander's shortcomings as a strategist, which "kept his mind fixed on the [prospect of a] great decisive battle fought in the classical, European way."

44. Hamilton to Philip Schuyler, February 18, 1781, Syrett and Cooke, *Papers of Hamilton*, 2:564, 566, 566n; Alden, *Lee*, 297; Freeman, *Washington*, 5:436.

45. Adams to Rush, February 8, 1778, *Adams Papers Microfilm*, (Boston, MHS, 1962), Reel 89. The "indispensable man" argument has been advanced most fully in recent years by James Thomas Flexner, *Washington: The Indispensable Man* (Boston, Little, Brown, 1969).

46. Washington, "Address to Congress," December 23, 1783, Fitzpatrick, *WW*,

27:284; Washington, "Address to Faculty," August 25, 1783, Fitzpatrick, *WW*, 27:115; Washington to Comte d'Estaing, May 15, 1784, Fitzpatrick, *WW*, 27:402; Washington, "Farewell Orders," November 2, 1783, Fitzpatrick, *WW*, 27:227.

Chapter 5:
Washington's Lieutenants and the American Victory

1. John R. Alden, *General Charles Lee: Traitor or Patriot?* (Baton Rouge, La., Louisiana State University, 1951), 7–25.

2. George F. Scheer and Hugh F. Rankin, *Rebels and Redcoats* (Cleveland, 1957), 76–78.

3. Ibid., 82.

4. *American Historical Record* 1 (December 1872): 547–48.

5. CHS *Collections* 7 (1899): 128–29.

6. *LP* 1:123.

7. *LP*, 1:36–78, 383–84, 398–400.

8. William Moultrie, *Memoirs of the American Revolution* (New York, 1802):141–42.

9. Ibid.

10. Ibid., 176; *LP*, 2:100.

11. John Shy, "Charles Lee: The Soldier as Radical," in George Billias, ed., *George Washington's Generals* (New York, William Morrow, 1964), 37–38.

12. *LP*, 2:345.

13. Ibid., 361–66; Alden, *Lee*, 177–79.

14. Elias Boudinot, *Journal of Historical Recollections of American Events during the Revolutionary War* (Philadelphia, 1894), 178–79.

15. *LP*, 2:435–38.

16. Alden, *Lee*, 242; *LP*. 2:420.

17. George A. Billias, "Horatio Gates: Professional Soldier," in Billias, *Washington's Generals*, 84–85.

18. Paul David Nelson, *General Horatio Gates: A Biography* (Baton Rouge, La., Louisiana State University, 1976), 58–73.

19. Billias, "Gates," in Billias, *Washington's Generals*, 89.

20. Nelson, *Gates*, 122–56.

21. Ibid., 155–77.

22. Samuel W. Patterson, *Horatio Gates: Defender of American Liberties* (New York, Columbia University 1941), 265–66.

23. Scheer and Rankin, *Rebels and Redcoats*, 404.

24. Nelson, *Gates*, 222–37.

25. Billias, "Gates," in Billias, *Washington's Generals*, 103.

26. Ibid., 104.

27. Theodore Thayer, *Nathanael Greene: Strategist of the Revolution* (New York, Twayne, 1960), 15–50.,

28. Alexander Garden, *Anecdotes of the American Revolution*, 2 vols. (Brooklyn, 1865): 1:66.

29. Thayer, *Greene*, 118.

30. Theodore Thayer, "Nathanael Greene: Revolutionary War Strategist," in Billias, *Washington's Generals*, 115.

31. George Washington Greene, *Life of Nathanael Greene, Major General in the Army of the Revolution*, 3 vols. (New York, 1867–71), 2:1–40.

32. Jared Sparks, ed., *Correspondence of the American Revolution*, 4 vols. (Boston, 1853): 3:189–92.

33. Hugh F. Rankin, *The North Carolina Continentals* (Chapel Hill, N.C., University of North Carolina, 1971), 269–318.

34. Greene to Chevalier La Luzerne, June 22, 1781, Nathanael Greene Papers, William L. Clements Library, University of Michigan, Ann Arbor.

35. Rankin, *North Carolina Continentals*, 337–90; Thayer, *Greene*, 67.

36. Scheer and Rankin, *Rebels and Redcoats*, 232–33.

37. Louis Gottschalk, *Lafayette Joins the American Army* (Chicago, University of Chicago, 1937), 92.

38. Howard H. Peckham, "Marquis de Lafayette: Eager Warrior," in Billias, *Washington's Generals*, 221–51.

39. Ibid., 223–51; Hugh F. Rankin, *The War of the Revolution in Virginia* (Williamsburg, 1979), 39–43.

40. Rankin, *War in Virginia*, 52–78; Peckham, "Lafayette," in Billias, *Washington's Generals*, 233–36.

41. North Callahan, *Henry Knox: George Washington's General* (New York, Rinehart, 1958), 3–60.

42. Ibid., 58–98.

43. *North American Review* 27 (October, 1826):427–28.

44. Callahan, *Knox*, 155–56.

45. Ibid., 175–90, 207.

Chapter 6:
Logistics and the American Victory

1. Louis Clinton Hatch, *The Administration of the American Revolutionary Army* (New York, Longmans, Green, 1904); Victor Leroy Johnson, *The Administration of the American Commissariat during the Revolution War* (Philadelphia, University of Pennsylvania, 1941). Other accounts of army logistics administration are found in Erna Risch, *Quartermaster Support of the Army: A History of the Corps, 1775–1939* (Washington, D.C., Center of Military History, United States Army, 1962), 1–73; Erna Risch, *Supplying Washington's Army*, (Washington, D.C., Center of Military History, United States Army, 1981). Special Studies Series (Washington, D.C., Center of Military History, United States Army, 1981); James A. Huston, *The Sinews of War* (Washington, D.C., Office of Military History, United States Army, 1966), 3–74.

2. E. James Ferguson, *The Power of the Purse: A History of American Public Finance, 1776–1790* (Chapel Hill, University of North Carolina, 1961); Anne Bezanson, *Prices and Inflation during the American Revolution: Pennsylvania, 1770–1790* (Philadelphia, University of Pennsylvania, 1951). Richard Buel, *Dear Liberty: Connecticut's Mobilization for the Revolutionary War* (Middletown, Conn., Wesleyan University, 1980). For a local study of similar import, see Adrian Leiby, *The*

Revolutionary War in the Hackensack Valley: The Jersey Dutch and the Neutral Ground, 1775–1783 (New Brunswick, N.J., Rutgers University, 1962); an important overview of the entire question is in Richard Buel, Jr., "Time: Friend or Foe of the Revolution?" in Don Higginbotham, ed., *Reconsiderations on the Revolutionary War: Selected Essays* (Westport, Conn., Greenwood Press, 1978), 124–43.

3. E. Wayne Carp, *To Starve the Army at Pleasure: Continental Army Administration and American Political Culture, 1775–1783* (Chapel Hill, N.C., University of North Carolina, 1984).

4. This is not to say that historians have not appreciated certain aspects of the American logistics effort. Quartermaster General Nathanael Greene, for instance, has received good marks, as have particular logistics operations. See Don Higginbotham, *The War of American Independence: Military Attitudes, Policies, and Practice, 1763–1789* (New York, Macmillan, 1971), 301–8; and Victor L. Johnson, "Robert Morris and the Provisioning of the American Army during the Campaign of 1781," *PH* 5 (1938):7–20. On British leeriness, see William B. Willcox, *Portrait of a General: Sir Henry Clinton in the War of Independence* (New York, Knopf, 1964); and Ira D. Gruber, *The Howe Brothers and the American Revolution* (New York, W.W. Norton, 1972); Whipple to John Langdon, January 17, 1779, Paul H. Smith, ed. *LD*, 11:479.

5. On the normal definitions and functions of logistics, see R. Arthur Bowler, *Logistics and the Failure of the British Army in America: 1775–1783* (Princeton, Princeton University, 1975), vii–viii; R. Arthur Bowler, "Logistics and Operations in the American Revolution," in Higginbotham, *Reconsiderations*, 54–71; Mark Mayo Boatner, III, *Encyclopedia of the American Revolution* (New York, David McKay, 1974), 1079–84.

6. On colonial preparations for war by early 1775, including attempts to procure arms and martial supplies, see Higginbotham, *War of Independence*, 50; Charles K. Bolton, *The Private Soldier under Washington* (New York, Scribners, 1902), 6–9; A. French, *The First Year of the American Revolution* (Boston, Little, Brown, 1934), 41–45; Richard Alan Ryerson, *The Revolution Is Now Begun: The Radical Committees of Pennsylvania, 1765–1776* (Philadelphia, University of Pennsylvania, 1978), chap. 6; David L. Salay, "The Production of War Material in New Jersey during the Revolution," in William C. Wright, ed., *New Jersey in the American Revolution, III* (Trenton, N.J. Historical Commission, 1976), 7–20; Hugh Jameson, "Equipment for the Militia of the Middle States," in *Military Analysis of the Revolutionary War: An Anthology by the Editors of Military Affairs* (Millwood, N.Y., KTO, 1977), 121–30.

7. Orlando W. Stephenson, "The Supply of Gunpowder in 1776," *AHR* 30 (1925): 271–80; Salay, "Production of War Material," in Wright, *New Jersey in the Am. Rev.*, 16–17; David L. Salay, "The Production of Gunpowder in Pennsylvania during the American Revolution," *PMHB* 99 (1975):422–42.

8. John Franklin Jameson, "St. Eustatius in the American Revolution," *AHR* 8 (1903): 683–708; Higginbotham, *War for Independence*, 233–34; Hatch, *Administration of the Army*, 100–102; John C. Fitzpatrick, ed., *WW*, 10–39.

9. Bowler, "Logistics and Operations," in Higginbotham, *Reconsiderations*, 55; Washington to Richard Henry Lee, July 10, 1775, Fitzpatrick, *WW*, 3:330; *Lee Papers*, Collections of the New York Historical Society, 4 vols. (New York, 1872–75), 1:376–77.

10. Charles P. Whittemore, *A General of the Revolution: John Sullivan of New Hampshire* (New York, Columbia University, 1961), 121–22; Mark Edward Lender, "The Battle of Monmouth in the Context of the American Revolution," in Mary R. Murrin and Richard Waldron, eds., *Conflict at Monmouth Court House*, New Jersey Occasional Papers, No. 2 (Trenton, N.J. Historical Commission, 1983), 13; Bowler, "Logistics and Operations in Higginbotham, *Reconsiderations*, 55.

11. The rebel supply departments could not even tap all of the experienced men they had. William Maxwell, for example, who had seen extensive supply service with the British during and after the Seven Years' War, elected instead to serve in the line as a New Jersey regimental (later brigade) commander.

12. The standard source on the subject is Bowler, *Logistics and the Failure of the British Army*. Except as noted, this essay follows Bowler's conclusions on British logistics.

13. Eric Robson, *The American Revolution in Its Political and Military Aspects, 1763–1783* (New York, W.W. Norton, 1966), 100; Johann Ewald, *Diary of the American War: A Hessian Journal*, Joseph P. Tustin, trans. and ed. (New Haven, Yale University, 1979), 132–36.

14. W. B. Wilcox, "British Strategy in America, 1778," *JMH* 19 (1947): 98–99; Gruber, *The Howe Brothers and the American Revolution*, 295.

15. Hatch, *Administration of the Army*, 88.

16. James A. Huston, "The Logistics of Arnold's March to Quebec," in *Military Analysis of the Revolutionary War*, 106–20.

17. Most studies of logistics have not emphasized combat or active campaigning as supply problems in and of themselves. Higginbotham, *War for Independence*, 308, and especially Bowler, *Logistics and the Failure of the British Army*, 1–11, are worthy exceptions, pointing out that even preindustrial warfare could run quickly through tons of munitions and supplies. Carl von Clausewitz saw the point as self-evident. Active operations, he argued in *On War*, edited by Anatol Rapoport (Baltimore, 1969), were inherently difficult to support; small and unpredictable details—which he termed "friction" (bad weather, poor roads, raids, accidents, etc.)—constantly eroded an army's resources, and thus upset its plans.

18. Higginbotham, *War for Independence*, 308; John W. Jackson, *The Pennsylvania Navy: The Defense of the Delaware, 1775–1781* (New Brunswick, N.J., Rutgers University, 1974), 273.

19. Washington repeatedly expressed his concerns over the state of his transport capabilities, issuing a series of regulations designed to prevent the unauthorized use of horses, wagons, and related equipment, and to make army personnel accountable for the care of teams and vehicles. See, for example, General Orders, December 26, 1777, January 12, 1778, January 18, 1778, Fitzpatrick, *WW*, 10:207, 291, 313.

20. Boatner, *Encyclopedia of the Revolution*, 1080; Risch, *Quartermaster Support*, 37; Washington to the President of Congress, December 23, 1777, Fitzpatrick, *WW*, 10:194, 198.

21. Adams to Samuel Mather, October 26, 1776, in Harry Alonzo Cushing, ed., *The Writings of Samuel Adams*, 4 vols. (New York, G. P. Putnam, 1904), 3: 317. See also John Adams to Samuel Adams, August 16, 1776, Cushing, *Writings of Samuel Adams*, 3: 310–11.

22. A true executive department, the War Office, headed by a secretary at war,

emerged only in 1781. Harry M. Ward, *The Department of War, 1781–1795* (Pittsburgh, University of Pittsburgh, 1962).

23. Risch, *Quartermaster Support*, 7; Risch, *Supplying Washington's Army*, 23–24.

24. Bowler, "Logistics and Operations," in Higginbotham, *Reconsiderations*, 57; Board of War to Washington, June 19, 1777, Smith, *LD*, 7:221; Risch, *Supplying Washington's Army*, 436.

25. Risch, *Quartermaster Support*, 23, 26.

26. Duane to Schuyler, June 19, 1777, Smith, *LD*, 7:226. There was similar maneuvering for the post of commissary general of forage; Smith, *LD*, 7:231.

27. Lovell to John Adams, December 30, 1777, Smith, *LD*, 8:507.

28. The most charitable view of Mifflin's resignation—one that accepts the quartermaster general's plea of poor health—is in Kenneth R. Rossman, *Thomas Mifflin and the Politics of the American Revolution* (Chapel Hill, University of North Carolina, 1952), 94–95; Carp, *To Starve the Army*, 236, n. 22.

29. Bowler, "Logistics and Operations," in Higginbotham, *Reconsiderations*, 59; Laurens to Livingston, December 30, 1777, Smith, *LD*, 8:506.

30. Washington's views, in this first instance, were related in a letter from Timothy Pickering to Joseph Trumbull, June 28, 1777, quoted in Bowler, "Logistics and Operations," in Higginbotham, *Reconsiderations*, 57; his missive to Congress is in Fitzpatrick, *WW*, 10:192–98; Roberdeau to Thomas Wharton, December 27, 1777, Smith, *LD*, 8:482–83.

31. Adams to Abigail Adams, July 19, 1777, Smith, *LD*, 7:350–51; Congress called on the states to pass laws allowing Washington to impress supplies, and later urged the commander-in-chief to use impressments broadly. See Ford *JCC*, 3:323–24; 8:752–53; 9:905, 1013–15; Board of War to Washington, November 7, 1777, Smith, *LD*, 8:240. Washington expressed his reticence on the matter frequently. See, for examples, Washington to David Forman, November 24, 1776, Fitzpatrick, *WW*, 6:307; Washington to the Board of War, November 11, 1777, Fitzpatrick, *WW*, 10:39; Washington to Henry Lee, August 24, 1780, Fitzpatrick, *WW*, 19:432. Carp deals with the matter in *To Starve the Army*, 77–98.

32. Washington to Putnam, February 6, 1778, Fitzpatrick, *WW*, 10:423.

33. Washington to William Heath, December 17, 1777, Fitzpatrick, *WW*, 10:166; Washington to Patrick Henry, December 19, 1777, Fitzpatrick, *WW*, 10:173; Washington to William Heath, December 20, 1778, Fitzpatrick, *WW*, 10:177.

34. On the role and impact of privateers, see Higginbotham, *War for Independence*, 345. For a representative sampling of reactions to and interest in prizes taken, see John Adams to Abigail Adams, September 30, 1777, Smith, *LD*, 8:27; Thomas McKean to Sarah McKean, May 16, 1778, Smith, *LD*, 9:688; Marine Committee to Richard Ellis, May 25, 1778, Smith, *LD*, 9:750; John Bradford to the Continental Marine Committee, September 25, 1777, in William James Morgan, ed., *Naval Documents of the American Revolution* (Washington, D.C., Government Printing Office, 1986–), 9:962.

35. Laurens to William Livingston, December 30, 1777, Smith, *LD*, 8:506.

36. The work of the committee is traced in Henry Laurens to the Marquis de Lafayette, January 12, 1778, Smith, *LD*, 8:572; Elbridge Gerry to Washington, January 13, 1778, Smith, *LD*, 8:575; Committee at Camp Minutes of Proceedings, January 28–31, 1778, Smith, *LD*, 8:673–75; Committee at Camp to Henry Laurens,

January 28, 1778, Smith, *LD*, 8:673–76; Committee at Camp to Henry Laurens, January 29, 1778, Smith, *LD*, 8:680.

37. For a small selection of examples in this regard, see Washington to Samuel Blagden, December 30, 1777, Fitzpatrick, *WW*, 10:229–30; Washington to William Livingston, December 31, 1777, Fitzpatrick, *WW*, 10:231–34; Washington to Henry Knox, January 15, 1778, Fitzpatrick, *WW*, 10:308.

38. Powers to Officers to Collect Clothing, Etc., November, 1777, Fitzpatrick, *WW*, 10:124–25; Washington to the President of Congress, December 14, 1777, Fitzpatrick, *WW*, 10:159–60. Risch, *Supplying Washington's Army*, 21; Carp, *To Starve the Army*, 77.

39. On the general British problem of foraging in the interior, see Bowler, *Logistics and the Failure of the British Army*, 68–72. New Jersey endured bitter fighting during enemy foraging attempts; skirmishing over the winter of 1776/77 served as a case study in Washington's efforts to sting the British as they tried to feed themselves. See Jared Lobdell, "Six Generals Gather Forage: The Engagement at Quibbletown, 1777," *NJH* 102 (1984): 35–50; Jackson, *Pennsylvania Navy*, 246–47; Washington to Nathanael Greene, February 12, 1778, Fitzpatrick, *WW*, 10:454.

40. Joseph Reed to Thomas Wharton, February 1, 1778, Smith, *LD*, 9:4–6; Committee at Camp to Henry Laurens, February 3, 1778, Smith, *LD*, 9:13–14.

41. Huston, *Sinews of War*, 22; Washington to the Board of War, November 27, 1777, Fitzpatrick, *WW*, 10:115–16; General Orders, December 18, 1777, Fitzpatrick, *WW*, 10:170; General Instructions for the Colonels and Commanding Officers of Regiments in the Continental Service, [December] 1777, Fitzpatrick, *WW*, 10:242; General Orders, January 10, 1778, Fitzpatrick, *WW*, 10:289.

42. General Orders, January 1, 1778, Fitzpatrick, *WW*, 10:243; Washington to the President of Congress, January 2, 1778, Fitzpatrick, *WW*, 10:250.

43. Robson, *American Revolution*, 159.

44. Committee at Camp to Henry Laurens, February 25, 1778, Smith, *LD*, 9:168–75; Ford, *JCC*, 11:554–55; Henry Lutterloh and Philip Schuyler also came under the consideration of Congress for the quartermaster's posts. See Committee at Camp to Henry Laurens, February 12, 1778, Smith, *LD*, 9:81–82; Joseph Reed to Jonathan Bayard Smith, February 13, 1778, Smith, *LD*, 9:92; William Duer to Francis Lightfoot Lee, February 14, 1778, Smith, *LD*, 9:97–98; Eliphalet Dyer to Jeremiah Wadsworth, February 10, 1778, Smith, *LD*, 9:66–79; Ford, *JCC*, 10:141, 210, 293, 327–28. Greene's droll comment came in a letter to Washington, April 24, 1779, in Richard K. Showman et al., eds., *PG*, 3:427.

45. Johnson, *American Commissariat*, 136–37; Huston, *Sinews of War*, 62–63; Risch, *Quartermaster Support of the Army*, 46; Bowler, "Logistics and Operations," in Higginbotham, *Reconsiderations*, 59. On the special efforts to supply Sullivan, see Greene to Washington, May 25, 1779, Showman, *PG*, 4:77–78; Charles Pettit to Greene, May 27, 1779, Showman, *PG*, 4:89–92; Greene to Robert L. Hooper, July 10, 1779, Showman, *PG*, 4:25.

46. The planning for Middlebrook is found in Greene to Washington, October 18, 1778, Showman, *PG*, 3:3–5; Estimate of Teams Required to Transport Provisions and Forage from Trenton to Kings Ferry, *ca.* October 27, 1778, Showman, *PG*, 3:19–21. Greene displayed similar skill in planning for Sullivan's expedition against the Indians. See Greene to Washington, March [17–20], 1779, Showman, *PG*, 3:346–50.

47. Committee at Camp to Henry Laurens, February 25, 1778, Smith, *LD*, 9:171; Carp, *To Starve the Army*, 3–5; Greene to Charles Pettit, November 23, 1778, Showman, *PG*, 3:82–83; Circular to Deputy Quartermasters General in Pennsylvania, March 26, 1779, Showman, *PG*, 3:366–68.

48. Greene to Catherine Greene, November 13, 1778, Showman, *PG*, 3:67; Greene to Nehemiah Hubbard, December 4, 1778, Showman, *PG*, 3:96.

49. Henry Marchant to Greene, November 30, 1778, Showman, *PG*, 3:36–37; Joseph Reed to Greene, November 5, 1778, Showman, *PG*, 3:40–41; Jeremiah Wadsworth to Greene, May 7, 1779, Showman, *PG*, 3:468.

50. Risch, *Quartermaster Support of the Army*, 61; John Gooch to Greene, October 25, 1778, Showman, *PG*, 3:17–18; Greene to John Cox, November 25, 1778, Showman, *PG*, 3:84; Nehemiah Hubbard to Greene, April 27, 1779, Showman, *PG*, 3:434.

51. On the commissions controversy, see Committee at Camp to Henry Laurens, February 25, 1778, Smith, *LD*, 3:169–72; Carp, *To Starve the Army*, 46–47; Greene to Joseph Reed, March 9, 1778, Showman, *PG*, 2:307.

52. Carp, *To Starve the Army*, 104–106. For examples of Greene's personal indignation, see Greene to John Jay, April 27, 1779, Showman, *PG*, 3:431–32; Greene to Jacob Greene, April [28–30], 1779, Showman, *PG*, 3:434–35; Greene to Jeremiah Wadsworth, May 7, 1779, Showman, *PG*, 3:468.

53. Huston, *Sinews of War*, 63–66; Johnson, *American Commissariat*, 143; Thomas L. Wells, "An Inquiry into the Resignation of Quartermaster General Nathanael Greene in 1780," *RIsH* 24 (1965):41–48.

54. On Pickering and Blaine, see Gerald H. Clarfield, *Timothy Pickering and the American Republic* (Pittsburgh, University of Pittsburgh, 1980); and John Ewing Blaine, comp. and ed., *The Blaine Family: James Blaine, Emigrant, and His Children* (Cincinnati, J. Blaine, 1920). On the changing role of the Quartermaster Department under Pickering, see Risch, *Quartermaster Support for the Army*, 62.

55. Risch, *Quartermaster Support for the Army*, 57–58. Alexander Hamilton noted that the "mode of supplying the army—by state purchases—is not one of the least considerable defects of our system." Harold C. Syrett and Jacob E. Cooke, eds., *The Papers of Alexander Hamilton*, 15 vols. (New York, Columbia University, 1961–1979), 2:406.

56. Carp, *To Starve the Army*, 172–73; Smith, *LD*, 10:471, n.3; Estimate of Teams Required to Transport Provisions and Forage from Trenton to Kings Ferry, October 1778, Showman, *PG*, 3:20; S. Sydney Bradford, "Hunger Menaces the Revolution, December 1779–January 1780," *MHM* 6 (1966):1–23.

57. Fitzpatrick, *WW*, 18:427–28; Fitzpatrick, *WW*, 18:470.

58. On Heath's effort to rally supplies in New England, see Washington to William Heath, May 9, 1781, Fitzpatrick, *WW*, 22:63–64; Circular letter to New England States, May 10, 1781, Fitzpatrick, *WW*, 22:68.

59. Tustin, ed., *Ewald Diary*, 244–46; Klein and Howard, *Robertson Letter Book*, 126–27; Thomas J. Fleming, *The Forgotten Victory: The Battle for New Jersey, 1781* (New York, Reader's Digest, 1973); Risch, *Supplying Washington's Army*, 22.

60. For views of Greene, see Theodore Thayer, *Nathanael Greene: Strategist of the Revolution* (New York, Twayne, 1960); and Theodore Thayer, "Nathanael

Greene: Revolutionary War Strategist," in George Billias, ed., *George Washington's Generals* (New York, William Morrow, 1964), 109–38.

61. Clarence L. Ver Steeg, *Robert Morris: Revolutionary Financier* (Philadelphia, University of Pennsylvania, 1954), 60–61; Morris to the President of Congress, March 13, 1781, in E. James Ferguson et al., eds., *The Papers of Robert Morris, 1781–1784* (Pittsburgh, University of Pittsburgh, 1973–), 1:18; Carp, *To Starve the Army*, 209–11.

62. Ver Steeg, *Robert Morris*, 73; Victor L. Johnson, "Robert Morris, and the Provisioning of the American Army," *PH 5* (1938):9.

63. Ver Steeg, *Robert Morris*, 68–77.

64. Carp, *To Starve the Army*, 211–12.

65. Johnson, "Robert Morris and the Provisioning of the American Army," *PH 5* (1938):7–20; Morris's correspondence on the Yorktown campaign is voluminous. See vols. 2 and 3 of Ferguson, *Morris Papers*.

66. Risch, *Supplying Washington's Army*, 22. On the move of Washington's and Rochambeau's armies, see Henry P. Johnston, *The Yorktown Campaign and the Surrender of Cornwallis, 1781* (1881; reprint, New York, 1971), 83–102.

67. Risch, *Supplying Washington's Army*, 418; Committee at Camp to Henry Laurens, February 11, 1778, Smith, *LD*, 9:74–75. Similar concerns had kept Washington from striking at Philadelphia in early 1778; see Joseph Reed to Thomas Wharton, February 1, 1778, Smith, *LD*, 9:6; Committee at Camp to Henry Laurens, February 3, 1778, Smith, *LD*, 9:13–14.

68. Johnston, *Yorktown Campaign*, 156, 177–78.

Chapter 7:
Frontier Warfare and the American Victory

1. John R. Alden, *A History of the American Revolution* (New York: Harper and Row, 1969), 423; Don Higginbotham, *The War of American Independence: Military Attitudes, Policies, and Practice, 1763–1789* (New York, Macmillan, 1971), 331. Modern studies on the frontier in the American Revolution include Jack Sosin, *The Revolutionary Frontier, 1763–1783* (New York, Holt, Rinehart, and Winston, 1967), and George M. Waller, *American Revolution in the West* (Chicago, University of Chicago, 1976).

2. Thomas Gage to John Stuart, September 12, 1775, CO, series 5, 76:187. Details of Stuart's activities during the Revolution may be found in James H. O'Donnell, III, *Southern Indians in the American Revolution* (Knoxville, Tenn., University of Tennessee, 1973).

3. Worthington C. Ford, et al., eds. *JCC*, 2:123.

4. John Allan to General Heath, January 25, 1778, Heath Manuscripts, MHS; Joseph M. Bourg to the Indians, September 15, 1778, Heath Manuscripts, MHS.

5. Ford, *JCC*, 2:175.

6. Ford, *JCC*, 2:182. Richard Henry Lee thought these actions of Congress sufficient "to secure the friendship of the Indians all along our extensive frontiers." See Lee to George Washington, August 1, 1775, in Jared Sparks, ed., *The Writings of George Washington*, 12 vols. (New York, 1847–48), 1:12–13.

7. Ford, *JCC*, 3:183, 192; Burnett, LMCC, 2:163n.

8. Henry Laurens to the Georgia Council of Safety, September 29, 1775, Henry Laurens Papers and Letterbooks, Bundle 50, SCHS.

9. O'Donnell, *Southern Indians*, 15; Deposition of Thomas Volmer, December 18, 1775, Miscellaneous Bound Manuscripts, MHS; and Nead Papers, HSP.

10. For a more complete discussion of the Cherokee War of 1776, see O'Donnell, *Southern Indians*, 34–53 and the relevant notes.

11. Ibid., 72, n. 8. Gist likewise had failed in an earlier attempt to recruit Cherokee warriors for Washington's army. See O'Donnell, *Southern Indians*, 56, n. 3.

12. For recent comments on Henry Hamilton, see Bernard Sheehan, " 'The Famous Hair Buyer General': Henry Hamilton, George Rogers Clark and the American Indian," *Indiana Magazine of History* 79 (1983): 1–28. A thorough treatment of Hamilton's career may be found in Orville John Jaebker, "Henry Hamilton: British Soldier and Colonial Governor" (PH.D. diss., Indiana University, 1954). For Clark's standard biography see James A. James, *The Life of George Rogers Clark* (Chicago, University of Chicago, 1928). A more recent study which includes a discussion of Clark's Illinois adventure is Waller, *Revolution in the West*.

13. Account of a Conference at Detroit, June 17, 1777, APS; Resume of Parties going out from Detroit, July-September, 1777, July 27, 1777, M.G. 12, B Series, W.O. 28, vol. 10, part 1, Public Archives of Canada, Ottawa; Samuel Moorhead to Edward Hand, August 19, 1777, Force Transcripts, Series 7E, Hand Papers, vol. 1, LC; and Deveraux Smith to Hand, September 2, 1777, ibid. Hereafter references to the Force materials will be as Force, 7E, Hand, vol. 1.

14. Patrick Henry to Colonel William Fleming, September 7, 1777, McIlwaine, *LGV*, 1:186. See also Hand to Jasper Yeates, August 25, 1777, Force, 7E, Hand, vol. 3; and Joseph Ogle to Hand August 2, 1777, Force, 7E, Hand, vol. 1.

15. Hand to Yeates, August 25, 1777, Force, 7E, Hand, vol. 3.

16. Minutes of the Virginia Council of State, January 2, 1778, McIlwaine, *LGV*, 1:222; Henry to George Rogers Clark, January 2 and 24, 1778, McIlwaine, *LGV*, 1:222, 235. See also Hand to Colonel David Shepherd, March 22, 1778, Force, 7E, Hand, vol. 4; Hand to Gates, April 21, 1778, Force, 7E, Hand, vol. 4; and Clark to Hand, April 17, 1778, Force, 7E, Hand, vol. 2. In the last cited letter Clark reported that he had recruited some men but had received no supplies.

17. Richard Butler's Journal, 1775, HSP; Ohio Indians to George Crohan, 1775, Henry Clinton Papers, William L. Clements Library, University of Michigan, Ann Arbor; William Trent to "Dear Sir," October 15, 1775, CO, Series 5, 40:51, 53.

18. Henry Hamilton's Journal, Houghton Library, Harvard University.

19. Clark to Henry, February 3, 1779, in William P. Palmer et al., eds., *CVSP*, 1:315; Bowman to Hite, June 14, 1779, Manuscript 2C5477b3, George Rogers Clark Papers, VSL.

20. Journal of Henry Hamilton; Bowman to Hite, June 14, 1779, MS 2C5477b3, Clark Papers, VSL.

21. The author's " 'National Retaliation:' ", based on an unpublished Jefferson note at the VSL, traces the development of Jefferson's argument for imprisoning Hamilton. See " 'National Retaliation:' Thomas Jefferson's Brief for the Imprisonment of Henry Hamilton," presented at the Duquesne History Forum, October, 1985, Pittsburgh, Pennsylvania.

22. George Washington to Lachlan McIntosh, January 31, and February 15,

1779, in Fitzpatrick, *WW*, 14:58–59, 114–15; Washington to Hand, February 7, 1779, Fitzpatrick, *WW*, 14:74–76.

23. Greene to Washington, January 5, 1779, Nathanael Greene Papers, HHL; Washington to Schuyler, February 28, 1779, Fitzpatrick, *WW*, 14:149–50.

24. Washington to John Sullivan, May 31, 1779, Greene Papers, HHL; H. W. Dwight to Theodore Sedgwick, February, 1779, Theodore Sedgwick Papers, MHS; Greene to Washington, March 23, 1779, Greene Papers, HHL.

25. Butler to Hand, February 11 and March 23, 1779, Force, 7E, Hand, vol. 2.

26. James Dean to Goose van Schaick, May 16, 1779, Force, 7E, Hand, vol. 2.

27. Washington to Gates, March 6, 1779, Fitzpatrick, *WW*, 14:198; Washington to Sullivan, March 6, 1779, Fitzpatrick, *WW*, 14:201; Gates to Washington, March 16, 1779, Fitzpatrick, *WW*, 14:200.

28. James Clinton to "Dear Wife," August 24, 1779, George and James Clinton Papers, 1776–89, LC.

29. Greene to Charles Pettit, July 29, 1779, Nathanael Greene Letters, 11:4, APS; William Henry Dearborn, Journal of the Sullivan Campaign, 1779, MHS.

30. A. Fowler to Hand, August 18, 1779, Force, 7E, Hand, vol. 2; Washington to Congress, October 21, 1779, Fitzpatrick, *WW*, 18:1; Précis of Brodhead's Campaign in George Washington's General Orders, October 18, 1779, Fitzpatrick, *WW*, 14:480; Washington to Brodhead, October 18, 1779, Fitzpatrick, *WW*, 14:485.

31. Washington to the Marquis de Lafayette, September 12, 1779, Fitzpatrick, *WW*, 16:268; Huntington to Schuyler, November 29, 1779, PCC, 12:237, NA.

32. Randolph C. Downes, *Council Fires on the Upper Ohio* (Pittsburgh, University of Pittsburgh, 1940), 248–76.

33. Thomas Jefferson to Clark, March 19, 1780, in Julian P. Boyd, ed., *The Papers of Thomas Jefferson* (Princeton, New Jersey, Princeton University, 1950–), 3:316–17; Jefferson to Clark, September 29, 1780, McIlwaine, *LGV*, 2:213.

34. Deposition of John Anderson, William Ward, and Richard Thomas, November 10, 1777, Force, 7E, Hand, vol. 4; Hand to Henry, December 9, 1777, Force, 7E, Hand, vol. 4; Hand to Peters, December 9, 1777, Force, 7E, Hand, vol. 4; Journal of the Council, March 27, 1778, McIlwaine, *LGV*, 1:256. The murder suspects were identified and rewards posted for their capture, but none were apprehended. See also Hamilton to Lord Dartmouth, August 24 to September 2, 1778, CO, ser. 5, 7:342–43.

35. DePeyster to McKee, April 4 and May 8, 1780, Daniel Claus Papers, vol. 2, Public Archives of Canada, Ottawa; Haldimand to Clinton, August 28, 1780, British Headquarters Papers, #595(7), microfilm at CWRL; DePeyster to McKee, September 8, 1780, Claus Papers, 2; Bird to McKee, August 16, 1780, Claus Papers, 2; Bowman to Brodhead, May 27, 1780, William H. English Collection, IHS; Worthington to Bowman, May 19, 1780, William H. English Collection, IHS; Autobiography of Colonel Cave Johnson, Filson Club Collections, Louisville, Kentucky.

36. Charles Shaw to Germain, September 18, 1780, CO, ser. 5, 81:171. James Wright to Germain, September 18, 1780, in G.W.J. DeRenne, ed., "Letters from Governor Sir James Wright to the Earl of Dartmouth and Lord George Germain, Secretaries of State for America, from August 24, 1774 to February 17, 1782," *Collections of the Georgia Historical Society*, 3:316–17; *Royal Georgia Gazette*, September 23, 1780; *Royal Gazette* (South Carolina), September 27, 1780; William

B. Stevens, *A History of Georgia*, 2 vols. (Philadelphia, 1859), 2:248; Elijah Clerk [*sic*] to General Sumpter [*sic*] October 29, 1780, Thomas Sumter Papers, vol. 1, LC.

37. Edward J. Cashin, " 'But Brothers, It is Our Land We Are Talking About': Winners and Losers in the Backcountry," in Ronald Hoffman, Thad W. Tate, and Peter J. Albert, eds. *An Uncivil War: The Southern Bankcountry during the American Revolution* (Charlottesville, University Press of Virginia, 1985), 268.

38. Alden, *History*, 458–59.

39. Armstrong to Gates, November 19, 1780, in William M. Saunders et al., eds., *The Colonial Records of North Carolina*, 30 vols. (Raleigh, N.C., 1886–1914), 14:744.

40. William Campbell to Major Edmiston, December 17, 1780, King's Mountain Papers, Lyman C. Draper Collections, 9:23, UNC microfilm. The Patriots believed that British agents had encouraged the Cherokee to renew warfare. See Joseph Martin to Jefferson, December 12, 1780, Tennessee Papers, Draper Coll., 1:41, UNC microfilm; John Sevier to Martin, December 20, 1780, King's Mountain Papers, Draper Coll., 11:91, UNC microfilm; and James Sevier, ed., "A Memoir of John Sevier," *American Historical Magazine* 6 (1900):40–45.

41. Arthur Campbell to Jefferson, January 15, 1781, *CVSP*, 1:434–37; Jefferson to the President of Congress, February 17, 1781, McIlwaine, *LGV*, 2:351.

42. Thomas Brown to Germain, August 9, 1781, CO, ser. 5, 82:252; Cameron to Germain, May 27, 1781, CO, ser. 5, 82: 204; Kenneth Coleman, *The American Revolution in Georgia* (Athens, GA., University of Georgia, 1958), 135; Clyde A. Ferguson, "General Andrew Pickens" (Ph.D. diss., Duke University, 1960), 209.

43. Brown to Germain, August 9, 1781, CO, ser. 5, 82:252; *Royal Gazette* (South Carolina), May 30, 1781.

44. Henry Lee, *Memoirs of the War in the Southern Department of the United States* (New York, 1870), 369; J. Burnet to Andrew Pickens, June 7, 1781, Revolutionary War Collection, Duke University Library; Pickens to Greene, June 7, 1781, Duke University Library; Pickens to Greene, June 7, 1781, in R. W. Gibbes, *Documentary History of the American Revolution, 1774–1782*, 3 vols. (New York, 1853–57), 3:91–92; Browne to Germain, August 9, 1781, CO, ser. 5, 82:252.

45. Clyde A. Ferguson, "Andrew Pickens—Partisan," (M.A. Thesis, Duke University, 1957), 221; John Twiggs to Greene, December 16, 1781, PCC, no. 155, 2:401–11; Nathan Brownson to Greene, December 15, 1781, PCC, no. 155, 2:401–11; Greene to Twiggs, December 25, 1781, Nathanael Greene Papers, Duke University.

46. Robert McCready's Orderly Book, 1778, LC; John Heckewelder, *The Narrative of John Heckewelder* (Cleveland, J. Heckewelder, 1907), 347–60.

47. Accounts of this unfortunate incident may be found in the Relation of Frederick Lineback, April 8, 1782, *CVSP*, 1:122; Depeyster to _____, May 13, 1782, British Museum Additional Manuscripts, #21781:78; and, [Anon]., *The Murder of the Christian Indians in North America in the Year 1782, A Narrative of Facts* (Dublin, 1823).

Chapter 8:
Politics and the American Victory

1. Merrill Jensen, ed., *English Historical Documents (American Colonial Documents to 1776)* (New York, Eyre and Spottiswoode, 1955), 9:696.

2. Lord Dartmouth to Thomas Gage, April 15, 1775, in Clarence E. Carter, ed., *The Correspondence of General Thomas Gage*, 2 vols. (New Haven, Yale University, 1931–1933), 2:190–96.

3. James Duane, Notes on the State of the Colonies, May 24, 1775, Burnett, *LMCC*, 1:100; Ford, *JCC*, 2:56, 69, 74; Connecticut Delegates to William Williams, May 31, 1775, Burnett, *LMCC*, 1:104.

4. Ford, *JCC*, 2:76–78; Jonathan G. Rossie, *The Politics of Command* (Syracuse, Syracuse University, 1975), 8, and *passim*.

5. Ford, *JCC*, 2:76–79.

6. Ibid., 2:76–79, 83–85.

7. Eliphalet Dyer to Joseph Trumbull, June 17, 1775, Burnett, *LMCC*, 1:127–29.

8. Rossie, *Politics of Command*, 13–16.

9. Lewis Henry Boutell, *Life of Roger Sherman* (Chicago, A.C. McClurg, 1896), 88.

10. Rossie, *Politics of Command*, 122–23.

11. John Adams to James Warren, July 6 and 23, 1775, Burnett, *LMCC*, 1:151–52, 173–74; Duane to Robert Montgomery, Burnett, *LMCC*, 1:171.

12. Ford, *JCC*, 2:190–91, 211–12.

13. John Adams to Warren, July 26, 1775, Burnett, *LMCC*, 1:177–78; Washington to Jonathan Trumbull, August 14, 1775, Fitzpatrick, *WW*, 3:419.

14. Washington to Richard Henry Lee, August 29, 1775, Fitzpatrick, *WW*, 3:450.

15. Caractacus, "On Standing Armies" (Philadelphia) August 21, 1775, in Peter Force, comp., *American Archives*, 4th ser., 6 vols. (Washington, 1837–46), 3:219–21.

16. President of Congress to Washington, September 26, 1775, Burnett, *LMCC*, 1:207–8.

17. L.H. Butterfield, ed., *The Diary and Autobiography of John Adams*, 4 vols. (Cambridge, Mass., Harvard University, 1961), 2:202.

18. Ibid., 2:203–4.

19. Samuel Ward to Henry Ward, October 11, 1775, Burnett, *LMCC*, 1:225; President of Congress to N.J. Prov. Cong, October 25, 1775, Burnett, *LMCC*, 1:240–41; Ford, *JCC*, 3:305, 335, 370, 416.

20. Rossie, *Politics of Command*, 45, *passim*; Howard H. Peckham, ed., *The Toll of Independence* (Chicago, University of Chicago, 1974), 11.

21. Rossie, *Politics of Command*, 97–99.

22. *PCC*, 1:16; 2:313; Josiah Bartlett to John Langdon, June 10 and 17, 1776, Whipple Papers, LC; Don R. Gerlach, *Proud Patriot: Philip Schuyler and the War of Independence* (Syracuse, Syracuse University, 1987), 144–45.

23. Ford, *JCC*, 5:448–51.

24. N.Y. Delegates to N.Y. Council of Safety, July 29, 1777, Burnett, *LMCC*, 2:429–30; James Lovell to William Whipple, August 1, 1777, Whipple Papers, LC.

25. Lovell to Whipple, September 17, 1777, Whipple Papers, LC; Sullivan to the President of Congress, September 17, 1777, 160, PCC, 57; Henry Laurens to John Laurens, October 10, 1777, Burnett, *LMCC*, 2:514–15; Jonathan Trumbull, Jr., to Jonathan Trumbull, Sr., November 18, and December 1, 1777, "Trumbull Papers," MHS *Collections*, 7th ser., 2:197–98, 200; Elbridge Gerry to John Adams, December 3 and 8, 1777, Gerry Papers, LC.

26. Rossie, *Politics of Command*, 188–202.

27. Washington to Officers of the Army, March 15, 1783, Fitzpatrick, *WW*, 26:227.

Chapter 9:
The French Alliance and the American Victory

1. Le ministre à M. de Vaudreuil, Versailles, 10 mai 1710. RAPQ 1946–1947, 377.

2. Adolph B. Benson, ed., *The America of 1750: Peter Kalm's Travels in North America*, 2 vols. (New York, Wilson-Erickson, 1966), 1:139–40; Gustave Schelle, ed., *Oeuvres de Turgot et documents le concernant*, 5 vols. (Paris, 1913–33) 1:141; Thomas Hutchinson to Dartmouth, December 14, 1773, Massachusetts Archives, Colonial Documents, 26:586–88, in Lawrence Henry Gibson, *The Coming of the Revolution, 1763–1775* (New York, Harper and Row, 1954), 215.

3. Memoire sur le Canada. 27 dec. 1758, C11A, vol. 103, f 488; Memoire Concernant les Colonies et Relatif à la Paix par le marquis de Capellis, 11 dec. 1758, *ibid*, ff 497–98.

4. Cited in Sir Julian S. Corbett, *England in the Seven Years' War*, 2 vols. (London, Navy Records Society, 1918), 2:173.

5. Memoire du marquis de Choiseul, dec. 1759. Paris, Bibliotheque Nationale. Manuscrits français. Nouvelles Acquisitions, vol. 1041, ff 44–63.

6. Choiseul à d'Ossun, Paris 23 fev. 1762. Paris, Archives de la ministère des affaires étrangeres. Memoires et documents. Espagne vol. 574, f 132.

7. Zenab Esmat Rashed, *The Peace of Paris 1763* (Liverpool, University Press, 1951), 209; Jonathan R. Dull, *A Diplomatic History of the American Revolution* (New Haven, Yale University, 1985), 63; John Richard Alden, *The American Revolution* (New York, Harper and Row, 1954), 179.

8. Orville T. Murphy, "The Comte de Vergennes, the Newfoundland Fisheries, and the Peace Negotiations of 1783: A Reconsideration," *CHR* 46 (1965):33; Piers Mackesy, *The War for America, 1775–1783* (Cambridge, Mass., Harvard University, 1964), 349; Rene Pinon, "Louis XVI, Vergennes et la grande lutte contre l'Angleterre," *Revue d'histoire diplomatique* 43 (1929):37–64.

9. Louis De Vorsey Jr., *The Indian Boundary in the Southern Colonies, 1763–1775* (Chapel Hill, N.C.: University of North Carolina, 1966), 39; B. A. Hinsdale, "The Western Land Policy of the British Government from 1763 to 1775," *Ohio Archeological and Historical Publications* 1 (1887):207–29.

10. Claude Van Tyne, "French Aid before the Alliance of 1778," *AHR* 31 (1925):120.

11. Marcel Trudel, *Louis XVI, le congres americain et le Canada 1774–1789*, (Quebec, Publications de l'Université Laval, 1949), 120.

12. Alden, *American Revolution*, 181.

13. Van Tyne, "French Aid," 20; Alden, *American Revolution*, 120.

14. Charles Royster, *A Revolutionary People at War: The Continental Army and American Character, 1775–1783* (Chapel Hill, University of North Carolina, 1979), 176.

15. See Robert McConnell Hatch, *Thrust for Canada: The American Attempt*

on Quebec in 1775–1776 (Boston, Little, Brown, 1979), 188–208; Alden, *American Revolution*, 149, n. 19.

16. Jonathan R. Dull, *The French Navy and American Independence* (Princeton, Princeton University, 1975), 90.

17. Henri Doniol, ed., *Histoire de la participation de la France à l'establissement des États-Unis d'Amerique: Correspondance diplomatique et documents*, 5 vols. (Paris, 1886–99), 2:274–5.

18. Hunter Miller, ed., *Treaties and Other International Acts of the United States of America*, 8 vols. (Washington, DC, United States Government Printing Office, 1931), 2:38–39.

19. Mackesy, *The War for America*, 490.

20. William C. Stinchcombe, *The American Revolution and the French Alliance* (Syracuse, Syracuse University, 1969), 88.

21. Dull, *A Diplomatic History*, 107–9.

22. Howard C. Rice, Jr., and Anne S. K. Brown, eds. and trans., *The American Campaigns of ROCHAMBEAU'S ARMY 1780, 1781, 1782, 1783*, 2 vols. (Princeton, N.J., Princeton University, 1972), 1:18, n. 9.

23. Stinchcombe, *The American Revolution and the French Alliance*, 2; Mackesy, *The War for America*, 349–50; Rice and Brown, *The American Campaigns of Rochambeau's Army*, 1:33, 78, 82–83; Royster, *A Revolutionary People*, 60.

24. Stinchcombe, *The American Revolution and the French Alliance*, 51–52.

25. Rice and Brown, *The American Campaigns of ROCHAMBEAU'S ARMY*, 1:22, 27.

26. Mackesy, *The War for America*, 349–50.

27. Royster, *A Revolutionary People*, esp. 295–308.

28. Doniol, *Histoire de la participation de la France*, 4:549–50; Mackesy, *The War for America*, 387.

29. Stinchcombe, *The American Revolution and the French Alliance*, 153–54.

30. Rice and Brown, *The American Campaigns of ROCHAMBEAU'S ARMY*, 1:26, n. 21; Mackesy, *The War for America*, 413.

31. Rice and Brown, *The American Campaigns of ROCHAMBEAU'S ARMY*, 1:133–34, 241–53.

32. Ibid., 39–40, n. 54.

33. Mackesy, *The War for America*, 419.

34. Rice and Brown, *The American Campaigns of ROCHAMBEAU'S ARMY*, 1:252, n. 77; 2:158–59.

35. Ibid., 1:64, 151.

36. See W. J. Eccles, *France in America* (New York, Harper and Row, 1972), 181; Mackesy, *The War for America*, 351, 491. For a discussion of the American military strategy of annihilation see the flawed but informative essay by Don Higginbotham, "The Early American Way of War: Reconnaissance and Appraisal," *WMQ* 44 (1987): 230–73.

37. Rice and Brown, *The American Campaigns of ROCHAMBEAU'S ARMY*, 1:64.

38. Ibid., 1:167–68.

39. Edward S. Corwin, *French Policy and the American Alliance of 1778* (Princeton, Princeton University), 1916):203–4.

---

40. W. J. Eccles, "Sovereignty-Association, 1500–1783," *CHR* 65 (1984):509–10.

41. The friends of the loyalists in Britain protested vigorously. There was an immediate riposte. A series of letters appeared in the *Boston Independent Chronicle* purporting to relate in horrifying detail the appalling cruelties inflicted on innocent American settlers by the Indian allies of the loyalists, in British pay. Copies of the newspaper were sent to the Netherlands by Franklin and from there disseminated throughout Europe. The French soon discovered that the letters had emanated from the pen of Franklin in his lodgings at Passy. See Philippe Sagnac, *La fin de l'ancien régime et la revolution americaine (1763–1789)* (Paris, Presses Universitaires de France, 1947), 374.

42. Murphy, "The Comte de Vergennes, the Newfoundland Fisheries," 42.

43. Trudel, *Louis XVI*, 217, n. 81.

44. Sagnac, *La fin de l'ancien régime*, 375.

45. Stinchcombe, *The American Revolution and the French Alliance*, 191; Dull, *French Navy*, 90.

46. Murphy, "The Comte de Vergennes, the Newfoundland Fisheries," 32–46.

47. Sagnac, *La fin de l'ancien régime*," 375.

48. Stinchcombe, *The American Revolution and the French Alliance*, 199, 204, 208–9.

Chapter 10:
British Armed Forces and the American Victory

1. John Shy, *Toward Lexington: The Role of the British Army in the Coming of the American Revolution* (Princeton, N.J., Princeton University, 1965), esp. 45–83, 376–98.

2. Charles Grieg Cruickshank, *Elizabeth's Army*, 2d ed. (London, Clarendon, 1966), esp. 6, 18.

3. Lois G. Schwoerer, *"No Standing Armies!" The Antiarmy Ideology in Seventeenth-Century England* (Baltimore and London, John Hopkins University, 1974), 21–28.

4. Ibid., 38.

5. Ibid., 51–56.

6. John Phillip Reid, *In Defiance of the Law: The Standing-Army Controversy, The Two Constitutions, and the Coming of the American Revolution* (Chapel Hill, N.C., University of North Carolina, 1981), 86; J. G. A. Pocock, "Machiavelli, Harrington and English Political Ideologies in the Eighteenth Century," *WMQ* 3d ser., 22 (1965):549–83; Lawrence Delbert Cress, *Citizens in Arms: The Army and the Militia in American Society to the War of 1812* (Chapel Hill, N.C., University of North Carolina, 1982), 18.

7. Quoted in Reid, *In Defiance of the Law*, 83–84; Schwoerer, *"No Standing Armies,"* 137–54.

8. For a detailed study of the history of the Declaration of Rights see Lois G. Schwoerer, *The Declaration of Rights, 1689* (Baltimore and London, Johns Hopkins University, 1981); Reid, *In Defiance of the Law*, 85.

9. Reid, *In Defiance of the Law*, 89; Cress, *Citizens in Arms*, 18; Schwoerer, "*No Standing Armies*," 137–54.

10. John Sweetman, *War and Administration: The Significance of the Crimean War for the British Army* (Edinburgh, Scottish Academic Press, 1984), 6.

11. Walter L. Dorn, "The Prussian Bureaucracy in the Eighteenth Century," *PSQ* 46 (1931): 403–23; 47 (1932):75–94, 259–73; Edward E. Curtis, *The Organization of the British Army in the American Revolution* (originally published 1926, reprint, St. Clair Shores, Michigan, Scholarly Press, 1972), 33; Sweetman, *War and Administration*, 77.

12. Curtis, *Organization of the British Army*, 39–41, 106–9; Sweetman, *War and Administration*, 41–42, 59–61.

13. Olive Gee, "The British War Office in the Later Years of the American War of Independence," *JMH* 26 (1954):123–36; Correlli Barnett, *Britain and Her Army 1509–1970: A Military, Political and Social Survey* (New York, William Morrow, 1970), 132, 175.

14. Sylvia R. Frey, *The British Soldier in America: A Social History of Military Life in the Revolutionary Period* (Austin, University of Texas, 1981), 29, 34, 36; Field Marshal Lord Carver, Michael, *The Seven Ages of the British Army* (New York, Beaufort, 1984), 60–61.

15. Cress, *Citizens in Arms*, 21–25; Schwoerer, "*No Standing Armies*," 188–200.

16. Barnett, *Britain and Her Army*, 166.

17. For a general survey of social and economic developments see C. P. Hill, *British Economic and Social History 1700–1982*, 5th ed. (London, E. Arnold, 1985), esp. 22–23.

18. Frey, *The British Soldier*, 7–8; John U. Nef, *War and Human Progress: An Essay on the Rise of Industrial Civilization* (New York, W.W. Norton, 1968), 10–11, 81–84, 212, 283–84, 291.

19. Tony Hayter, *The Army and the Crowd in Mid-Georgian England* (Totowa, N.J., Rowman and Littlefield, 1978), esp. 20–35; Reid, *In Defiance of the Law*, 111–20. Later troops also were used to control polling at elections, quell opposition to the revised Poor Laws, and deal with Chartism. See Sweetman, *War and Administration*, 16.

20. Curtis, *Organization of the British Army*, 51.

21. Cruickshank, *Elizabeth's Army*, 27–28; Frey, *The British Soldier*, 6.

22. Frey, *The British Soldier*, 3–4. See also Edward E. Curtis, "The Recruiting of the British Army in the American Revolution," *American Historical Association Annual Report* 1 (1922):311–22.

23. Frey, *The British Soldier*, 25–26.

24. Ibid., 15, 16; Walter Hart Blumenthal, *Women Camp Followers of the American Revolution* (Philadelphia, G.S. MacManus, 1952), 42; Nef, *War and Human Progress*, 95, 210–11; Sylvia R. Frey, "Between Slavery and Freedom: Virginia Slaves During the American Revolution," *JSH* 49 (1983):375–89; Sylvia R. Frey, "The British and the Black: A New Perspective," *The Historian* 38 (1976):225–38.

25. James Hayes, "Scottish Army Officers in the British Army," *Scottish Historical Review* 37 (1958):23–33; James Hayes, "The Social and Professional Backgrounds of the Officers of the British Army, 1714–1763" (M.A. thesis, University of London, 1956).

26. Stephen Conway, "British Army Officers and the American War for Independence," *WMQ*, 3d ser., 46 (1984):271.

27. Shy, *Toward Lexington*, 351; Frey, *The British Soldier*, 66; Conway, "British Army Officers," 275; see also Eric Robson, "Purchase and Promotion in the British Army in the Eighteenth Century," *History* 36 (1951):57–72.

28. For a more detailed biographical sketch of Howe, see Ira D. Gruber, *The Howe Brothers and the American Revolution* (Chapel Hill, N.C., University of North Carolina, 1972), 45, 46, 56–59. For Clinton see William B. Willcox, *Portrait of a General: Sir Henry Clinton in the War of Independence* (New York, Knopf, 1964), 3–39.

29. Larry H. Addington, *The Patterns of War Since the Eighteenth Century* (Bloomington, Ind., Indiana University, 1984), 2; Hayes, "Scottish Officers," 27.

30. Shy, *Toward Lexington*, 69; Carver, *Seven Ages*, 156; Sweetman, *War and Administration*, 6.

31. Carver, *Seven Ages*, 60.

32. Nef, *War and Human Progress*, 95, 96, 205; Frey, *The British Soldier*, 121–22.

33. Frey, *The British Soldier*, 118, 119.

34. Ibid., 123.

35. Ibid., 124.

36. Ibid., 118–19, 125–26; Arthur N. Gilbert, "Law and Honour among Eighteenth-Century British Army Officers," *The Historical Journal* 19 (1976):75–87; Shy, *Toward Lexington*, 19, n.39.

37. Carver, *Seven Ages*, 74; Frey, *The British Soldier*, 97–98; Barnett, *Britain and Her Army*, 177.

38. Quoted in Barnett, *Britain and Her Army*, 192.

39. Frey, *The British Soldier*, 127–29; 139–44.

40. Quotes from John S. Pancake, *This Destructive War: The British Campaign in the Carolinas, 1780–1782* (Tuscaloosa, Ala., University of Alabama, 1985), 21, 244; Jerome J. Nadelhaft, *The Disorders of War: The Revolution in South Carolina* (Orono, Maine, University of Maine, 1981), 51. See also Ira D. Gruber, "Lord Howe and Lord George Germain: British Politics and the Winning of American Independence," *WMQ*, 3d ser., 22 (1965):225–43, which discusses the changing attitudes of the British government.

41. Gruber, *The Howe Brothers*, 156–57, 129–80, 189–212; Piers Mackesy, *The War for America, 1775–1783* (Cambridge, Mass., Harvard University, 1964), 105–12.

42. Barnett, *Britain and Her Army*, 217–18.

43. Cress, *Citizens in Arms*, 39–40; Shy, *Toward Lexington*, 376–86.

44. Stephen Conway, "To Subdue America: British Army Officers and the Conduct of the Revolutionary War," *WMQ*, 3d ser., 43 (1986):381–406.

45. Joseph S. Tiedeman, "Patriots By Default: Queens County, New York, and the British Army, 1776–1783," *WMQ*, 3d ser., 43 (1986):35–63.

46. Sylvia R. Frey, "Bitter Fruit from the Sweet Stem of Liberty: Georgia Slavery and the American Revolution," unpublished paper presented at the annual meeting of the American Historical Association, December 27–30, 1985, New York.

47. Frey, *The British Soldier*, 32, 74–75. The most detailed study of logistical

problems is R. Arthur Bowler, *Logistics and the Failure of the British Army in America, 1775–1783* (Princeton, Princeton University, 1975).

48. Sylvia R. Frey, "Liberty, Equality, and Slavery: The Paradox of the American Revolution," in Jack P. Greene, ed., *The American Revolution: Its Character and Limits* (New York, New York University, 1987).

Chapter 11:
Naval Warfare and the American Victory

1. William M. Fowler, Jr., *Rebels under Sail* (New York, Scribners, 1976), 263.

2. Ibid., 87–91.

3. R. Arthur Bowler, *Logistics and the Failure of the British Army in America, 1775–1783* (Princeton, Princeton University, 1975), 212–25. For pertinent documents see also William Bell Clark, et al, eds., *Naval Documents of the American Revolution*, 9 vols. to date (Washington, Government Printing Office, 1964–86), 6:*passim*. For a full account of the action see Fowler, *Rebels*, 153–86.

4. Arbuthnot to Germain, No. 17, May 27, 1778: PRO, CO 217/54, quoted in John D. Faibisy, "The Greening of A. Crabtree: The Downeast Adventures of a Revolutionary Privateersman," *The American Neptune* 42 (1982):18.

5. Fowler, *Rebels*, 103–9.

6. Report of the Committee on the Penobscot Expedition, October 7, 1779: *Documentary History of the State of Maine*, 24 vols. (Portland, 1869–1916), 17:358–60. The Saltonstall quotation is in John D. Faibisy, "Penobscot, 1779: The Eye of a Hurricane," *MHSQ* 19 (1979): 97.

7. Faibisy, "Penobscot," 103–11.

8. William B. Willcox, *The Age of Aristocracy 1688 to 1830*, 3d ed. (Lexington, Mass., D.C. Heath, 1976), 143.

9. Abundant evidence of the bad state of the fleet and storehouses is present in Mary B. Wickwire, "Lord Sandwich and King's Ships: British Naval Administration, 1771–1782" (unpublished MS). Hawke's depletion of store is mentioned in Sir Oswyn A. R. Murray, "The Admiralty, VI," *Mariner's Mirror* 24 (1938):331. Even a historian who has little good to say of Sandwich's naval administration admits the bad state of the fleet that Sandwich inherited and the "general decay" that prevailed in 1771. See Robert G. Albion, *Forests and Sea Power: The Timber Problem of the Royal Navy, 1652–1862* (Cambridge, Mass., Harvard University, 1926), 12, 286. See also navy board directive to dockyard officers, November 16, 1773; PRO, Adm. 106/2508; "List of the Navy," July 1, 1770: PRO, T. 1/478; and memorandum endorsed 1780, in William L. Clements Library, Shelburne Papers, vol. 146, No. 84. Between 1771 and 1776, forty ships of the line and frigates were found to be so decayed that they were broken up or sold: see navy bd. to Stephens, March 27, 1782, in National Maritime Museum, ADM/B.P./3.

10. Account of the timber in store on December 31, 1770: PRO, Adm. 49/124; adm. bd. to navy bd., July 31, 1771: PRO, Adm. 2/240, 475–480; Account of oak in store on December 31, 1774: PRO, Adm. 49/124; navy bd. to Philip Stephens, January 28, 1778: National Maritime Museum, ADM/B/195. Also see numerous orders of the navy bd. to officers of all dockyards, 1771–1773: PRO, Adm. 106–2508.

11. Navy bd. to Stephens, March 25, 1771: PRO, Adm. 106–2200, 306–9; Sandwich to Admiral Samuel Barrington, August 5, 1779: *The Private Papers of John, Earl of Sandwich*, 4 vols. (London, 1932–1938), 2:365.

12. Rodney to Sandwich, February 16, 1780: *Sandwich Papers*, 3:201.

13. Ira Gruber, "Richard Lord Howe," in George Athan Billias, ed., *George Washington's Opponents* (New York, William Morrow, 1969), 233–59; Ira Gruber, *The Howe Brothers and the American Revolution* (New York, Atheneum 1972).

14. William B. Willcox, "Arbuthnot, Gambier, and Graves: The 'Old Women' of the Navy," in Billias, *Washington's Opponents*, 260–90.

15. The King to Sandwich, September 23, 1779, *Sandwich Papers*, 3:135.

16. *Sandwich Papers*, 1:334.

17. Jonathan Dull, *The French Navy and American Independence: A Study of Arms and Diplomacy, 1774–1787* (Princeton, N.J., Princeton University, 1975), 97–98, 126, 149.

18. For Sandwich's opinions of April 4, 1778 and August 3, 1777, see *Sandwich Papers*, 2:22–23; 1:236–37.

19. Gerald Saxon Brown, *The American Secretary: The Colonial Policy of Lord George Germain, 1775–1778* (Ann Arbor, University of Michigan, 1963), 149–73; *Sandwich Papers*, 2:23. Much of the following discussion of the differences between Germain and Sandwich regarding strategic considerations is based upon Brown's study.

20. The King to Lord North, May 6, 1778, in Sir John Fortescue, ed., *The Correspondence of King George the Third from 1760 to December 1783*, 6 vols. (London, Macmillan, 1927–1928), vol. 4, No. 2328. Although this particular quotation did not refer to strategy, Brown points out that the King was not prepared to disregard the ideas of top naval officers on marine matters, including strategy. See Brown, *American Secretary*, 168.

21. Minute of cabinet, January 1, 1781, Fortescue, *Correspondence of George III*, vol. 5, No. 3229.

22. Lord Barrington to Sandwich, September 17, 1779, *The Barrington Papers, Selected from the Letters and Papers of Admiral the Hon. Samuel Barrington*, 2 vols. (London, Navy Records Society, 1937–1941), 2:316–17.

23. William Cobbett, ed., *The Parliamentary History of England, from the Earliest Period to the Year 1803*, 36 vols. (London, 1806–1820), 22:866, 996.

24. *Sandwich Papers*, 4:126–27, 143n; "List Disposition & Condition of His Majestys Ships & Vessels employed under the orders of Vice Admiral Arbuthnot Commander in Chief in North America &c &c &c," June 12, 1781, PRO, Adm. 1/486.

25. For a detailed account of the naval actions, see Harold A. Larrabee, *Decision at the Chesapeake* (New York, C. N. Potter, 1964). For a brief but highly critical account, see William B. Willcox, "The British Road to Yorktown: A Study in Divided Command," *AHR* 52 (1946–1947):1–35. See also Robert Beatson, *Naval and Military Memoirs of Great Britain, from 1717 to 1783*, 6 vols. (London, 1804), vol. 5. Other accounts are in *Sandwich Papers*, 4:162–200, and in the letters from Graves to Stephens, August 30, and September 14, 1781, PRO, Adm. 1/489.

Many critics of admiralty policy have charged that Graves was unfit for command. Yet the admiralty had not appointed Graves to command the fleet; rather as second in command he took over from Arbuthnot, pending Digby's arrival. Furthermore, a study of the signals issued during the Chesapeake Bay encounter tends to dispel the totally unfavorable impression of Graves. While he lacked genius, he did not lack ability, intelligence, or experience. Two things seem clear. The confusion in interpreting his signals was fatal. Moreover, Hood's guilt at least equalled that of Graves. For but one example of the condemnation of Graves, see the old work by W. M. James, *The British Navy in Adversity: A Study of the War of American Independence* (London, Longmans, Greene, 1926), 300. For a "new" view of Graves, see Julian S. Corbett, ed., *Signals and Instructions, 1776–1794* (London, Navy Records Society, 1908), 53–57, 260–61. See also the analysis by Larrabee, *Decision at the Chesapeake*, 274–76.

26. Christopher Ward, *The War of the Revolution*, 2 vols. (New York, Macmillan, 1952), 1:96. For general accounts, see William B. Willcox, ed., *The American Rebellion; Sir Henry Clinton's Narrative of his Campaigns, 1775–1782* (New Haven, Conn., Yale University, 1954); and William B. Willcox, *Portraits of a General: Sir Henry Clinton in the War of Independence* (New York, Knopf, 1964).

27. For information on the riceboats, I am grateful to Franklin B. Wickwire, who has a forthcoming book on the irregular warfare during the Revolution. See also Harvey H. Jackson, "The Battle of the Riceboats: Georgia Joins the Revolution," *GHQ* 58 (1974):229–43. See also Allen D. Chandler, *The Revolutionary Records of the State of Georgia*, 2 vols. (Atlanta, State Printers, 1908), 1:113; Peter Force, ed., *American Archives*, 4th ser., 6 vols. (Washington, 1837–46); and *Naval Documents*, vol. 3, which print most of the exchanges between Wright, the British naval commander, and Savannah's council of safety. Wright's description of Savannah as an "open, straggling, defenseless, and deserted town" is in McIntosh to George Washington, March 8, 1776, Force, *American Archives*, 4th ser., 5:119–20. The "Never before attempted" quotation is from Major John Maitland to Germain, March 26, 1776: PRO, CO 5/93, ff. 428–29.

28. McIntosh to Washington, March 8, 1776, Force, *American Archives*, 4th ser., 5:119–20.

29. Wright to Clinton, March 10, 1776, Sir Henry Clinton Papers, 14:24, William L. Clements Library, University of Michigan, Ann Arbor.

30. Martin to Dartmouth, July 6, 1775, in William L. Saunders, ed., *The Colonial Records of North Carolina*, 10 vols. (Raleigh, N.C., 1886–1907) 10:70.

31. Eric Robson, "The Expedition to the Southern Colonies, 1775–1776," *EHR* 66 (October 1951):535–60; Willcox, *Clinton's Narrative*, 24, 24n.

32. Hugh F. Rankin, "The Moore's Creek Bridge Campaign, 1776," *NCHR* 30 (1953):23–60. Unpublished loyalist narratives of the campaign can be found in the William L. Clements Library and in "A Narrative of the Proceedings of a Body of Loyalists in North Carolina," PRO, CO 5/93, ff. 143–47. See also Martin to Germain, March 21, 1776, Saunders, Col. Rec. N.C., 10:489.

33. Ward, *War of the Revolution*, 2:665–78. Richard Reeve, Clinton's secretary, wrote a detailed account of the Sullivan's Island fiasco. See Clinton Papers, 15:48, Clements Library. The latter source also contains the letters exchanged by Clinton and Parker. See also Parker to Clinton, June 5, 1776, *Sandwich Papers*, 1:136. Francis, Lord Rowdon's letter about the incompetence of local pilots is to the 10th Earl of Huntingdon, July 3, 1776, in HMC, *Report on the Manuscripts of the late Reginald Rawdon Hastings*, 3 vols. (London, Navy Records Society, 1928–1934), 3:175.

34. *Naval Documents*, 9:255.

Bibliographic Essay

The past few decades have witnessed enormous scholarly activity in the history of the War of Independence. This work has not been characterized by what used to be called "drum and bugle" history, the story of flanking maneuvers and battlefield charges, narratives of the heroism of officers and the glorification of the martial spirit. Instead, academic historians have entered an area once monopolized by armchair historians and professional soldiers, and the result has been groundbreaking studies on such topics as the lives of the common soldiery, scrutiny of civil-military relations, and research into the impact of society upon warfare as well as of war's imprint on society. So vast has been this outpouring of scholarship, in fact, that numerous historiographical evaluations have appeared to keep us abreast of the deluge. Among the best of the summaries and assessments are: Don Higginbotham, "The Early American Way of War: Reconnaissance and Appraisal," *William and Mary Quarterly* 3d ser., 44 (1987):230–73; Peter Karsten, "The 'New' American Military History: A Map of the Territory, Explored and Unexplored," *American Quarterly* 36 (1984):389–418; Edward M. Coffman, "The New American Military History," *Military Affairs* 48 (1984):1–5; E. Wayne Carp, "Early American Military History: A Review of Recent Work," *Virginia Magazine of History and Biography* 94 (1986):259–84; Paul David Nelson, "British Conduct of the American Revolutionary War: A Review of Interpretations," *Journal of American History* 65 (1978):623–53; and David Syrett, "American and British Naval Historians and the American Revolutionary War, 1875–1980," *American Neptune* 42 (1982):179–92. The fear of standing armies has received separate historiographical appraisal in Reginald C. Stuart, " ' Engines of Tyranny': Recent Historiography on Standing Armies during the Era of the American Revolution," *Canadian Journal of History* 19 (1984):183–99.

For those wishing to understand the War of Independence, it might be wise to first explore the history of warfare in Colonial America. The best general account is that of Douglas E. Leach, *Arms for Empire: A Military History of the British*

Colonies in North America, 1607–1763 (New York, Macmillan, 1973). Leach also has authored a more analytical account that seeks to tie this early warfare to the origins of the American Revolution. The reader should see Leach, *Roots of Conflict: British Armed Forces and Colonial America, 1677–1763* (Chapel Hill, University of North Carolina, 1986). For a brief, general account of the intercolonial wars, one might peruse Howard H. Peckham, *The Colonial Wars, 1689–1762* (Chicago, University of Chicago, 1964). Other works that explore varied aspects of early American warfare include: Fred Anderson, *A People's Army: Massachusetts Soldiers and Society in the Seven Years' War* (Chapel Hill, University of North Carolina, 1984); John E. Ferling, *A Wilderness of Miseries: War and Warriors in Early America* (Westport, Conn., Greenwood Press, 1980); William Pencak, *War, Politics & Revolution in Provincial Massachusetts* (Boston, Northeastern University, 1981); Alan Rogers, *Empire and Liberty: American Resistance to Britain, 1755–1763* (Berkeley, University of California, 1974). On the colonial militia, see the relevant essays in John Shy, *A People Numerous and Armed: Reflections on the Military Struggle for American Independence* (New York, Oxford University Press, 1976).

Before proceeding to general histories of the revolutionary war, it might be wise to consult Don Higginbotham, "American Historians and the Military History of the American Revolution," *American Historical Review* 70 (1964):18–34. There are many excellent general histories of this conflict. Perhaps the liveliest and most enjoyable are those by Marshall Smelser, *The Winning of Independence* (New York, Franklin Watts, 1973); Willard M. Wallace, *Appeal to Arms* (New York, Harpers, 1951); and Robert Middlekauff, *The Glorious Cause: The American Revolution, 1763–1789* (New York, Oxford University Press, 1982). Although constructed less along the lines of narrative history than the above works, no reader will go wrong with any of the following: John R. Alden, *The American Revolution, 1775–1783* (New York, Harper and Row, 1954); Don Higginbotham, *The War of American Independence: Military Attitudes, Policies, and Practice, 1763–1789* (New York, Macmillan, 1971); Piers Mackesy, *The War for America, 1775–1783* (Cambridge, Mass., Harvard University, 1964); John C. Miller, *Triumph of Freedom, 1775–1783* (New York, Little, Brown, 1948); George F. Scheer and Hugh F. Rankin, *Rebels and Redcoats* (Cleveland, World Publishing, 1957); or Christopher Ward, *The War of the Revolution*, 2 vols. (New York, Macmillan, 1952). For a succinct treatment of the conflict, Howard H. Peckham, *The War for Independence: A Military History* (Chicago, University of Chicago, 1958) is excellent. A stimulating interpretive analysis of the outcome of the war is offered by Eric Robson, *The American Revolution in its Political and Military Aspects, 1763–1783* (New York, W. W. Norton, 1966).

There are numerous biographies of the most important military commanders in the War of Independence. The most recent study of George Washington is John Ferling, *The First of Men: A Life of George Washington* (Knoxville, Tenn., University of Tennessee, 1988). For longer works on the American commander, see: Douglas Southall Freeman, J. A. Carroll, and M. W. Ashworth, *George Washington: A Biography*, 7 vols. (New York, Scribners, 1948–1957), and James T. Flexner, *George Washington*, 4 vols. (Boston, Little, Brown, 1965–1972). On Washington in this war, see: Marcus Cunliffe, *George Washington: Man and Monument* (Boston, Little, Brown, 1957); Don Higginbotham, *George Washington and the American Military Tradition* (Athens, Ga., University of Georgia, 1985); and Dave Richard Palmer,

The Way of the Fox: American Strategy in the War of Independence (Westport, Conn., Greenwood Press, 1975).

Excellent essays on Washington's principal officers can be found in George Athan Billias, ed., *George Washington's Generals* (New York, William Morrow, 1964). The best full biography of Charles Lee is that by John R. Alden, *Charles Lee: Traitor or Patriot?* (Baton Rouge, Louisiana State University, 1951). On Horatio Gates one should consult Paul David Nelson, *General Horatio Gates: A Biography* (Baton Rouge, Louisiana State University, 1976). Theodore Thayer, *Nathanael Greene: Strategist of the Revolution* (New York, Twayne, 1960), remains the standard work on Washington's important subordinate, while North Callahan, *Henry Knox: General Washington's General* (New York, Rinehart, 1958) is still the best biography of the artillery commander. Nothing has yet equaled Louis R. Gottschalk, *Lafayette Comes to America*, 4 vols. (Chicago, University of Chicago, 1935–1942) as a biography of Washington's young general officer. For good treatments of other important American leaders, see: Charles P. Whittemore, *A General of the Revolution: John Sullivan of New Hampshire* (New York, Columbia University, 1961); Willard M. Wallace, *Traitorous Hero: The Life and Fortunes of Benedict Arnold* (New York, Books for Libraries, 1954); and Paul David Nelson, *Anthony Wayne: Soldier of the Early Republic* (Bloomington, Ind., Indiana University, 1985).

A companion piece to Billias's collection of essays on America's principal general officers, George Athan Billias, ed., *George Washington's Opponents* (New York, William Morrow, 1969), will serve as a good introduction to Great Britain's leading army and navy commanders. Those wishing to study the controversial Sir William Howe might start with Troyer S. Anderson, *The Command of the Howe Brothers during the American Revolution* (New York, Oxford University, 1936); and Ira D. Gruber, *The Howe Brothers and the American Revolution* (New York, Atheneum, 1972). On the Earl of Cornwallis, the best study remains Franklin B. Wickwire and Mary Wickwire, *Cornwallis: The American Adventure* (London: Faber and Faber, 1971). Richard Hargrove, *General John Burgoyne* (Newark, Del., University of Delaware, 1983) is a fine treatment of that important figure.

A good place to begin one's study of the common soldiery is with the overview provided in Richard H. Kohn, "The Social History of the American Soldier: A Review and Prospectus for Research," *American Historical Review* 86 (1981):553–67. From there the reader might wish to proceed to Charles K. Bolton, *The Private Soldier under Washington* (New York, Scribners, 1902); and Benjamin Quarles, *The Negro in the American Revolution* (Chapel Hill, University of North Carolina, 1961). On the militiamen's efforts, one will profit from Don Higginbotham, "The American Militia: A Traditional Institution with Revolutionary Responsibilities," in Don Higginbotham, ed., *Reconsiderations on the Revolutionary War* (Westport, Conn., Greenwood Press, 1978), a volume that contains several good essays on this war. In a similarly important collection of essays, Ronald Hoffman and Peter Albert, eds., *Arms and Independence: The Military Character of the American Revolution* (Charlottesville, Va., University Press of Virginia, 1984), one should see the essay by James Kirby Martin, "A 'Most Undisciplined, Profligate Crew': Protest and Defiance in the Continental Ranks, 1776–1783." For an excellent account of the British counterparts of the American soldiers, see Sylvia R. Frey, *The British Soldier in America: A Social History of Military Life in the Revolutionary Period* (Austin, Tex., University of Texas, 1981).

There are many good books on the various armies in this conflict. For the American army, it might be wise to start with James Kirby Martin and Mark Edward Lender, *A Respectable Army: The Military Origins of the Republic, 1763–1789* (Arlington Heights, Ill., Harlan Davidson, 1982). One also should consult Charles Royster, *A Revolutionary People at War: The Continental Army and the American Character, 1775–1783* (Chapel Hill, University of North Carolina, 1979), a magisterial work that treats far more than just the Continental army. Also good is Robert K. Wright, *The Continental Army* (Washington, Center of Military History, United States Army, 1983). Many of the works previously cited contain excellent treatments of the British armed forces. Other important works include volume three of John W. Fortescue, *A History of the British Army*, 13 vols. (London, Macmillan, 1899–1935) and John Shy, *Toward Lexington: The Role of the British Army in the Coming of the American Revolution* (Princeton, Princeton University, 1965). The best treatment of the French army in this war remains Lee Kennett, *The French Forces in America, 1780–1783* (Westport, Conn., Greenwood Press, 1977).

Students who wish to explore the Continentals' problem of supply should consult E. Wayne Carp, *To Starve the Army at Pleasure: Continental Army Administration and American Political Culture, 1775–1783* (Chapel Hill, University of North Carolina, 1984). Other useful accounts are: James A. Huston, *The Sinews of War: Army Logistics, 1775–1783* (Washington, Office of Military History, United States Army, 1966); Victor L. Johnson, *The Administration of the American Commissariat during the Revolutionary War* (Philadelphia, University of Pennsylvania, 1941); and Erna Risch, *Supplying Washington's Army* (Washington, Center of Military History, United States Army, 1981). On the problems Britain faced in supplying its armies, see David Syrett, *Shipping and the American War, 1775–1783: A Study of British Transport Organization* (London, Athlone, 1970); and R. Arthur Bowler, *Logistics and the Failure of the British Army in America, 1775–1783* (Princeton, Princeton University, 1975).

The literature on the frontier warfare in this conflict is enormous. Excellent accounts include Barbara Graymont, *The Iroquois in the American Revolution* (Syracuse, Syracuse University, 1972); James H. O'Donnell, III, *Southern Indians in the American Revolution* (Knoxville, Tenn., University of Tennessee, 1972); and Jack M. Sosin, *The Revolutionary Frontier, 1763–1783* (New York, Holt, Rinehart, and Winston, 1967).

The available general treatments of the naval war are rather dated. One might look into the following: Gardner W. Allen, *A Naval History of the American Revolution*, 2 vols. (Boston, Little, Brown, 1913); and Alfred T. Mahan, *A Naval History of the American Revolution*, 2 vols. (Boston, Little, Brown, 1913); The American navy is treated in William M. Fowler, *Rebels under Sail: The American Navy during the Revolution* (New York, Scribners, 1976); and Nathan Miller, *Sea of Glory: The Continental Navy Fights for Independence, 1775–1783* (New York, David McKay, 1974). An excellent account of the French navy is that of Jonathan R. Dull, *The French Navy and American Independence: A Study of Arms and Diplomacy, 1774–1787* (Princeton, Princeton University, 1975).

The squabbling among the general officers, as well as Congress's involvement in the conflicts over command, is capably covered in Jonathan G. Rossie, *The Politics of Command in the American Revolution* (Syracuse, Syracuse University, 1975). On

Congress and the war, one should see Edmund C. Burnett, *The Continental Congress* (New York, Macmillan, 1941); Jack N. Rakove, *The Beginnings of National Politics: An Interpretive History of the Continental Congress* (New York, Knopf, 1979); or H. James Henderson, *Party Politics in the Continental Congress* (New York, McGraw-Hill, 1974).

Those wishing to explore the role of France in the American Revolution should consult Edward S. Corwin, *French Policy and the American Alliance* (Princeton, Princeton University, 1916); and William C. Stinchcombe, *The American Revolution and the French Alliance* (Syracuse, Syracuse University, 1969).

For additional secondary literature on the War of Independence, as well as for citations of important primary source materials that relate to this conflict, see the notes that accompany this study.

Index

Douglas, Charles, 186
Douw, Volkert P., 117
Dryden, John, 5
Duane, James, 134–35, 140
Dyer, Eliphalet, 53

Elizabeth I, Queen, 2, 4, 166, 172, 201
Emerson, Ralph Waldo, 1
England. *See* Great Britain
Estaing, Charles Hector, comte d', 190–91
Eutaw Springs (South Carolina), battle of, 84
Ewing, George, 38

Fabius Cunctator, 24
Fairfax, George William, 55
Farnsworth, Amos, 43
Ferguson, Patrick, 29, 83, 126–27, 131
Fisher, Elijah, 47
Fitch, Jabez, 44
Floridablanca, Jose Monino y Redondo, comte de, 154
Fontenoy, battle of, 179
Fort Detroit, 120–22, 126, 129
Fortescue, Sir John, 181
Fort George, 187
Fort Niagara, 125
Fort Pitt, 121, 124, 129–30
Fort St. Johns, 142
Fort Ticonderoga, 22, 61, 77, 88, 95, 101, 134, 143–45, 186
Fort Washington, battle of, 23, 62–63, 66, 73, 81–82, 85
Fort William Henry, 6
France, 14, 67–68; historic warfare with England, 171; policy toward Great Britain, 148–49; treaties of alliance with United States, 152–53
Francis, Turbot, 117
Franco-American Alliance. *See* France
Franklin, Benjamin, 117, 143, 150, 161
Franklin, William, 54
French and Indian War, 6, 8, 12, 16–17, 58, 94, 136, 149, 162

Gage, Thomas, 20–21, 61, 115, 131, 134–35, 174, 197
Galphin, George, 117
Galvez, Bernardo de, 156
Gambier, James, 190
Gates, Horatio, 27, 29, 32, 54, 65, 70–71, 73, 90, 124, 126, 136; favors invasion of Canada, 67–68, 78; Saratoga campaign, 76–79, 144–45, 151–52; Schuyler command controversy, 143–45; in the South, 79–80
George III, King, 27, 150, 162, 192, 232
Georgia, 20, 117–18, 128, 182, 195–96
Germain, George, Lord, 28, 31, 179–80, 188, 191–92
Germantown, battle of, 64, 79, 89, 105
Gist, Christopher, 119–20
Glorious Revolution, 167–68, 170
Gnadenhutten Massacre, 129–30
Governor Dummer's War, 6
Grasse, Francois Joseph Paul, comte de, 30, 87, 155–56, 190; at Yorktown, 192–93
Graves, Thomas, 157, 190, 193–94, 232–33
Great Britain: economic growth of, 170–72; eighteenth century army of, 172–79; evolution of army in, 166–70; failure of army in War of Independence, 179–83; militia system in, 2–3, 166–67; navy in War of Independence, 185–98
Great Kanawha River, 121
Great Meadows (Pennsylvania), battle of, 56
Greene, Nathanael, 29–30, 34, 70–71, 88, 90, 123, 179; on militia, 36–37, 41, 66; as quartermaster-general, 106–8, 114; in the South, 83–85, 111–12, 128   9
Greenman, Jeremiah, 37, 45, 47
Green Spring Farm (Virginia), battle of, 45
Guilford Court House (North Carolina), battle of, 30, 84, 128

About the Editor and Contributors

FRED ANDERSON is Assistant Professor of History at the University of Colorado, Boulder. He is the author of *A People's Army: Massachusetts Soldiers and Society in the Seven Years' War* (1984).

W. J. ECCLES is Professor of History Emeritus, University of Toronto. His publications include *Frontenac: The Courtier Governor* (1959), *Canada under Louis XIV* (1964), *The Canadian Frontier, 1534–1760* (1969), *France in America* (1972), and *Essays on New France* (1987). He is presently working on a study of imperialism in North America.

JOHN FERLING is the author of *The Loyalist Mind* (1977), *A Wilderness of Miseries: War and Warriors in Early America* (1981), and *The First of Men: A Life of George Washington* (1988). Professor of History at West Georgia College, he is writing a biography of John Adams.

SYLVIA R. FREY is a member of the Department of History at Tulane University. Her works include *The British Soldier in America: A Social History of Military Life in the Revolutionary Period* (1981), *New World: New Roles: A Documentary History of Women in Pre-Industrial America* (coeditor, 1986), and numerous scholarly articles. She is currently at work on a study of the impact of the American Revolution on slavery.

MARK EDWARD LENDER is Director of Grants at Kean College of New Jersey. He is coauthor of *A Respectable Army: The Military Origins of America* (1982) and *Citizen-Soldier: The Revolutionary War Journal of Joseph Bloomfield* (1982). He is editor of *New Jersey History*.

JAMES KIRBY MARTIN is Professor of History at the University of Houston. His writings include *Men in Rebellion* (1973), *In the Course of Human Events* (1979), and *A Respectable Army* (with Mark E. Lender, 1982). He is presently writing a biography of Benedict Arnold.

PAUL DAVID NELSON is Professor of History at Berea College. He is the author of *General Horatio Gates: A Biography* (1976), *Anthony Wayne: Soldier of the Early Republic* (1985), and *William Alexander: Lord Sterling* (1987). He is currently writing a biography of William Tryon, an eighteenth-century British soldier and American colonial governor.

JAMES H. O'DONNELL, III, is Professor of History and chair of the Department of History, Philosophy, Political Science, and Religion at Marietta College. His publications include *The Southern Indians and the American Revolution* (1973) and *Southeastern Frontiers: Europeans, Africans, and American Indians, 1513–1840* (1982). He is completing a study of the Northern Indians in the American Revolution.

HUGH F. RANKIN is Professor Emeritus of History at Tulane University. His publications include *Rebels and Redcoats* (with George F. Scheer, 1957), *The American Revolution* (1964), *The Theater in Colonial America* (1965), *The Golden Age of Piracy* (1969), *The North Carolina Continentals* (1971), and *Francis Marion: The Swamp Fox* (1973).

JONATHAN G. ROSSIE is the author of *The Politics of Command in the American Revolution* (1975) and "Daniel Claus: A Personal History of Militant Loyalism," in *The Human Dimensions of Nation Making* (James Kirby Martin, editor, 1976). Vilas Professor of History at St. Lawrence University in Canton, New York, he is currently writing a history of Loyalism in Central New York.

MARY B. WICKWIRE is Professor of History at the University of Massachusetts in Amherst. Her research and teaching interests include the British Empire and Commonwealth, the history of Canada, and European history. She is the coauthor of *Cornwallis: The American Adventure* (1970) and *Cornwallis: The Imperial Years* (1971).